Fully Roman Catholic

Fully Roman Catholic

Pope Francis in Protestant Perspective:
A Selection of Articles

Leonardo De Chirico

compiled and edited by
Skyler Hamilton

co-edited by
Casey Cheney

WIPF & STOCK · Eugene, Oregon

FULLY ROMAN CATHOLIC
Pope Francis in Protestant Perspective: A Selection of Articles

Copyright © 2025 Leonardo De Chirico. All rights reserved. Except for brief quotations in critical publications or reviews, no part of this book may be reproduced in any manner without prior written permission from the publisher. Write: Permissions, Wipf and Stock Publishers, 199 W. 8th Ave., Suite 3, Eugene, OR 97401.

Wipf & Stock
An Imprint of Wipf and Stock Publishers
199 W. 8th Ave., Suite 3
Eugene, OR 97401

www.wipfandstock.com

PAPERBACK ISBN: 979-8-3852-5745-4
HARDCOVER ISBN: 979-8-3852-5746-1
EBOOK ISBN: 979-8-3852-5747-8

VERSION NUMBER 10/14/25

Three chapters ("Evangelicals and Catholics: A New Era?"; "Mission: Did Pope Francis Say Mission?"; "Atonement-free Mercy") have been published in Leonardo De Chirico, *Same Words, Different Worlds. Do Roman Catholics and Evangelicals Believe the Same Gospel?* (London: IVP, 2021), pp. 9–15, 83–86 and 55–58, respectively.

Scripture quotations are from the ESV® Bible (The Holy Bible, English Standard Version®), copyright 2001 by Crossway, a publishing ministry of Good News Publishers. Used by permission. All rights reserved.

Dedicated to the listeners of the Distinctive Christianity Podcast and anybody who has been misled by pretended charismatic authority.

Contents

Foreword by Skyler Hamilton | ix

1. Introduction: The Early Days | 1
2. Official Theology | 13
3. General Themes | 63
4. Big Picture: The Theology of Pope Francis | 84
5. The Tridentine Paradigm | 125
6. Mariology | 140
7. Universalism | 157
8. Ecumenism | 186
9. Morals | 222
10. Miscellaneous | 235
11. Future Impact and Legacy | 247

Obituaries | 269
Bibliography | 277

Foreword

In September 2024, when Pope Francis taught that "every religion is a way to arrive at God,"[1] many were surprised. Indeed, Francis goes on to affirm the universal fatherhood of God and brotherhood of man: "We are all God's children." Though not surprising from an apostle or prophet of Mormonism, surely the "Vicar of Christ" wouldn't say such a thing.[2] Or *mean* such a thing. Yet, the Pope has both said and meant this very thing, both officially and less officially, for the entirety of his pontificate—and

---

1. As translated live on-scene into English, see full official transcript here: Francis, "Address of His Holiness: 'Catholic Junior College.'" This occurred multiple times that same week. He stated in Tirana, Albania, "Contemplate the diversity of your traditions as a wealth, willed by God . . . Unity is not uniformity, and the diversity of our cultural and religious identities is a gift from God" See Brockhaus, "Diverse Religious Identities," para. 1. Francis then, the following week, stated, "We need to keep meeting, to weave bonds of fraternity and to allow ourselves to be guided by the divine inspiration present in every faith, in order to join in 'imagining peace' among all peoples." Francis, "Message of the Holy Father Francis to Participants," para. 7.

2. In LDS-Mormon theology, the Creator-Creation distinction is denied. Man and Gods are of the same species at different places or stages of eternal progression, in a context of eternally-existing matter. As two of their prophets, Brigham Young and Lorenzo Snow, taught respectively, "As God was, we shall be. As we are God was," and "As man is God once was; as God is, man may become." Indeed, "the great secret" according to their founding prophet Joseph Smith in his most famous sermon is that "God himself, who sits enthroned in yonder heavens, is a man like unto yourselves." Moreover, when LDS prophets and apostles speak of all mankind being the sons of daughters of god—it is in the context of affirming "heavenly parents." At least one heavenly mother is implied. Thus, when LDS prophets and apostles have affirmed the "universal fatherhood of god and brotherhood of man" (or something similar), it is often more literal in their view than many outsiders may suppose. See, for example, President Joseph Smith's "King Follett Discourse," Elder John Taylor's "Man," Elder Ezra Taft Benson's "Life is Eternal," President Howard W. Hunter's "The Gospel—A Global Faith," and President Russell M. Nelson's "The Second Great Commandment."

in continuity with Rome's most recent Ecumenical Council. If that's not *magisterial*, then what is?[3]

Speaking from an American context, there are many Roman Catholic apologists (RCa) who have made careers giving the impression of a very provincial *Roman* church—with the image of stability, tradition, and being impervious to any sort of innovation. There appears to be truth to some of this impression in a "bubble" (even a curated social media bubble) that avoids and ignores the flip side of Roman *Catholicism*: an ever-widening embrace of more and more, while never explicitly renouncing anything else. Roman *Catholicism* is an ever-expanding global reality beneath a *Roman*-imperial umbrella. The whole world is to be embraced, not confronted—and thus, the "sacred tradition" that widened to include Marian dogmas and the veneration of icons has simply continued to widen, upon the same principle, to include provincial Aztec and Mayan worship as well as a global charismatic movement.

Thus, when Pope Francis makes comments like the ones cited above—is it really that surprising? When Pope Francis states, for example, that "people are fundamentally *good*. We are all fundamentally good. Sometimes we are a little mischievous, sinners, but the heart is good,"[4] is that really such a deviation?

The evangelical response to many of the seemingly shocking comments by Pope Francis has often seemed to imitate the RCa, many of whom have been making ad hoc excuses and pretending not to see the obvious since the pontificate of Francis began, perhaps even since Vatican II. Similarly, sometimes even seeing the obvious and yet minimizing it based on what was perceived as "historic teaching." Though likely motivated to see the best in a traditional Catholic political base with whom we are so often co-belligerents, Protestants should know better than to protect Roman Catholics from their own Pope. Even using the *Catechism of the Catholic Church* as if it functions for the magisterium of Rome the way the Westminster Standards function for confessional Presbyterianism obscures the fact that "tradition" has always been a hollow term, seemingly designed for aesthetically pretending the new and novel are

---

3. Surely this is more magisterial than any Roman Catholic apologist on YouTube, who all combined have little to no "ecclesial authority."

4. O'Donnell, "Pope Francis Tells 60 Minutes." See also, De Chirico, *Engaging*, 52–53.

ancient and apostolic.[5] Too often, what is claimed to be based on history is simply a masquerade for the mystical.

The Protestant-Rome divide may have initially been a clear divide over the relation and priority of Scripture relative to church authority and the doctrine of Justification by Grace through Faith alone—and it has indeed, at base, stayed there. What the Roman Catholic decision on those fundamental points has developed into is what *appears* so different, even to "traditional Catholics," especially in the American context. Yet, it is that very choice of fundamentals that has come home to roost. Now that "tradition," papal supremacy, and *sola ecclesia* has come to include universalism, secular environmentalism, Pachamama, and Marian dogmas that consistently obfuscate the Lord Jesus and minimize (if not replace) God the Holy Spirit[6]—the moment calls for theological and pastoral clarity, not acting as if we are likewise surprised.[7] Once Scripture is abandoned as sole *infallible* authority, Christianity becomes less faithful and consistent—not more. And it doesn't just become apparent on Justification, but that same unfaithfulness will spread until every doctrine of the faith decays into an alien substance—even while retaining the now fossilized historic terminology.

Watching RCa pretend that Protestants are the problem strains credulity when the religion they claim is now dependent on a Bishop who affirms that all religions have "divine inspiration," that hell is nothing to worry about, who opposes "proselytism," and feels they have the authority to dedicate the world to Mary.[8] One may almost need a Calvinist view of sin to avoid utter confusion while seeing the obvious. To understate the problem, these RCa "strain at a gnat and swallow a camel." Far too often, they aren't defending and promoting Rome *as it truly is*—but rather, their fantasy of what it is as they imagine it. The rare reaction of surprise at comments by the "Vicar of Christ" give the false impression that this theology is somehow out of the norm or unexpected today. They are wrong. Pope Francis is not only expected but a faithful exponent of

---

5. Allison, *Roman Catholic Theology*; see also Monergism, "John Calvin to Cardinal Sadoleto."

6. De Chirico, *Pocket Guide to the Papacy*; De Chirico, *Pocket Guide to Mary*.

7. See De Chirico, *Tell Your Catholic Friend*.

8. All these are key examples of how Roman Catholic apologetic claims of Scripture being *an* authority (even if not the sole authority) are hollow, at best. God is not a partial authority—and his Word won't be, either. Apparently, for those paying attention, these apologists' Pope care less for their priorities when it comes to official doctrine and practice than their evangelical interlocutors do.

Roman Catholic theology and practice, as it *actually* is today. Holding Pope Francis to Tridentine standards, as if the church that developed *into* them couldn't develop further, demonstrates a fundamental misunderstanding of the Roman Catholic Church.

Roman Catholicism has developed and innovated through many ecumenical councils, such as Vatican I and Vatican II, as well as through dogmatic assertions such as the papal bulls on Mary's alleged Immaculate Conception and bodily assumption.[9] To truly understand Rome one must not only see discontinuity but continuity, and those who have followed official documents should not have been that surprised.[10] Those who followed the work of Dr. Leonardo De Chirico would not be surprised. As he has stated, "Rome never changes, and always changes."[11]

Going all the way back to his book concerning Vatican II,[12] Dr. De Chirico has been a consistent voice of scholarly clarity and thoroughness, as well as pastoral care. De Chirico sees the root of the problem: a Rome that uses talk of "tradition" to mask a radical ability for those in power to fundamentally change the faith, a "magisterium" unaccountable and non-responsive to the correcting authority of Scripture, and that this has not only happened—but should have been expected. Perhaps a Reformation *was* needed.

Dr. De Chirico's work bridges the gap between the scholar and the layman and combines academic rigor with pastoral faithfulness. This has been apparent throughout his work—from his book on Thomas Aquinas[13] to the Reformanda Initiative and Vatican Files blog. De Chirico has been educating Protestants on the root problems with Rome, as well as reminding Protestants why they are Protestant and why it should matter.[14] If there ever was a pastor-theologian, De Chirico is one.

This book is a compilation of his work. There is no one better to educate the Evangelical Protestant about Pope Francis than a scholar of the very "ecumenical council" that Francis represents so faithfully. With De Chirico's gift of understanding also comes a gift of communicating

---

9. On Immaculate Conception, see Pius IX, "Ineffabilis Deus." On bodily assumption, see Pius XII, "Munificentissimus Deus." See also De Chirico, "Vatican File 182."

10. For one interesting example of an evangelical response to Vatican II, see Wells, *Revolution in Rome*.

11. De Chirico, "Leonardo De Chirico on Pope Francis."

12. De Chirico, *Evangelical Theological Perspectives*.

13. De Chirico, *Engaging*.

14. De Chirico, *Same Words*. See also Wells, *Courage*.

such an understanding, and editing this volume was a joy. We look forward to the reader having a similar experience of De Chirico aiding our minds to put the pieces of the puzzle together so we can accurately see the box-top of the state of Rome, today.

The editors have tried to structure this book in a way that is helpful to the reader. We have attempted to balance a structure that is topical while also attempting to preserve the chronology of De Chirico's work. One will see that he has not only documented the clear problems along the way or analyzed in retrospect—but has also forecasted and foreseen the very career of a Pope he understood from the start. Please note that in the "official documents" section, we have included a couple posts dealing with news items that, if responded to at all, were often treated as at odds with the official position of Rome—contrary to the evidence as found in the official documents themselves.

Perhaps the pontificate of Pope Francis can be seen as an opportunity. If Jesus is Lord, and is "the Way, the Truth, and the Life" as he said, and he refers to Scripture as "the word of God" that is authoritative against and despite a claimed authority for "traditions of men" (oral or otherwise)—the choice is clear.[15] If there is apostolic authority around today, not lost from a church Jesus promised would be preserved, then where is it? If not in Holy Scripture, where? Surely it is not in a man who literally speaks out against evangelizing, on the basis of the dogmatic assertion of everyone being "children of God" *by nature*—and sees "every faith" as having "divine inspiration."

Reading De Chirico's work in this volume, we suspect the true Christian will feel a sense of relief at the doses of sanity provided. The clarity and sanity herein documented could only come based upon the actual authority of the what the Triune God has spoken (and continues to speak), based on the real apostolic authority preserved in Scripture.

Thanks be to the Triune God that we Christians are not left as orphans. God has spoken, and his word *is* Truth. The gospel is not about what we do but about what God has done in and as Christ Jesus of Nazareth. The message is Christ and him crucified, not Popes and them enthroned! We pray that all people—Protestant, Roman Catholic, or any other religion—will hear what he has said. There is a judgment coming. The antithesis between the seed of the serpent and the seed of the woman

---

15. One of the numerous examples is Mark 7. Was there ever a case where Jesus in fact sided with an unwritten text or tradition, from any group, against the text of the Old Testament? Wenham, *Christ and the Bible*.

will eventually, by God's mercy *and justice*, be revealed in the fate of the blessed and the damned. Christ is our only hope from a hell we all, in Adam, deserve and will receive apart from faith in the atoning substitutionary blood of Jesus *alone*.

Trusting in Christ and his work alone: that is the apostolic gospel, and the message that believing, faithful, truly *conservative* Christians have heard and proclaimed and will hear and spread until Christ comes again.

Come quickly, Lord. *Soli Deo Gloria!*

Skyler Hamilton
April 10, 2025

1

Introduction
The Early Days

The Three Tasks of Pope Francis
(March 18, 2013, Number 54)

THE ELECTION OF CARDINAL Bergoglio to the papacy responds to three basic concerns that the conclave felt it necessary to address. These concerns helped to sketch the profile of the new Pope and Cardinal Bergoglio fit it.

The Transitional Task

No one in the curia will ever say Benedict XVI's reign was a failure. Yet the impression is that the election of Pope Bergoglio is an implicit admission that the previous papacy achieved less than what was expected, especially as far as the main point of its agenda was concerned, i.e., the relationship with the secular West. After eight years of Benedict's reign, the secular West has become more distant from the church and critical of it. Moreover, the curial church has given the poorest performance in terms of lack of Christian standards. The church needed therefore a *different* Pope.

Between the traditional yet secularized West and the vibrant yet still "young" Global South, the conclave has chosen the classical "via media," or "middle way." Pope Bergoglio is an Argentinian born of an Italian family. He is Latin American but with a European background.

He embodies the transition between the Western establishment and the Southern fervor. Perhaps the conclave thought that choosing an African Pope or an Asian Pope would have been a too long and unwarranted stretch. On the other hand, sticking to another European Pope would have been too much of a geopolitical conservative move that the church could not bear. Pope Bergoglio is an in-between figure. Different but not so strange. Similar but not a replica.

He is also a transitional figure in terms of his age. At seventy-six, he is not a "young" Pope with the expectation of a long papacy. Neither is he an "old" Pope with not much time in front of him. His papacy will test the willingness of the Church of Rome to move beyond the standstill position of recent years, but perhaps it will not have enough time to see changes implemented. The conclave did not commit the Catholic Church to a long papacy (like that of John Paul II) but has instead opted to keep the future in sight, waiting to see how this papacy will unfold. All the while the hierarchy will retain the right to make changes if they deem it necessary.

Pope Bergoglio is presented as an outsider, but in fact he is not. Supported by Cardinal Martini, Bergoglio was the runner up in the 2005 conclave, the one in which Joseph Ratzinger became Benedict XVI. He is well known to the cardinals and was apparently considered "reliable" by the conclave. In the top list of candidates prior to the conclave was the Brazilian Scherer, another transitional figure. Scherer, however, was apparently perceived as being too involved in the politics of the Roman curia to be able to free himself from its maneuvering. Bergoglio is integrated but not organic to the curial world.

The Apologetic Task

The name chosen by the Jesuit Pope is Francis. He mentioned that Francis is a reference to Francis of Assisi (1181–1226). The international press put a lot of stress on this Franciscan symbolism and apparently liked it. Apparently, he will combine the Jesuit wit with the emphasis on poverty and frugality. The choice has to do with the willingness to mark an apologetic transition in dealing with the modern world. Ratzinger addressed it by lecturing as a professor, but the West does not like detached, top-down teachers. Ratzinger argued his positions in a very clever and intellectual way, but the West is looking more to celebrities who can ignite imagination. Ratzinger denounced the moral relativism of our day, but the West does not like people who do not practice the "political correctness" of accepting everything. Ratzinger's strategy ended at a standstill.

Pope Francis began his papacy with a very different apologetic style. Approachable, normal, and ordinary, he likes to be with the people, speaking their language and making his message simple. Ratzinger stressed "faith and reason"; Francis is likely to stress "mercy and simplicity." While Ratzinger addressed the West as a theologian, Francis is likely to underline the common humanity of all. The difference is significant.

Will the church become poor and meek? Will it give priority to a simpler lifestyle? Will it put a stronger emphasis on its spiritual tasks than its secular interests? One thing is to be remembered: Francis of Assisi did not want to reform the whole church but wished to receive from the official church the right for his circle of friends to live in poverty. He wanted a niche to pursue his evangelical ideals, leaving untouched the apparatus of the imperial church. The church of his time readily gave him what he wanted because she did not feel threatened by him. We will see whether Pope Francis will transition evangelical poverty from being a niche of the few idealists to being the standard of the worldwide church. If this is the case, he will have to look at Peter Waldo (1140–1218) who, like Francis, practiced evangelical poverty but challenged the official church to do the same. Francis was integrated; Waldo was persecuted.

The Geo-political Task

A final thought on the geopolitical significance of the election. Pope Bergoglio comes from a country where, in recent decades, the secular *status quo* that saw Roman Catholicism being the dominant religion has been shaken by the growth of evangelical churches and new religious movements of various kinds. This phenomenon designed a new spiritual geography of the country. The same can be said for other Latin American countries. It is interesting that the Catholic Church chose a Pope from Latin America giving him the task of monitoring and presiding over this continental religious border that has become fluid if not weak. The traditional response to the numerical growth of evangelicals has been labeling them as "sects" and "cults," but this derogatory approach did not stop millions of people from leaving the Catholic Church. Now, the Pope himself will be directly involved in rescuing the continent. Something important is taking place in Latin America and the risk of losing the continent was considered in need of being addressed at the highest level.

Pope Francis is a transition figure. Time will show how Latin American, how curial, how Jesuit, and how Franciscan he will be. In his first short speech in front of the applauding crowd in St. Peter's Square, the most-quoted figure was the Virgin Mary to whom he committed himself and his predecessor. His first appointment in his first day of papacy was visiting the Marian basilica of St. Mary Major in Rome to pray to Mary for guidance and help. More of a Jesuit than a Franciscan way of beginning a papacy.

A Papal Honeymoon . . . Until When?
(March 21, 2013, Number 55)

A honeymoon is a special time when two lovers live their newly established relationship in a sentimental way, i.e., romantically and enchantingly. In such times, one partner only perceives and highlights the best traits of the loved one but does not see the defects. Honeymoons generally last for a short time and are followed by more realistic and critical appreciations of one another.

What is interesting to notice is what happens in the public domain. In our celebrity culture, honeymoons with global figures are frequent and passionate. Once a person is elected to an important office, the public opinion tends to begin an "affair" with the new powerful figure, selecting and praising all his merits and overlooking the rest, at least at the beginning. This is what has been happening with Pope Francis after his election to the papacy. A global honeymoon is taking place. Among the many sides of it (e.g., in Catholic inner circles, in ecumenical circles), two main angles are worth considering.

The Secular Honeymoon

Comments from the international press have been very generous if not enthusiastic so far. Francis's image was perceived as "real," "down to earth," "personal," "non-presuming," very different from a "regal" arrogance of more traditional popes. His references to the care of the environment, poverty, and tenderness were highly praised and understood as being very politically correct. His insistence on "mercy" was understood as an open door to different sexual lifestyles and moral choices, moving away from a judgmental attitude on the church's side. His willingness to intermingle with people and his relaxed behavior as far as protocols are concerned were seen as proofs of his desire to be identified with normal people and with ordinary life.

The international press decided to bypass and consider irrelevant Cardinal Bergoglio's relationship with the Argentinian political past. No further press investigation was pursed concerning the "dark" years of the totalitarian regimes and the role of the Catholic Church in Latin America. His strong stance against gay marriages in his country was forgotten. His rather conservative positions on moral issues were simply overlooked. Unlike his predecessor, who was a published and public theologian, Pope Bergoglio does not have a record of being a Catholic *maitre-à-penser*. People that know all his staff say that Pope Francis is on the same page as Benedict XVI in defending the traditional position of the Catholic Church in these areas. Yet the secular press fell in love with Francis. Why?

There may be a sociological explanation to this phenomenon. In this time marked by social crisis, cultural disruption, and economic uncertainty, people are eager to find someone that inspires trust and injects hope. Someone who is powerful but nonetheless gives the impression that he is on the same boat as us. A positive father-like figure that can speak simple words of love and distribute psychological caresses. Someone who can identify with the people, sending the message that "I am with you," struggling with the same challenges and helping everyone to overcome them. A secular "messiah" that proclaims a "soft gospel" of compassion and resilience. In his first days as Pope, Pope Francis has met expectations. The secular world strongly dislikes the church but loves the celebrity Pope. What is going to happen when he begins to speak the "hard" sayings of the Catholic Church? The irony of it all is that the cynical, suspicious, and disenchanted modern world was re-enchanted by a man using the name of a medieval, primitive, and deeply religious saint.

The Evangelical Honeymoon

Comments from the evangelical world were also marked by the honeymoon attitude. Official statements and the social networks sent out enthusiastic reactions to his election. "Man of God," "friend of Jesus," "man of prayer." . . . these were some of the most common remarks. Francis was also acclaimed as the new national or even continental hero to be proud of, the new Diego Armando Maradona (of my generation) or another Lionel Messi, i.e., a man that embodies the expectations of an entire nation, someone that evangelical people too want to identify with.

With all due respect, the idea of a Christ-centered man of God praying to Mary and the saints, bowing in front of an icon and committing himself and his audience to the care of Mary, is difficult to accept from an evangelical point of view. But this was exactly what Pope Francis did on the first day of his papacy. No one is denying the deep spirituality of Francis or his godly devotion. The problem lies with the evangelical discernment that tends to select few apparently positive aspects and forgets the negative ones. The outcome is a truncated picture at best, a false assessment at worst.

The global evangelical movement does not have celebrities that can compare with those stemming from the worlds of music, sport, and politics. Pope Francis apparently filled the gap. Unlike his cerebral predecessor, he knows how to speak to the heart. He knows how to embrace people.

Evangelical comments were largely based on past personal acquaintances with the former Cardinal Bergoglio. Again, no one for a moment doubts the integrity and warmth of the Pope, but the man can never be separated from his role and his loyalty to his Jesuit mission, which is now Papal as well. The Jesuits were founded in 1534 by Ignatius of Loyola, and in their turbulent history they have always been committed to serve as "soldiers" of the Pope to fight against the (Protestant) heresy and to promote the Catholic mission in the world. Francis is the first Jesuit to become Pope, and time will tell just how Jesuit his papacy will be, especially in Latin America, where the evangelical-Catholic border is moving. Will the Jesuit Pope be able to stop the evangelical expansion? Will he manage to take it back into the Catholic fold? Will he be able to enchant evangelicals with his manners without changing the doctrinal points of controversy? Will biblical doctrine still be an issue for evangelicals in dealing with the Roman Catholic Church at the highest level?

Anyone who is aware of history should carefully consider these questions. The Spirit is surely able to work miracles even in traditional institutions, but the Bible warns us to not be forgetful of history. Personal relationships are important, but biblical discernment is bigger than that. It calls for theological awareness, historical alertness, and spiritual vigilance.

The honeymoon with Pope Francis continues. Yet the mood of the public's opinion can suddenly change when the fuller mission of the Pope is put on fuller display. What seemed to be a promising marriage may turn into a painful divorce. As for Christians who are experiencing the honeymoon, let the warning of not forsaking the "first love" (Rev 2:4) of Jesus be a constant reminder of the need to love and to follow Christ and Christ alone.

The Catholicity of Pope Francis (March 9, 2014, Number 76)

One year ago (March 13th) Cardinal Bergoglio was elected as Pope Francis. Different evaluations of the first year are mushrooming everywhere in the form of books and editorials. They suggest various interpretations of what the Pope has been doing, saying, and implementing thus far. As his first anniversary approaches, several questions seem appropriate to ask, and all of them assume that something significant has been happening. What has been the "Francis effect" on the church? The simplest answer is that he is envisaging a different kind of catholicity.

Roman Catholic Catholicity

In the Roman Catholic understanding, catholicity has to do simultaneously with unity and totality. The basic premise is that multiplicity should be brought into a unity. The church is seen as an expression, a guarantor and a promoter of true unity between God and humanity and within humanity itself. In Vatican II terms, the church is a "sacrament of unity." As long as the institutional structure which preserves this unity remains intact (i.e., the Roman element), everything can and must find its home somewhere within its realm (i.e., the catholic element).

The catholic mindset is characterized by an attitude of overall openness without losing touch with its Roman center. It is inherently dynamic and comprehensive, capable of holding together doctrines, ideas, and practices that in other Christian traditions are thought of as being mutually exclusive. By way of its inclusive *et-et* (both-and) epistemology, in a catholic system, two apparently contradicting elements can be reconciled into a synthesis which entail both. In principle, the system is wide enough to welcome everything and everyone. The defining term is not the Word of God written (*sola Scriptura*) but the Roman Church itself. From a catholic point of view then, affirming something does not necessarily mean denying something else but simply means enlarging one's own perspective of the whole truth. In this respect, what is perceived as being important is the integration of the part into the catholic whole by way of relating the thing newly affirmed with what is already existing.

Catholicity allows doctrinal development without a radical breach from the past and allows different kinds of catholicity to coexist. Each Pope has his own catholicity project. John Paul II pushed the church to become a global player, thus expanding the geographical catholicity and its profile with the media. Benedict XVI tried to define catholicity in terms of its adherence to universal "reason," thus trying to reconnect the chasm between faith and reason that Western Enlightenment had introduced. These catholicity projects are not mutually exclusive, but they all contribute to the overall dynamic catholicity of the church. They were all organically related to the Roman element that safeguards the continuity of the system.

Mapping Francis's Catholicity

After one year of his pontificate, it is becoming apparent what kind of catholicity Francis has in mind. He wants to build on John Paul II's global catholicity while shifting emphases from Wojtyła's doctrinal rigidity to more inclusive patterns. He pays lip service to Ratzinger's rational catholicity but wants to move the agenda from Western ideological battles to "human" issues which find appeal across the global spectrum. If Ratzinger wanted to mark the difference between the church and the world, Francis tries to make them overlap. In shaping the new catholicity he seems closer to the "pastoral" tone of John XXIII, who will be canonized (i.e., declared a "saint") next April. So, there is continuity and development. This is the gist of catholicity.

Francis has little time for "non-negotiable" truths and gives more attention to the variety of people's conscience. He is more interested in warmth than light, more in empathy than judgment. He focuses on attitude rather than identity, and on embracing rather than teaching. He underlines the relational over the doctrinal. For him proximity is more important than integrity. Belonging together has priority over believing differently. Reaching out to people comes before calling them back. Of course, all these marks are not pitted against each other, but their relationship is worked out within a new balance, whereby the first one determines the overall orientation. Roman catholicity works this way: never abandoning the past, always enlarging the synthesis by repositioning the elements around the Roman center.

Francis calls this catholicity "mission." The word is familiar and intriguing for Bible-believing Christians, yet one needs to understand what he means by it beyond what it appears to mean on the surface.

The Intellectual Journey of J. M. Bergoglio, Now Pope Francis (April 1st, 2018, Number 148)

Five years ago, Jorge Mario Bergoglio was elected Pope Francis. Since then, several biographies have been published to make his life known to the general public. For example, Austen Ivereigh's *The Great Reformer: Francis and the Making of a Radical Pope*[1] sticks out as perhaps the most comprehensive window onto Bergoglio's life. As he was not a major figure in global Roman Catholic circles prior to his election, let alone in the wider world, these accounts have helped many to better understand the main events of Bergoglio's personal story before becoming Pope.

One recent book by Massimo Borghesi, *Jorge Mario Bergoglio: Una biografia intellettuale*[2] looks at Bergoglio's life from a particular angle. Borghesi focuses on the intellectual influences (e.g., books, journals, authors, friendships, networks) that have shaped Bergoglio's thought. In so doing, it provides a fruitful perspective on the genesis and development of the vision that Bergoglio embodies and promotes as Pope. In addition to surveying all the relevant literature, Borghesi has also worked on a questionnaire that Pope Francis responded to, giving further details and filling in the blanks of previous attempts. According to this well-researched analysis, Bergoglio's intellectual biography seems to be marked by three main influences.

The French Jesuit Starting Point . . .

The formative years of Bergoglio as a student in philosophy and theology were profoundly impacted by his reading of French Jesuit intellectuals like Henri de Lubac, Gaston Fessard, and Michel de Certeau. They introduced the young Bergoglio to the Catholic dialectical thought, away from

1. See Ivereigh, *Great Reformer*.
2. See Borghesi, *Bergoglio*.

rigid Thomism and towards the dynamic synthesis of embracing opposites and enlarging the overall vision. In this Jesuit school of thought—which, by the way, became the matrix of the theology of the Second Vatican Council (1962–65)—what are perceived as oppositions become "tensions," at times painfully disruptive but also potentially creative and always to be maintained as such. Bergoglio became persuaded that human thought is always "in tension," never fixed or stable. He distanced himself from abstract definitions and propositions. He learned to always think in programmatically "open" and "loose" thought-forms.

Intertwined with this dialectical tendency was Bergoglio's early exposure to liberation theology. Since his first attempts at coming to terms with its growing popularity in Latin America, Bergoglio was not interested in the Marxist ideological and political framework of much of the liberation theology of those years. He was definitely attracted to the "theology of the people" that is a side aspect of liberation theology. According to this particular way of theologizing, the people's concerns, preoccupations, aspirations, etc., need to be the starting point. Rather than considering folk devotions and beliefs as a pre-modern stage that will be overcome by political liberation, the "theology of the people" assumes them as vital and central. Marian devotions and practices become the most appreciated expressions of the people's heart, even if they are contrary to Scripture. Theology and pastoral practice must therefore be developed only in a bottom-up way. In this view there is no sense in which the Bible can be the supreme norm for faith and life. In Borghesi's terms, the future Pope embraced "a liberation theology without Marxism."[3] This is the context of Bergoglio's important emphasis on the "people" being the principal subject of theology and church life.

. . . Mediated Through the Uruguayan Alberto Methol Ferré . . .

Bergoglio's early fascination with French Jesuit thought was further consolidated by his reading of the lay Uruguayan Catholic philosopher Alberto Methol Ferrè (1929–2009). From Methol Ferré he learned that human thought is always unstable, mobile, and ever-renewing. This was yet another injection of Catholic dialecticism that moved Bergoglio further away from static and traditional Thomism.

3. Borghesi, *Bergoglio*, 71.

Methol Ferrè is also the intellectual who suggested that with the Second Vatican Council, the Roman Catholic Church had finally overcome both the Protestant Reformation and the Enlightenment. After fiercely fighting them up front (from the 16th century to the 19th century), Rome eventually came to terms with its ability to assimilate and absorb the Reformation and the Enlightenment rather than opposing them. At Vatican II, the Catholic Church took the "best" of both and launched a "new" Reformation and a "new" Enlightenment. They were no longer adversaries but parts of the "catholic" accomplishment of their positive contributions. This is the background of both Francis's recent kind words toward the Reformation on the occasion of the 5th centenary[4] and his low-key approach towards controversial lifestyles[5] (e.g., homosexuality) marked by modern individual autonomy. What this basically means is that after Vatican II, the Reformation as such is over and has been absorbed within the ongoing renewal of the Church of Rome.

. . . Leading to the Italian-German Romano Guardini

Building on these two important phases of his intellectual life, Bergoglio grew in his conviction that the Catholic Church is the "complexio oppositorum" (the whole that makes room for opposites). His study of German theologian Romano Guardini (1885–1968) corroborated the Catholic dialectical dimension of his thought. Guardini argued that Roman Catholicism is a "Weltanschauung," an all-embracing worldview, the only one that is capable of handling multiple tensions between diverging poles and bringing them to a "catholic" unity. From Guardini, Bergoglio developed his idea of unity as being a "polyhedron." The polyhedron is a geometric figure with different angles and lines. All different parts have their own peculiarity. It's a figure that brings together unity and diversity, and Roman Catholicism is the home of unity as a polyhedron. This explains Francis's commitment to ecumenical and interreligious unity that downplays differences and concentrates on generic commonalities. In this view unity is not governed by biblical truth and biblical love but by the embracing view of Rome, which holds together all angles and lines of life.

---

4. De Chirico, "Vatican File 131."
5. De Chirico, "Vatican File 93."

On March 13, 2013, Jorge Mario Bergoglio became Pope Francis, marking a significant transition in the Roman Catholic Church. What he has been saying and doing since being elected, e.g., his affirming attitudes towards all,[6] his noisy silences over doctrine,[7] his thoroughgoing Marianism, and his lack of clarity on several key issues, has caused many to wonder where his thought came from. Borghesi's intellectual biography makes it clear that Francis's pontificate comes from afar. It is the result of a long series of developments within Catholic thought, from Jesuit sources to Latin American influences up to the Vatican II matrix of contemporary Rome, without having been corrected by the Word of God. One needs to immerse oneself in what happened at the Second Vatican Council to begin to make sense of what Francis is saying and doing now. All analyses of Francis being an "evangelical" or a "kerygmatic" Pope are simplistic and short-sighted. He is much more than that, in ways that are dialectical, open-ended, and at the service of the Catholic vision to embrace the whole world.

---

6. De Chirico, "Vatican File 65."
7. De Chirico, "Vatican File 134."

2

Official Theology

Lumen Fidei. The First Encyclical by Pope Francis (July 8th, 2013, Number 61)

As SUPREME TEACHERS OF the Roman Catholic Church, popes write encyclicals to expound aspects of Christian belief that they deem particularly relevant or important for their time. Encyclicals mark the theological profile of a given pontificate and provide a helpful interpretative grid to it. It is, therefore, interesting to read Pope Francis's first encyclical which was officially presented today (July 5, 2013) and is titled *Lumen Fidei* (LF), the Light of Faith. It is Bergoglio's first theologically articulate work since becoming Pope Francis.

Benedict XVI's Blueprint

The first element worth noting is that it is actually a work that comes from Benedict XVI, now Pope Emeritus. Ratzinger had planned a trilogy of encyclicals on the theological virtues of Love, Hope, and Faith (in this order). In this respect he wrote "God is Love" and "Saved in Hope." His unexpected resignation brought everything to a halt. Evidently, he passed the manuscript on to Francis, who thought it would be a good idea to release it as part of his own teaching after adding "a few contributions" of his own.¹ We are therefore confronted with an encyclical signed by Francis but largely shaped by Benedict XVI.

Ratzinger's contribution is evident throughout the text. Nearly all the quotations come from either the German tradition² or the larger European culture.³ It is clear that a scholar like Ratzinger stands behind these discussions. The beloved Augustine is by far the most quoted church father.⁴ It was Augustine's theology that was the subject of Ratzinger's doctorate. The themes and the tone of Ratzinger's thought are also powerfully reflected in how this encyclical deals with the issue of truth and relativism,⁵ or modernity and its "totalitarianism" that excludes faith.⁶

Apparently, Francis is at ease with all this and therefore makes no changes or modifications. LF recalls "the gift of apostolic succession" through which the church's memory is granted continuity and the encyclical itself testifies to the unbroken succession of the Papacy even as far as doctrine is concerned.⁷

Evangelical Language But . . .

LF is a long reflection on faith which is divided into four parts. It starts with the biblical character of Abraham and the subsequent story of the people of Israel. The language is biblical (e.g., faith departs from idolatry) and the tone is evangelical (e.g., faith is a "personal encounter").⁸ At one point the text goes as far as saying that "we believe in Jesus when we personally welcome him into our lives and journey towards him, clinging to him in love and following in his footsteps along the way."⁹ Stopping here, one might think this is an evangelical document which stresses the personal language of faith. This is not the whole story, however.

---

1. Francis, "Lumen Fidei," 7.
2. Francis, "Lumen Fidei," see e.g., F. Nietzsche, 2; M. Buber, 13; R. Guardini, 22; L. Wittgenstein, 27; H. Schlier, 30.
3. Francis, "Lumen Fidei," see e.g., Dante, 4; J.-J. Rousseau, 14; F. Dostoevsky, 16; J.H. Newman, 48; T.S. Eliot, 75.
4. Francis, "Lumen Fidei," see e.g., 10, 15, 19, 23, 31, 33, 43, 48.
5. Francis, "Lumen Fidei," see e.g., 25.
6. Francis, "Lumen Fidei," see e.g., 54.
7. Francis, "Lumen Fidei," 49.
8. Francis, "Lumen Fidei," 13.
9. Francis, "Lumen Fidei," 18.

Continue reading, however, and one finds a section entitled "Salvation by Faith." Notice the absence of the adverb "alone," which is of course foundational for an evangelical understanding of salvation. The 16th century Protestant Reformation insisted that salvation is "by faith alone," but ever since the Council of Trent, the Roman Catholic Church has not accepted the doctrine of salvation by grace alone through faith alone. In fact, Francis writes that "the beginning of salvation is openness to something prior to ourselves."[10] Faith, suggests the Pope, is only the beginning of the process, but the journey of the believer requires faith plus works, faith through the sacraments, and faith with the church that imparts the sacraments. In other words, the faith of the LF is the faith that the Council of Trent defined in its decrees and canons. Part of the language has become evangelical, but at its core the theological substance is Roman Catholic.

Sacramental Faith

The third part of LF explains in further detail. Here Francis (and Benedict) want to underline the fact that the church is "the mother of our faith."[11] Our faith is never originated in ourselves as individuals but precedes us and follows us. It is through "the apostolic Tradition preserved in the Church" that faith is born and nurtured. Quoting Vatican II, Francis writes that "the Church, in her doctrine, life and worship, perpetuates and transmits to every generation all that she herself is, all that she believes."[12] It is no longer the Word of God that leads the way but the church. The way it does so is through the sacraments. In one revealing passage, LF says that "faith itself possesses a sacramental structure."[13] According to LF, faith is a personal encounter, but faith is also received through the sacraments. These are the two sides of the same coin. What follows is a brief explanation of the Roman Catholic doctrine of baptismal regeneration[14] and the Eucharist,[15] which are the gateway of faith and its highest expression. The Pope goes on to say that this doctrine is one

---

10. Francis, "Lumen Fidei," 19.
11. Francis, "Lumen Fidei," 37–38.
12. Francis, "Lumen Fidei," 40.
13. Francis, "Lumen Fidei," 40.
14. Francis, "Lumen Fidei," 41–43.
15. Francis, "Lumen Fidei," 44–45.

and the same, i.e., the personal and the sacramental dimensions of faith are undivided.[16]

As it is common in encyclicals, LF also ends with an invocation to Mary, "Mother of the Church, Mother of our faith."[17] While the disciples asked Jesus to increase their faith (Luke 17:5), LF ends with a prayer to Mary: "Mother, help our faith!"

Lumen Fidei well depicts the current appropriation of evangelical language by important sectors of the Roman Catholic Church. It started with "evangelization" and now continues with faith as "personal encounter." Pope Francis seems to be leading the way in this process. This appropriation, however, must be put in the context of the traditional Roman Catholic doctrine that is Tridentine, sacramental, and Marian.

The Joy of the Gospel: A Window into Francis's Vision (December 2, 2013, Number 69)

Five chapters, 288 paragraphs, and more than 220 pages. This is the apostolic letter of Pope Francis titled *The Joy of the Gospel* (*Evangelii Gaudium*), the second magisterial document of his Pontificate (the previous being the encyclical *Light of Faith*). It is the first, however, to come entirely from his own pen (and was originally written in Spanish). In 2010 Benedict XVI launched the idea of the "new evangelization" and in 2012 convened a Synod of Bishops to discuss it. Now we have Francis's interpretation of the new evangelization in an authoritative statement which is also a compendium to interpret most of what the Pope has been saying and doing so far. Here are some selected highlights.

Missionary Conversion

Although *Evangelii Gaudium* comes one year after the Synod and is quoted twenty-seven times, Francis's whole approach to the topic is more dependent on the 2007 Latin American document of Aparecida than from it. More than the "new evangelization," this Pope loves to speak about "mission." The former attempts at reaching the un-practicing Catholics; the latter is a style of the whole church going in all directions. The former is particularly relevant for the ever-more-secular West; the latter is

---

16. Francis, "Lumen Fidei," 47–49.
17. Francis, "Lumen Fidei," 58–60.

a "catholic" agenda for the world. According to the Pope, "missionary outreach is paradigmatic to all the church's activity."[18] Evangelization is a part of mission, not the other way around. Here we are confronted with a programmatic statement of the Papacy: the church cannot afford to stay in a "simple maintenance" mode—she needs to be in a "permanent state of mission," going out, being always engaged in involving others, and being constantly focused on reaching out.[19] Maintenance culture and self-referential attitudes are the "internal" enemies that Francis is willing to fight. The vision of Pope Francis is an outward one, and "mission" (whatever it may mean) is at the center of it. His church will not be on the defensive but will be proactively engaged in promoting its vision.

A Conversion of the Papacy?

In calling others to change, the Pope is also aware of the need for the Papacy to be converted. At times, some "ecclesial structures" may become a burden and should therefore be open to transformation.[20] In a telling passage, he goes as far as to say that he is willing to see a "conversion of the papacy."[21] For those who may wonder what this expression means, this conversion does not entail a deconstruction of the dogmatic outlook of the Papacy nor the radical questioning of the Papal claims about the Petrine office. It has to do more with how the Vatican bureaucracy functions than with the doctrinal substance of the Papacy. The document in fact speaks of "decentralization"[22] over against "excessive centralization"[23] or the growing role of the Episcopal Conferences.[24] There is no sign of "real" conversion of the Papacy in the biblical sense. The change that is foreseen is in the realm of internal church governance.

---

18. Francis, "Evangelii Gaudium," 15.
19. Francis, "Evangelii Gaudium," 25.
20. Francis, "Evangelii Gaudium," 26.
21. Francis, "Evangelii Gaudium," 32.
22. Francis, "Evangelii Gaudium," 16.
23. Francis, "Evangelii Gaudium," 32.
24. Francis, "Evangelii Gaudium," 32.

More Joy than Gospel

The word "joy" is repeated fifty-nine times and is the common theme of the document. The Pope wants to give a joyful flavor to mission. The gospel is also part of the title but has a lesser role in it. The "heart" of the gospel is summarized in this way: "the beauty of the saving love of God made manifest in Jesus Christ who died and rose from the dead."[25] In this apparently evangelical definition of the gospel, something is missing: while the objective good news of God is rightly related to the narrative of Jesus Christ, the subjective part of it (i.e., repentance from one's own sin and personal faith) is omitted. The tragedy of being lost without Jesus Christ is also downplayed. For this reason, nowhere in the document are unrepentant unbelievers called to repent and believe in Jesus Christ. Non-Catholic Christians are already united in baptism,[26] Jews don't need to convert,[27] and with believing Muslims the way is "dialogue" because "together with us they adore the one and merciful God."[28] Other non-Christians are also "justified by the grace of God" and are associated to "the paschal mystery of Jesus Christ."[29] The gospel appears not to be a message of salvation from God's judgment but instead access to a fuller measure of a salvation that is already given to all mankind. According to Francis, therefore, mission is the joyful willingness to extend the fullness of grace to the world that is already under grace.

Roman Catholicism in Pill Form

The document provides interesting comments by the Pope on preaching ("homily" in Catholic language),[30] special consideration for the poor,[31] and the "evangelizing power of popular piety,"[32] i.e., the various forms of the cult of the saints and Mary. What is even more noteworthy, however, is the section where Francis refers to various slogans that mark the

---

25. Francis, "Evangelii Gaudium," 36.
26. Francis, "Evangelii Gaudium," 244.
27. Francis, "Evangelii Gaudium," 247.
28. Francis, "Evangelii Gaudium," 252; a quotation from *Lumen Gentium*, 16.
29. Francis, "Evangelii Gaudium," 254.
30. Francis, "Evangelii Gaudium," 135–59.
31. Francis, "Evangelii Gaudium," 186–216.
32. Francis, "Evangelii Gaudium," 122–26.

Roman Catholic worldview as it opens up to the missionary task. Here are just two of them:

1. "Unity prevails over conflict."[33] The Pope encourages Catholics to find ways in which "conflicts, tensions, and oppositions can achieve a diversified and life-giving unity."[34] This resolution "takes place on a higher plane and preserves what is valid and useful on both sides" (idem). The "reconciled diversity" is the traditional *et-et* (both-and) approach that makes a synthesis of opposing views and beliefs, holding them in a "catholic" equilibrium.[35]

2. "The whole is greater than the parts."[36] The Pope here encourages Catholics to see the big picture of things. "The whole is greater than the part, but it is also greater than the sum of its parts."[37] This "principle of totality"[38] recalls another distinctive aspect of the Roman Catholic vision in that the Church is "a sign and instrument both of a very closely knit union with God and of the unity of the whole human race."[39]

A final question needs to be asked: is not the mission envisaged by Francis an attempt by the Roman Catholic Church to increase its catholicity and to expand its being the ultimate sign of unity for all mankind?

Laudato Si': A "Green" Pope? (July 1, 2015, Number 110)

As expected, the release of the encyclical *Laudato Si'* (*Praise Be to You*) by Pope Francis was acclaimed as a major contribution to the urgent need for a sustained effort in environmental care. Given the breadth of the issues discussed, with this document the Pope wishes to engage not only the Christians or the like-minded people but "every *person living* on this *planet*."[40] It is possible that *Laudato Si'* will have an echo in wider circles

---

33. Francis, "Evangelii Gaudium," 226–30.
34. Francis, "Evangelii Gaudium," 228.
35. Francis, "Evangelii Gaudium," 230.
36. Francis, "Evangelii Gaudium," 234–37.
37. Francis, "Evangelii Gaudium," 235.
38. Francis, "Evangelii Gaudium," 237.
39. Second Vatican Council, "Lumen Gentium," 1.
40. Francis, "Laudato Si,'" 3.

of public opinion (e.g., green movements and left-wing political sectors) and for a more prolonged time than a usual Papal encyclical. Certainly, it is the highest authoritative document that the present Pope has written so far, given that his 2013 first encyclical *Lumen Fidei* (*The Light of Faith*) was essentially drafted by his predecessor Benedict XVI and that his 2013 exhortation *Evangelii Gaudium* (*The Joy of the Gospel*) is hierarchically inferior in the ranking of magisterial documents. More than expounding traditional doctrinal points, Francis wants to underline widespread concerns and to show the open-mindedness of the Roman Catholic vision to address them. The reference to a well-known prayer by Francis of Assisi in the title reinforces the intention to recall a long tradition and to attract wide attention.

Environmental Concerns and Roman Catholic Emphases

In 192 pages (a fairly long length for an encyclical), six chapters, the usual invocation to Mary "the Mother and Queen of all creation," and two closing prayers, Pope Francis delineates his concerns for the deteriorating health of planet Earth and calls humanity to take action in order to stop the degenerating process. The remedy to the downgrade trajectory is the adoption of an "integral ecology" which will lead to a "sustainable and integral development." After analyzing what is happening at our "common home" in terms of pollution and climate change, access to water, loss of biodiversity, decline in the quality of human life, and global inequality, the Pope touches on the cultural and social distortions that cause the present-day ecological crisis (e.g., pervasive technocracy and distorted anthropocentrism) and suggests the "gospel of creation" based on "common good" principles and applied to the social and cultural levels as the solution for it.

The document strikes the chords of the widespread environmentalist mentality. At the same time, it is part and parcel of the Social Doctrine of the Roman Catholic Church. This means that its analyses and proposals are interspersed with typically Roman Catholic elements. For instance, apart from the Marian title of "Mother and Queen of creation," there is a strong sacramental language in the final part of the document whereby the Eucharist is presented as the "greatest exaltation" of creation: "Joined to the incarnate Son, present in the Eucharist, the whole cosmos gives thanks to God. Indeed, the Eucharist is itself an act of cosmic love." "In the bread of the Eucharist, creation is projected towards divinization, towards the holy wedding feast, towards unification with the Creator himself."[41] Another specific Catholic emphasis in calling for an "ecological conversion" is the insistence on the role of global agencies and organizations while there is little stress on personal conversion. In the Papal document sin has more social than individual dimensions. The thoroughgoing reference to the role of education in overcoming the ecological crisis tends to be more wishful humanistic thinking than a sober Christian comment that has a realist view of humanity's ability to deal with its problems.

Evangelical Parallel Resources

Laudato Si' will prove to be a useful reading to penetrate what is central in the Pope's vision: the poor, universal brotherhood, a sacramental vision of the world, and an appeal to the secular public opinion. In coming to terms with this encyclical, evangelicals should be aware of what their own tradition has already produced on these pressing issues.

The 1980 Lausanne Occasional Paper "An Evangelical Commitment to Simple Life-style"[42] is a compelling reminder of our biblical vocation to live soberly and to promote justice. The 2008 document by the World Evangelical Alliance "Statement on the Care of Creation"[43] tackles the challenges of being faithful stewards of God's creation in a biblically responsible way. Finally, the 2010 Cape Town Commitment[44] is a passionate call to a Christian lifestyle marked by humility, integrity, and simplicity.

These documents are much better grounded in the biblical doctrine of creation, the fall, and Christ's redemption than the Papal encyclical. They are also framed in the context of an evangelical concern for evangelism and mission, thus reflecting a more biblical and holistic approach than *Laudato Si'*. A comparative study between these evangelical documents and Francis's encyclical will be a good exercise for all those who want to come to terms with what the two main global Christian families are saying and doing about the environment.

---

41. Francis, "Laudato Si,'" 236.
42. Nichols, "Occasional Paper."
43. World Evangelical Alliance, "On the Care of Creation."
44. Lausanne Movement, "Cape Town Commitment."

Pope Francis Fears for the Planet, But Where Is the Gospel? (September 1, 2019, Number 166)

Europe, sovereignism (the "us-first" type of politics), migrants, glaciers, the Amazon . . . these are the topics covered in a recent interview[45] given by Pope Francis to the Italian daily newspaper *La Stampa* (August 8, 2019). It is a fairly long conversation that mirrors the concerns the Pope has in looking at today's global world: he begins with Europe and stretches to the Amazon, touching on social, political, environmental, and ecclesiastical issues. Some of the topics are politically controversial and divisive, even among the Roman Catholic constituency. Beyond confirming stances on which the Pope is strongly convinced, however, what is striking in the interview are his silences.

The Biggest Fear for the Planet

None of the things that Francis said were really new. There have been multiple occasions at all levels in which the Pope has expressed his views on sovereignist ideology ("it leads to war"), the populist tendency in the public opinion ("it leads to sovereignism"), the migrant issue (the four imperatives are to "receive," "accompany," "promote," and "integrate"), the exploitation of natural resources ("the Overshoot Day: On July 29th, we used up all the regenerative resources of 2019 . . . It's a global emergency"); the challenges that the Amazon region is facing ("deforestation means killing humanity," "the issue of open-cast mines which are poisoning water and causing so many diseases," "the issue of fertilizers," "the economic and political interests of society's dominant sectors").

These are all serious points, most of which the Pope touched on in his 2015 encyclical *Laudato Si*[46] on "care for our common home." They have to be thought through and acted upon. They are real emergencies. However, something is missing in the answers of the Pope. Reaching the climax of the interview, the question comes up: "Your Holiness, what do you fear most for our planet?" The Pope's answer is striking. Here it is: "The disappearance of biodiversity. New lethal diseases. A drift and devastation of nature that can lead to the death of humanity."[47]

---

45. Agasso, "Pope Francis Warns."
46. Francis, "Laudato Si."
47. Agasso, "Pope Francis Warns," para. 23.

The disappearance of biodiversity, new lethal diseases, and the devastation of nature. These are the things that the Pope fears the most for the world. Again, these are real and scary threats. But isn't there something missing from a Christian point of view? If Jesus were asked such a question, what would his response be? If Paul, John, Peter, and James were asked such a question, what would their response be? In the Pope's answer, there is no mention of Christ, sin, the cross, repentance, conversion, God's judgement, grace, the gospel. And yet he claims to be the "vicar of Christ"!

The question opened up wonderful opportunities to reply in such a way that those fears could be approached and framed in terms of the gospel, rather than in terms of a merely humanistic worldview. In what he said and what he didn't say, Pope Francis acted as if he were the spokesperson of a secular NGO focused on humanitarian and environmental issues, rather than a Christian who is passionate to tell the whole world the biblical message of God's creation, human sin, and redemption in Christ alone and to work out its implication for the church and the world.

Where Is Christ in All This?

Actually, Christ is not only missing in this answer—he is never mentioned in the whole interview. Greta Thunberg, the young ecologist activist, is referred to by name, but Jesus isn't. One might say: but the Pope wasn't asked direct questions about Christ. That's true, but it was a long interview with lots of questions, full of entry points for the gospel to be announced. These opportunities were all missed by the Pope. In reading the interview, the reader is not at all challenged by the gospel. He or she is instead alerted to some pressing environmental and political issues that an informed and cunning politician could have raised. Does his silence say tell something about the kind of "gospel" the Pope has in mind?

Expressing concerns for the Amazon region, the interviewer talked about the upcoming Roman Catholic Synod of Bishops for the Pan-Amazon that is going to take place at the end of October 2019. At this point the Pope shared what is going to be the highlight of the Synod: "The important thing will be the ministries of evangelisation and the different ways of evangelising."[48]

---

48. Agasso, "Pope Francis Warns," para. 20.

Evangelization and evangelizing. One is left wondering what evangelization even means to Francis. In the long interview the Pope does not spell it out. The only hint he gives is to "dialogue":

> This is crucial: starting from our own identity we must open to dialogue in order to receive something greater from the identity of others. Never forget that 'the whole is greater than the parts.' Globalisation, unity, should not be conceived as a sphere, but as a polyhedron: each people retains its identity in unity with others.[49]

This is what the Pope says: we open up dialogue in order to form a polycentric unity with the people we dialogue with. Again, there is no reference to the biblical content of the "good news" (i.e., the message of salvation in Jesus Christ), nor the biblical expectation that conversions to Christ will result out of dialogue. For the Pope, the outcome of dialogue is an expanded, polymorphic unity among people. In the Bible, however, evangelization entails dialogue but also proclamation, preaching, persuading, etc. (e.g., Acts 17:16–31). These elements are totally missing in the Pope's view of evangelization. Moreover, the Bible is also soberly aware that when and where evangelization takes place, some refuse the gospel and some believe it (e.g., Acts 17:32–34). No greater unity within humanity is expected, but the conversion of the lost is the goal of evangelism. This should be the greatest concern for all Christians: taking the gospel to the ends of the world so that those who believe in Jesus Christ will have eternal life. Unfortunately, this does not seem to be the Pope's vision, although he claims to be the highest representative of Christ on earth.

Querida Amazonia: A Reinforcement of Pope Francis's Missiology (March 1, 2020, Number 173)

Progressives were disappointed. Traditionalists were perplexed. In the end, *Querida Amazonia* (*Beloved Amazon*), the 2020 Apostolic Exhortation of Pope Francis following the Synod on the Pan-Amazon region, was neither the revolutionary push that many were fearful of nor the reaffirmation of the well-established Roman Catholic discourse on mission that others could have desired. *Querida Amazonia* was rather a reinforcement of Pope Francis's own missiology. Its tenets had been already enshrined in *Evangelii Gaudium*, with its call to his church to be "outgoing," and further affirmed in *Laudato Si'*, with its ecological concerns elevated to

---

49. Agasso, "Pope Francis Warns," para. 8.

missiological primary focus. In the latest Papal document, these threads are interwoven and more strongly knitted together as they are applied to the Amazon region. Initial reactions to it show the fact that the Pope did not go left or right but followed *his* path.

Different Expectations

As already mentioned, the Pope did not back up progressive voices expecting his approval for the consecration to the priesthood of the *viri probati* (married "men of proven virtue") and for women to join the diaconate. These measures had been foreshadowed in the Final Document of the Synod (*The Amazon: New Paths for the Church and for an Integral Ecology*),[50] but the Pope kept silent on them. Perhaps the silence was due to awareness of the fact that, if approved, they would have caused further disruption to a Roman Catholic Church already in turmoil. Both the celibacy of priests and the exclusion of women from the diaconate belong to the Latin tradition to which Rome is committed. Progressive sectors of the Roman Church (i.e., some Latin American bishops and the majority of the German bishops) supported the relaxation of the vetoes and the eventual admission of married men to the priesthood and of women to the diaconate. Pope Francis did not mention these points, although the Final Document of the Synod makes reference to them. In this respect, Francis wrote that he did not want his exhortation to replace or duplicate the Final Document[51]—indeed, he called the "entire Church" to apply it.[52] So, even though he does not treat the two critical points explicitly, the Final Document does, and his exhortation somehow validates it. Francis's silence is, at best, an ambiguous silence.

While breathing a sigh of relief for not seeing the intentional undoing of well-established traditions, Catholic conservatives were disturbed to find in the Papal document a powerful reaffirmation of some idiosyncratic elements of the "outgoing" missiology of the reigning Pope. Apparently weak in doctrinal emphases and overflowing with a "merciful" tone, the exhortation insists on globalist and nativist themes and focuses on the practice of theological and liturgical inculturation: twenty-five paragraphs are dedicated to inculturation, one-fourth of the whole document.

---

50. Synod of Bishops, "Amazon."
51. Francis, "Querida Amazonia," 2.
52. Francis, "Querida Amazonia," 4.

The kind of inculturation that is envisaged is basically open to syncretism with indigenous cultures. *Querida Amazonia* tends to have a very positive view of indigenous cultures—at times somewhat naïve—and in so doing it lacks biblical realism. According to the Bible, cultures are not to be idealized nor demonized: they are mixed bags of idolatry and common grace in need of redemption. Pope Francis tends to idealize native cultures, seeing them as already infused by the grace of God.

The Pope's "Dreams"

Querida Amazonia presents four dreams that the Pope has for the region. Talking about dreams is very evocative and emotionally engaging. First, Francis has a "social dream" in which he deals with themes such as injustice and crime, a sense of community, broken institutions, and social dialogue. Second, there is a reference to a "cultural dream" whereby the Pope talks about caring for roots, intercultural encounters, endangered cultures, and peoples at risk. Third, reference is made to an "ecological dream" in which the preservation of water reservoirs and the contemplation of the environment are treated together with the need for ecological education and habits. More than half of the document is dedicated to the first three dreams.

Finally, the Pope also has an "ecclesial dream." In this section he talks about the "message" that the Amazon region needs to hear. The gospel is summarized in this sentence:

> "God who infinitely loves every man and woman and has revealed this love fully in Jesus Christ, crucified for us and risen in our lives."[53]

This is the Papal *kerygma*. It is a message of love manifested in Jesus Christ who died and rose and lives in us. This is all biblically right though selective at best, flawed at worst. There is no reference to sin, the need for repentance and faith, salvation in Christ alone, God's holiness and righteousness in salvation and judgement, or the biblical framework of the Christian faith. Francis's gospel is a proclamation of a divine love that falls on all and is already in all. While it contains elements of the gospel, it is not the biblical gospel. Jesus' *kerygma* was "the kingdom of God is at hand: repent and believe in the gospel" (e.g., Mark 1:15). Here God's

---

53. Francis, "Querida Amazonia," 64.

action (i.e., his kingdom) and man's lostness (i.e., our need to repent) are explicitly stated and interwoven. The need to believe in the gospel is also essential, and that implies a transition, a conversion on our part. Without it we are lost and continue to be lost. Unlike the Pope's truncated message, this is the biblical *kerygma*.

It is true that the Pope encourages readers of *Querida Amazonia* to refer to "the brief summary of this great message found in Chapter Four of the Exhortation *Christus Vivit*," i.e., the 2019 document issued after the Vatican Synod on the young people. Even there, the gospel is summarized under three headings: "God is love; Christ saves you; the Spirit gives life." The outlook is Trinitarian, but the content misses the reference to our sinful condition and our responsibility to respond in repentance and faith to God's love. Again, the Papal gospel looks like an objective and historical message, although void of covenantal premises and consequences, i.e., God's righteous judgement on sinners. It seems that all have already received God's love and are saved by Christ and live in the Spirit. Is this universalist message what the biblical gospel teaches? Given the fact that *Querida Amazonia* is addressed to "all persons of good will," therefore Christians and non-Christians alike, the ambiguity of the account of the gospel contained in the exhortation is even more striking. The non-Christian reader of the document is not challenged to repent and believe but is assured that God is love in spite of what she/he believes and stands for.[54]

A Word to Evangelicals: "All This Unites Us"?

In the final paragraphs, *Querida Amazonia* makes reference to "ecumenical co-existence," i.e., a word to evangelicals and Pentecostals who have become a strong presence in the Amazon region, subtracting people and influence from the Roman Catholic Church. After having summarized his account of the kerygma, Francis writes:

> "All this unites us. How can we not struggle together? How can we not pray and work together, side by side, to defend the poor of the Amazon region, to show the sacred countenance of the Lord, and to care for his work of creation?"[55]

---

54. Francis, "Querida Amazonia," 109.
55. Francis, "Querida Amazonia," 110.

Does all this unite us? If "all this" refers to the Papal gospel as it is presented earlier, the answer is no. Many words and themes are the same, but they are understood and lived out differently, and what is missing is as important as what is said. Then, the Pope invites evangelicals and Catholics to "pray and work" together. These two activities do not overlap and need to be distinguished. Certainly, there is room for "co-belligerence,"[56] i.e., common action in advocating for the poor and caring for creation. This is both possible and necessary, open to all peoples sharing these concerns. However, common prayer is a spiritual activity requiring unity in the biblical gospel and involvement from born-again Christians.

Does all this unite us? What comes after adds further reasons to answer in the negative. The following paragraph is a heartfelt invocation to Mary by Pope Francis:

> Mother whose heart is pierced, who yourself suffer in your mistreated sons and daughters, and in the wounds inflicted on nature, reign in the Amazon, together with your Son. Reign so that no one else can claim lordship over the handiwork of God. We trust in you, Mother of life. Do not abandon us in this dark hour.[57]

Why is the Pope so selective and ambiguous in the presentation of the biblical gospel, and why does he spend so many words in the invocation to Mary? Does all this unite evangelicals and Roman Catholics? No. Is a truncated *kerygma* and an invocation to Mary (who is said to reign and in whom we are called to trust) the foundation for being united in the gospel? No. After all, *Querida Amazonia* consolidates the blurred and confusing missiology of Pope Francis.

Towards a Politically Correct Apologetics? (October 3, 2013, Number 66)

Secular people and media are praising Pope Francis for being open to "dialogue" with the modern world in a way that is personally engaging and fresh in style. On his side, the Pope is taking more and more pleasure in entertaining editors, journalists, and opinion-makers with interviews, personal meetings, and direct phone calls. The last instance of such Papal strategy for communication is a long interview that was published on

---

56. Search "co-belligerence" at vaticanfiles.org: https://vaticanfiles.org/it/?s=co-belligerence.

57. Francis, "Querida Amazonia," 110.

October 1 by the Italian daily newspaper *La Repubblica*, with its former editor Eugenio Scalfari, an outspoken atheist. The interview follows an exchange of letters and a personal meeting between the two men.

What seems to emerge from all these pieces is a specific apologetic strategy by Francis. Here are three steps that form the apologetic backbone of what the Pope said in the course of the conversation and few biblical remarks about them.

First Step: Disparaging Proselytism to Avoid the Hard Question About Conversion

At the beginning of the conversation, Scalfari says, "My friends think you want to convert me," and here is how Francis replies: "Proselytism is solemn nonsense, it makes no sense. We need to get to know each other, listen to each other and improve our knowledge of the world around us. Sometimes after a meeting I want to arrange another one because new ideas are born and I discover new needs. This is important: to get to know people, listen, expand the circle of ideas."[58]

As is well known, proselytism is a "bad" word and has an even worse press. It is associated with fanaticism, unethical methods, and religious extremism. The Pope wants to reaffirm the negative understanding of it, and in so doing he wants to build a bridge with his secular interlocutor, who has a terrible opinion of it. Notice, though, that Scalfari had not asked his opinion on proselytism. He wanted to know if the Pope desired his conversion. Instead of answering, Francis speaks of proselytism, knowing that Scalfari agrees with him. Is it ethical for a Christian not to give an answer about his conversion? Is not conversion a biblical word? Is not conversion the goal that should inspire all Christian mission? Moreover, Francis's description of what it means for a Christian to engage in dialogue is a biblically flawed account. He speaks of "knowing, listening, expanding the circle of ideas," but what about telling, witnessing, preaching, proclaiming the good news? In Athens, the apostle Paul did the former but also the latter (Acts 17:16–31). Why does Francis affirm the former and omit the latter?

---

58. Scalfari, "Pope," para. 9.

Second Step: Offering a "Lovely" Summary of the Gospel to Soften the Secular Prejudices

In the course of the conversation, the Pope provides a summary of the gospel that suits the expectations of the secular intellectual. Here it is: "The Son of God became incarnate in the souls of men to instill the feeling of brotherhood. All are brothers and all children of God."[59] A little later he says, "Agape, the love of each one of us for the other, from the closest to the furthest, is in fact the only way that Jesus has given us to find the way of salvation and of the Beatitudes."[60]

Strangely enough, this language is very similar to the old liberal account of the gospel: a God of love wishing the brotherhood of all men. According to theological liberalism, this is the "essence" of Christianity. But, biblically speaking, it is not. In this summary there is no reference to justice, sin, judgment, atonement, death and resurrection, conversion . . . not surprisingly words that are unpalatable to the secular mind. Is not the summary offered by the Pope at best a seriously truncated gospel, at worst *another* gospel? Is pleasing the dialogue partner and matching his expectations the primary task of apologetics?

Third Step: Reinforcing the Role of the Individual Conscience to Eschew Confrontation

At another point, Scalfari asks, "Is there is a single vision of the Good? And who decides what it is?" Here is Francis's reply: "Each of us has a vision of good and of evil. We have to encourage people to move towards what they think is Good." Scalfari: "You wrote that in your letter to me. The conscience is autonomous, you said, and everyone must obey his conscience. I think that's one of the most courageous steps taken by a Pope." Francis: "And I repeat it here. Everyone has his own idea of good and evil and must choose to follow the good and fight evil as he conceives them."[61]

The Pope agrees that "the conscience is autonomous" and following its indications is one's own task. No reference, however, to the lies that subjugate the conscience and to sin that mars it. No reference to

---

59. Scalfari, "Pope," para. 15.
60. Scalfari, "Pope," para. 15.
61. Scalfari, "Pope," para. 10.

the guilty conscience or the misguided one that needs the power of the gospel to free it from bondage.

Later on, Scalfari asks, "Do you feel touched by grace?" Francis: "No one can know that. Grace is not part of consciousness, it is the amount of light in our souls, not knowledge nor reason. Even you, without knowing it, could be touched by grace." Scalfari: "Without faith? A non-believer?" Francis: "Grace regards the soul."[62]

Is grace really an experience beyond knowledge, reason, and even faith? Are all men, for their being men, already graced, even without knowing it and without believing in the biblical God? To this question the Bible would say no (e.g., Eph 2:1–10).

The dialogue was politically correct, and the outcome of the conversation was the following: the secular thinker is no longer nervous about his need to be converted. He is also confirmed in the idea that the gospel is about love and human brotherhood. He is also reinforced in his conviction that his conscience is what really matters. Unfortunately, the Pope seems to agree on all three points. Is this good apologetics?

Mission. Did Pope Francis Say Mission? (January 1, 2018, Number 145)

"Throughout the world, let us be permanently in a state of mission."[63] These programmatic words epitomize the missionary vision that Pope Francis has been expounding and implementing since becoming Pope in 2013. Without a doubt, mission is central to his thought and action and is a defining mark of his pontificate. Having said that, it is not always clear what he means when he talks about "mission." Indeed, in today's religious language, "mission" is one of those words which can have multiple "shades of gray," and discovering its meaning can become a conundrum. Pope Francis adds his own complexities and nuances to the already variegated semantic range of the word "mission."

The recent Papal journey to Myanmar and Bangladesh (November 28–30) provides an entry point into the applied missiology of the Pope. Here Francis was visiting two countries where Christians are minorities and where mission, however definable, is the top priority of the church.

---

62. Scalfari, "Pope," para. 36.
63. Francis, "Evangelii Gaudium," 25.

What a great opportunity for him to embody and exemplify the vigorous call to his church to be permanently "in a state of mission"!

Omitting to Speak of Christ?

What took place there—or, should we say, what did not take place—sheds light on the whole issue. The Pope's public speeches were about peace and harmony, solidarity, and dialogue and were centered on a generic faith in "God" which could have been understood in all kinds of ways. Any references to Jesus Christ were omitted. As Italian journalist Sandro Magister put it:

> There was only one moment in which Jesus was named and his Gospel proclaimed, in the speeches on the first day of Pope Francis's visit to Myanmar. Only that the one who spoke these words was not the pope, but the Burmese state counsellor and foreign minister Aung San Suu Kyi, who is of the Buddhist faith.[64]

This is a strange way of doing mission, one might think. The gospel was vaguely proclaimed by a Buddhist politician rather than by the Pope. As far as Francis is concerned, important omissions of this kind are not new. For example, acute observers like Chris Castaldo have already pointed out the lack of Christ-related language in other public speeches.[65] In 2015, visiting US Congress[66] and the United Nations,[67] the Pope delivered Christ-less speeches, however interfaith and ecumenically friendly they were. As Castaldo soberly commented, "Sadly, he failed to do so much as mention the name 'Jesus' or 'Christ.'"[68]

This omission looks like a pattern in Francis's mission. It is true that even the apostle Paul in the Areopagus speech at Athens did not explicitly mention the name of Jesus Christ, though he referred to the "man" (Acts 17:31), which is a clear reference to the Lord Jesus, the risen One and the coming Judge. Paul's speech, nonetheless, challenged the belief system of his hearers and presented the reality of God's righteous judgment overall, calling people to repent. All these elements also seem to be missing in the Pope's missiology. When he is in interfaith and political

64. Magister, "Pope in Mission Territory," para. 1.
65. Costaldo, "Why I Am Disappointed."
66. "Transcript: Speech to Congress."
67. "Transcript: Remarks to the United Nations."
68. Costaldo, "Why I Am Disappointed," para. 1.

contexts, he seems reluctant to boldly and clearly proclaim the name of Jesus as the only Savior and Lord. Unlike Paul the missionary, who faced pushback and criticism because of his presentation of the gospel, Francis is normally liked by his hearers, who feel affirmed in what they already believe rather than challenged by the message of Jesus Christ. What kind of mission are we talking about then?

Mission Without Apologetics?

Is this critical assessment based on reading too much into the Pope's gospel omissions? One way of answering this question is to allow the Pope to speak for himself in explaining his missionary vision. Luckily, in flying back from Myanmar and Bangladesh, Francis gave a telling comment on what had just happened. Here is the script of the in-flight press conference,[69] during which Francis replied to a question posed by a French journalist. The Q&A is worth quoting at length:

> Etienne Loraillere (KTO): Holiness, there is a question from the group of journalists from France. Some are opposed to inter-religious dialogue and evangelization. During this trip you have spoken of dialogue for building peace. But, what is the priority? Evangelizing or dialoguing for peace? Because to evangelize means bringing about conversions that provoke tension and sometimes provoke conflicts between believers. So, what is the priority, evangelizing or dialoguing? Thanks.
>
> Pope Francis: First distinction: evangelizing is not making proselytism. The Church grows not for proselytism but for attraction, that is for testimony, this was said by Pope Benedict XVI. What is evangelization like? Living the Gospel and bearing witness to how one lives the Gospel, witnessing to the Beatitudes, giving testimony to Matthew 25, the Good Samaritan, forgiving 70 times 7 and in this witness the Holy Spirit works and there are conversions, but we are not very enthusiastic to make conversions immediately. If they come, they wait, you speak, your tradition... seeking that a conversion be the answer to something that the Holy Spirit has moved in my heart before the witness of the Christians.
>
> During the lunch I had with the young people at World Youth Day in Krakow, 15 or so young people from the entire world, one of them asked me this question: what do I have to

---

69. Francis, "Press Conference from Bangladesh."

say to a classmate at the university, a friend, good, but he is atheist . . . what do I have to say to change him, to convert him? The answer was this: the last thing you have to do is say something. You live your Gospel and if he asks you why you do this, you can explain why you do it. And let the Holy Spirit activate him. This is the strength and the meekness of the Holy Spirit in the conversion. It is not a mental convincing, with apologetics, with reasons, it is the Spirit that makes the vocation. We are witnesses, witnesses of the Gospel. "Testimony" is a Greek word that means martyr. Every day martyrdom, martyrdom also of blood, when it arrives. And your question: What is the priority, peace or conversion? But when you live with testimony and respect, you make peace. Peace starts to break down in this field when proselytism begins and there are so many ways of proselytism and this is not the Gospel. I don't know if I answered.[70]

With this answer one is projected into the missiological vision of the Pope. Let's briefly mention its main points. First, there is a negative reference to proselytism without defining it. As it stands, his words discourage the expectation for conversions and put a stigma on the missionary activity that looks forward to seeing people embracing Christ out of their religious or secular background (see instead Mark 1:15; Acts 2:37–38). Second, there is an unnecessary polarization between good deeds/attitudes and the verbal proclamation of the gospel. Nowhere in the Bible is such a polarization between the content of the message and the behavior of the messenger maintained. We are instead called to always join what we say, what we do, and how we do it (e.g., 1 Pet 3:15–17). Third, there is a distrust of apologetics in dealing with unbelief. The missionary is not expected to give reasons for what she believes and to challenge the belief system of her friend. In this way, the Pope seems to discourage engaging in meaningful apologetics (evidently against 1 Pet 3:15).

According to Pope Francis then, mission does not look forward to making disciples, refrains from verbally proclaiming the good news, and is skeptical about apologetics. How different this is to the standard evangelical understanding of evangelization given by the 1974 Lausanne Covenant:

> To evangelize is to spread the good news that Jesus Christ died for our sins and was raised from the dead according to the Scriptures, and that as the reigning Lord he now offers the forgiveness of sins and the liberating gifts of the Spirit to all who repent and believe. Our Christian presence in the world is indispensable to

70. Francis, "Press Conference from Bangladesh."

evangelism, and so is that kind of dialogue whose purpose is to listen sensitively in order to understand. But evangelism itself is the proclamation of the historical, biblical Christ as Savior and Lord, with a view to persuading people to come to him personally and so be reconciled to God. In issuing the gospel invitation we have no liberty to conceal the cost of discipleship. Jesus still calls all who would follow him to deny themselves, take up their cross, and identify themselves with his new community. The results of evangelism include obedience to Christ, incorporation into his Church and responsible service in the world.[71]

In this evangelical definition, almost everything the Pope warns against is instead strongly affirmed: the verbal proclamation of the gospel of Jesus Christ and the necessity of Christian persuasion in the context of lives marked by integrity. This is not what Pope Francis has in mind when he refers to mission.

"Baptized and Sent": Is This the Biblical Mission? (November 1, 2019, Number 169)

"Baptized and Sent: The Church of Christ on Mission in the World."[72] This is the theme chosen by Pope Francis for the Missionary Month that he called for this past June. "For the month of October 2019," he said in the homily that opened the month on October 1st, "I ask the whole Church to live an extraordinary time of missionary activity."[73]

This special initiative marked the 100th anniversary of Pope Benedict XV's apostolic letter *Maximum Illud*,[74] a document on the church's mission to the world, and was run in conjunction with the Synod of Bishops of the Pan-Amazon region. Pope Francis argued that "It will help us in our mission," which is not about spreading a "religious ideology" or a "lofty ethical teaching." Instead, he continued, "through the mission of the Church, Jesus Christ himself continues to evangelize and act; her mission thus makes present in history the *Kairos*, the favorable time of salvation."

The Message by Pope Francis for World Mission Day (20th October) contains some important aspects of Roman Catholic missiology

---

71. Lausanne Movement, "The Lausanne Covenant," para. 4.
72. Francis, "Message for World Mission Day."
73. Francis, "Homily (Vatican Basilica)."
74. Benedict XV, "Maximum Illud."

that deserve critical attention, especially on the importance that Rome attributes to baptism for mission.[75]

Is Baptism the Foundation of Mission?

The title of the Message indicates a causative link between baptism and mission. The background of the Pope's appeal to a renewed missionary effort by his church is given by the presentation of the standard Roman doctrine of baptism and by extension, of the sacramental life. Mission begins with a sacrament and unfolds in a sacramental journey. This is what the Pope said:

> This life is bestowed on us in baptism, which grants us the gift of faith in Jesus Christ, the conqueror of sin and death. Baptism gives us rebirth in God's own image and likeness, and makes us members of the Body of Christ, which is the Church. In this sense, baptism is truly necessary for salvation for it ensures that we are always and everywhere sons and daughters in the house of the Father, and never orphans, strangers or slaves. What in the Christian is a sacramental reality—whose fulfillment is found in the Eucharist—remains the vocation and destiny of every man and woman in search of conversion and salvation. For baptism fulfils the promise of the gift of God that makes everyone a son or daughter in the Son. We are children of our natural parents, but in baptism we receive the origin of all fatherhood and true motherhood: no one can have God for a Father who does not have the Church for a mother (cf. Saint Cyprian, De Cath. Eccl., 6).[76]

Here we find the traditional Roman Catholic view of baptism in a nutshell. Baptism is thought of as bestowing the gift of faith, giving new birth, incorporating into the church, granting salvation, enacting adoption, making accessible the promise of God, and making it possible to enter into the sacramental reality which finds its climax in the Eucharist. The church administers God's grace through the sacrament of baptism and nurtures it through the sacrament of the Eucharist. In the Roman Catholic view, this sacramental life, beginning with baptism, is what is offered in mission to all people.

In passing, notice that even when Rome speaks the seemingly evangelical language of mission, it does so in its own sacramental

---

75. Francis, "Message for World Mission Day."
76. Francis, "Message for World Mission Day," 5.

understanding. Baptism, and therefore the sacraments, and therefore the church, are central to the Roman Catholic gospel. Rome cannot be and will never be committed to the gospel truth that salvation is by faith alone. One is not saved by believing in Jesus Christ as Lord and Savior but by receiving the sacrament of baptism by the church. Rome finds it hard to accept the straightforward biblical message that "if you confess with your mouth that Jesus is Lord and believe in your heart that God raised him from the dead, you will be saved. For with the heart one believes and is justified, and with the mouth one confesses and is saved" (Rom 10:9–10). Whatever view of baptism churches might hold (and notoriously, Protestants disagree on the meaning of baptism), the gospel is clear that it is by confessing and believing (in other words, by faith and by faith alone) that one is saved.

"Every baptized man and woman is a mission."

According to Francis, then, mission stems from baptism. One is sent into mission because he/she is baptized. One who is baptized is a missionary by definition. Here is what he said to reinforce the point: "Our mission is rooted in the fatherhood of God and the motherhood of the Church. The mandate given by the Risen Jesus at Easter is inherent in Baptism."[77] In this Roman Catholic view, there is something intrinsic and objective in baptism that makes it foundational to the missionary mandate. This conviction was further elaborated when Francis affirmed:

> Today too, the Church needs men and women who, by virtue of their baptism, respond generously to the call to leave behind home, family, country, language and local Church, and to be sent forth to the nations, to a world not yet transformed by the sacraments of Jesus Christ and his holy Church.[78]

"By virtue of their baptism" people become missionaries, thus the theme of the Missionary Month: "Baptized and Sent." Later Pope Francis made the point again when he said, "Every baptized man and woman is a mission." So, mission is rooted in baptism, and the missionary calling derives from baptism. Once baptized, one is sent.

There are severe problems here. First, baptism, i.e., a sacrament of the church, is elevated to an importance that makes personal faith second;

77. Francis, "Message for World Mission Day," 6.
78. Francis, "Message for World Mission Day," 7.

it therefore highlights the centrality of the institution that administers it and the physical objects that the church uses (i.e., water), rather than the personal response to the gospel of Jesus Christ.

Secondly, most baptized people in the Catholic Church don't show any evidence of this missionary awareness; indeed, many don't believe in the biblical gospel at all. Many Catholics in majority-Catholic contexts have never professed a personal faith in the biblical Jesus and fall short of any biblical qualifications to be missionaries because they are not believers in Jesus Christ in the first place! How is it possible to maintain such a view that runs contrary to Scripture and the empirical evidence? From both theological and sociological grounds, the link between baptism and mission is not causal and linear as the Pope thinks.

Again, Rom 10 is helpful here: "How then will they call on him in whom they have not believed? And how are they to believe in him of whom they have never heard? And how are they to hear without someone preaching? And how are they to preach unless they are sent?" (10:14–15). The Bible teaches that mission requires *believers* in Jesus Christ to be sent, not baptized people by the church. This is a significantly *different* view than that of Pope Francis! One wonders if the link between baptism and mission actually suffocates the gospel rather than propelling it.

The language of Roman Catholic missiology may look like the evangelical understanding of it but, despite the common language, the theological meaning of the words and the overall theological framework are different. The Roman Catholic Missionary Month promoted by Pope Francis is not good news for evangelical mission.

"All Brothers": The Unbearable Cost of Roman Catholic Universalism (November 1, 2020, Number 181)

It has been rightly called the "political manifesto" of Pope Francis's pontificate. In fact, there is a lot of politics and a lot of sociology in the new encyclical *All Brothers*,[79] a very long document (130 pages) that looks more like a book than a letter. Francis wants to plead the cause of universal fraternity and social friendship. To do this, he speaks of borders to be broken down, of waste to be avoided, of human rights that are not sufficiently universal, of unjust globalization, of burdensome pandemics,

---

79. Francis, "Fratelli Tutti."

of migrants to be welcomed, of open societies, of solidarity, of peoples' rights, of local and global exchanges, of the limits of the liberal political vision, of world governance, of political love, of the recognition of the other, of the injustice of any war, of the abolition of the death penalty. These are all interesting "political" themes which, were it not for some comments on the parable of the good Samaritan that intersperse the chapters, could have been written by a group of sociologists and humanitarian workers from some international organization, perhaps after reading, for example, Edgar Morin and Zygmunt Bauman.

Much Politics, Little Theology

These are the themes that Pope Francis has disseminated in many speeches and in his other encyclical, *Laudato Si'*,[80] on the care for the environment. Not surprisingly, he himself is by far the most cited author in the work (about 180 times), which evidences the circular trend of his thinking (the need to be self-strengthening) and the "novelty" of his teaching with respect to the traditional themes of the social doctrine of the Roman Catholic Church. The vision proposed by *All Brothers* is the way in which Rome sees globalization with the eye of a South American Jesuit Pope.

It is only in the eighth (last) chapter of the encyclical that the Pope deals with the theme of fraternity with religions, and here the document becomes more "theological." This section can be considered to be an interpretation of the "Document on Human Fraternity for World Peace and Living Together" that Francis himself signed in Abu Dhabi with the Grand Imam of Al-Azhar Ahmad Al-Tayyeb in 2019.[81] More than just a reflection, this section is a jumble of quotations (better: self-quotations) which, by overlapping plans and juxtaposing issues, end up confusing rather than clarifying. Despite this, its basic message is sufficiently clear: we are all brothers as children of the same God. This is Pope Francis's theological truth. The best comment on this aspect of the encyclical comes from Judge Mohamed Mahmoud Abdel Salam, who spoke at the official presentation at the Vatican. Here is what he said: "As a young Muslim scholar of Shari'a (law), Islam, and its sciences, I find myself—with much love and enthusiasm—in agreement with the Pope, and I share

---

80. Francis, "Laudato Si'."
81. Francis and Al-Tayyeb, *Document on Human Fraternity*.

every word he has written in the encyclical. I follow, with satisfaction and hope, all his proposals put forward in a spirit of concern for the rebirth of human fraternity."[82] If a convinced and sincere Muslim shares "every word" of the Pope, it means that the writing is deist, at best theistic, but not in line with biblical and Trinitarian Christianity.

When *All Brothers* talks about God, it does so in general terms that can fit Muslim, Hindu, and other religions' accounts of god, as well as the Masonic reference to the Watchmaker. To further confirm this, *All Brothers* ends with a "Prayer to the Creator" that could be used both in a mosque and in a Masonic temple. Having removed the "stumbling block" of Jesus Christ, everyone can turn to an unspecified divinity to experiment with what it means to be "brothers"—brothers in a divinity made in the image and likeness of humanity, not brothers and sisters on the basis of the work of Jesus Christ, who has died and risen for sinners. *All Brothers* has genetically modified the biblically understood meaning of fraternity by transferring it to common humanity.[83] In doing so, it has lost the biblical boundaries of the word and replaced them with pan-religious traits and contents. Is this a service to the gospel of Jesus Christ?

What Is at Stake Theologically?

Many people, the vast majority of people, will not read Pope Francis's long encyclical *All Brothers*. They will only hear a few sentences or lines repeated here and there as slogans. However, what everyone will retain lies in the effective opening of the document: "All brothers"—we are all brothers (and sisters). It is a very powerful universalist and inclusive message that communicates the idea that the lines of demarcation between believers and nonbelievers, atheists and agnostics, Muslims and Christians, evangelicals and Catholics, are all so fluid and relative that they do not undermine the bonds of fraternity that they all share. The French Revolution had already launched "fraternity" as a secular belonging to human citizenship (together with "freedom" and "equality"), but now the Pope defines it in a theological sense. We are "brothers" not because we are citizens but as children of the same God. According to Pope Francis, we are all children of God, therefore brothers and sisters among us.

---

82. Holy See, "Conference on the Encyclical Letter 'Fratelli Tutti.'"
83. De Chirico, "Vatican File 86."

In *All Brothers* there is the understandable anxiety aimed at dissolving conflicts, overcoming injustices, and stopping wars. This concern is commendable, even if the analyses and proposals are political and therefore can be legitimately discussed. What is problematic is the theological key chosen to overcome divisions: the declaration of human fraternity in the name of the divine sonship of all humanity. The Pope uses a theological category ("all brothers as all children of God") to create the conditions for a better world.

What are the theological implications of such a statement? Here are a few. Firstly, *All Brothers* raises a soteriological question. If we are all brothers as we are all children of God, does this mean that all will be saved? The whole encyclical is pervaded by a powerful universalist inspiration that also includes atheists.[84] Religions in the broad sense are always presented in a positive sense, and there is no mention of a biblical criticism of religions nor of the need for repentance and faith in Jesus Christ as the key to receiving salvation.[85] Everything in the encyclical suggests that everyone, as brothers and sisters, will be saved.

Then there is a christological issue. Even though Jesus Christ is referred to here and there, his exclusive and "offensive" claims are kept silent. Francis wisely presents Jesus Christ not as the "cornerstone" on which the whole building of life stands or collapses but as the stone only for those who recognize him. Above Jesus Christ, according to the encyclical, there is a "God" who is the father of all. We are children of this "God," even without recognizing Jesus Christ as Lord and Savior. Jesus is thus reduced to the rank of the champion of Christians alone, while the other "brothers" are still children of the same "God," regardless of faith in Jesus Christ.

Thirdly, there is an ecclesiological issue. If we are all "brothers," there is a sense in which we are all part of the same church that gathers brothers and sisters together. The boundaries between humanity and church are so nonexistent that the two communities become coincident. Humanity is the church and the church is humanity. This is in line with the sacramental vision of the Roman Catholic Church which, according to Vatican II, is understood as a "sign and instrument of the unity of the whole human race."[86] According to the encyclical, the whole of the hu-

---

84. Francis, "Fratelli Tutti," 281.
85. Francis, "Fratelli Tutti," 277–79.
86. Second Vatican Council, "Lumen Gentium," 1.

man race belongs to the church not on the basis of faith in Jesus Christ but on the basis of a shared divine sonship and human fraternity.

The theological cost of *All Brothers* is enormous. The message that it sends is biblically devastating. The public opinion inside and outside the Roman Catholic Church will see the consolidation of the idea that God ultimately saves everyone, that Jesus Christ is one among many, and that the church is inclusive of all on the basis of a common and shared humanity, not on the basis of repentance and faith in Jesus Christ. This is *not* the gospel of Jesus Christ.

Roman Catholic Ecumenism Embraces the Whole World

The tragic irony of this Pope is that if, on the one hand, he presents himself as the herald of the relaunch of "mission" and the "church which goes forth," on the other hand, he is the pope who, with his Jesuit ambiguity and now with his Roman Catholic universalism, has made authentic Christian mission more complicated than it was. He uses the words "mission," "announcement," and "missionary church," but he has emptied them of their evangelical meaning, removing their biblical reference and filling them with empty and harmless content. *All Brothers* shows that the mission that Pope Francis has in mind is not the preaching of the gospel in words and deeds but the extension to all a message of universal fraternity.

After the Council of Trent (1545–63) and up to Vatican II (1962–65), Roman Catholicism related to the "others" (be they Protestants, other religions, or different cultural and social movements) through its "Roman" claims and called them to return to the fold. The "brothers" were only Roman Catholics in communion with the Roman Pope. The others were "pagans," "heretics," and "schismatics": excluded from sacramental grace, which is accessible only through the hierarchical system of the Roman Catholic Church. With Vatican II, it was Rome's "catholicity" that prevailed over its "Roman" centeredness. Protestants have become "separated brothers," other religions have been viewed positively, people in general have been approached as "anonymous Christians." Now, according to Francis's encyclical, we are "all brothers." The expansion of catholicity has been further stretched. From being excluded from the "Roman" side of Rome, we are now all included by the "catholic" side of Rome.

After *All Brothers*, will evangelicals better understand that Roman Catholic ecumenism is within an even greater plan that embraces everyone and everything so that the whole world comes *cum et sub Petro* (with and under Peter, the Roman center)?

"The Diversity of Religions is the Will of God." A Window into Pope Francis's Theology of Religions (May 1, 2025, Number 240)

Many Roman Catholics raised their eyebrows when they read, "The pluralism and the diversity of religions, color, sex, race, and language are willed by God in His wisdom, through which He created human beings." The one who was saying this was Pope Francis in the 2019 Abu Dhabi Statement on "Human Fraternity for World Peace and Living Together," co-signed with Ahmad Al-Tayyeb, the Grand Imam of Al-Azhar.[87]

That God willed (and therefore created) the diversity of color, sex, and race is unquestionable: these are all good traits of God's creation. One could argue that as far as language is concerned, the account of the tower of Babel (Gen 9) should be taken into account to realize that the multiplicity of languages is also the result of sin. But what about the diversity of religions? Is it really the will of God that men and women should worship gods and goddesses other than the One and True God, i.e., the Triune God of the Bible? The straightforward biblical answer is no. Period. However, Pope Francis says yes.

How is it possible? Does the Roman Catholic Church now accept that all religions lead to God? Where does this new view of religions come from? These are all legitimate questions. According to Alberto Caccaro,[88] in order to grasp the present-day theological debate on religions within Roman Catholicism, one needs to be aware of the work of the Jesuit theologian Jacques Dupuis (1923–2004). This Belgian theologian, who spent part of his life as a missionary in India, is an important voice that forms the Pope's theological framework. Pope Francis, himself a Jesuit, does not quote him either in the Abu Dhabi Statement or in the encyclical *All Brothers*[89] on fraternity among all peoples, but Dupuis's thoughts are part of the backbone of his positive and "fraternal" approach to religions.

Questioning the existing models for thinking about the role of religions (i.e., exclusivism = Christ excludes other religions; inclusivism =

---

87. Francis and Al-Tayyeb, *Human Fraternity for World Peace*.
88. Caccaro, *Jacques Dupuis*.
89. De Chirico, "Vatican File 181."

Christ includes all religions; pluralism = Christ is one among many religions), Dupuis explored new "frontiers" in light of what he believed to be the "surplus" of the mystery of Christ over the linguistic and institutional forms of Christianity. His theology of religious pluralism was a response to what he considered an oversimplification of traditional accounts and an invitation to rework Christology by recognizing the "space" of religions as a constitutive part of Christ and the gospel. In Dupuis's view, religions are convergent and complementary mediations of salvation, and therefore the task of theology is to elaborate a Christology of religions that corresponds to their role.

This study by Caccaro, a Roman Catholic theologian and missionary working in Cambodia, takes up the themes of Dupuis's reflection precisely from the christological question and considers Dupuis's three books on the subject: *Jesus Christ at the Encounter of World Religions*,[90] *Towards a Christian Theology of Religious Pluralism*,[91] and *Christianity and the Religions. From Confrontation to Dialogue*.[92]

These works caused debate not only in the theological academies but also in the Vatican Congregation for the Doctrine of Faith (at the time presided over by Cardinal Joseph Ratzinger), so much so that the congregation sent him a "notification," a yellow card for having entered minefield territory, for "serious doctrinal errors" and "ambiguities" in his thinking. Although it generated some heat, this "notification" had no disciplinary outcome. After Dupuis's death, the trial was dropped.

In Dupuis's thought, the distinction between *Logos énsarkos* (incarnate Word) and *Logos ásarkos* (non-incarnate Word) is central. While the former coincides with the person of Jesus Christ and the biblical account of him and his work, the latter is by its very nature open, spacious, and irreducible to any closed codification. On the side of the Holy Spirit, while the Spirit of Christ is associated with the historical person of the God-man Jesus (i.e., the hypostatic union), the Spirit of God "blows where He wills"—and possibly in all religions.

As a Roman Catholic theologian, Dupuis glimpses the problems raised by these insights, and in his theology, one can see the struggle to keep Christology anchored to the incarnate Person of Jesus Christ while opening the non-incarnate Logos to accommodating and welcoming the different religions. The underlying question is, Can one find salvation

---

90. Dupuis, *Jesus Christ at the Encounter*.
91. Dupuis, *Theology of Religious Pluralism*.
92. Dupuis, *Christianity and the Religions*.

beyond the historical and embodied revelation of Jesus Christ? If yes, as argued by Dupuis, there is room for "differentiated and complementary revelation" and salvation offered by other religions, since Dupuis wants to affirm both that Jesus Christ is the final revelation in his embodied Person and the possibility for other religions to be revelatory and salvific in his non-incarnate reality. Roman Catholic theology, a master in holding tensions together (*et-et*), must open its synthesis to the maximum exercise of its catholicity, i.e., its ability to embrace two opposites at the same time.

Dupuis speaks of "polarities at play." In the unresolved polarity between the incarnate Word (biblically attested) and the non-incarnate Word (spacious enough as to include other religions), there would be room for the salvific role of religions. Compared to traditional models (i.e., exclusivism, inclusivism, and pluralism), Caccaro claims that Dupuis's thought can be understood as "inclusive pluralism" or "pluralistic inclusivism."

Even on a first reading, the problems with this position are evident. If the non-incarnate Word is pitted against the incarnate revelation of God in Jesus Christ, doesn't one devalue the necessary scandal of the incarnation and the cross? If the Spirit and the Father operate outside of and without Jesus Christ, isn't the unity and harmony of the Trinity endangered? If salvation can be found outside of the incarnate Word, doesn't conversion to Christ become redundant?

Caccamo is helpful at exploring the "acrobatics" of Dupuis's theology of religions, especially as far as his concepts of "surplus" and "superabundance" of the mystery of the Word, which cannot be contained in closed and pre-defined schemes of thought.

What is perhaps most interesting is to see how his work influenced Pope Francis's claim that the diversity of religions is the will of God. Dupuis is only the latest development of a long-term process within Roman Catholicism that the Pope echoed. In fact, the theology of religions was given a shock at Vatican II (1962–65) when it was argued that the plan of salvation includes people who don't profess faith in Jesus Christ and that those who don't know the gospel can attain salvation.[93] Then, *Redemptoris Missio*, the 1990 encyclical by John Paul II, stated that "participated forms of mediation of different kinds and degrees are not excluded."

---

93. Second Vatican Council, "Lumen Gentium," 16.

A lot of water has passed under the bridges of Roman Catholic theology: from the "anonymous Christianity" of Karl Rahner to the "all brothers" of Pope Francis. Of course, there have been pushbacks here and there (e.g., the 2000 critical declaration *Dominus Iesus*[94] signed by Cardinal Joseph Ratzinger), but the direction seems to be clear. The theology of religions is fertile ground in post-Vatican II Roman Catholicism. It is therefore not by chance that Pope Francis could write that "the pluralism and the diversity of religions, color, sex, race, and language are willed by God in His wisdom, through which He created human beings."[95] In this sense, the spirit if not the letter of Dupuis's work is at play in the Pope's mind.

One glimpses a pattern: Dupuis broke new ground in his work, the immediate Vatican reaction was fairly negative, then his main concerns were accepted and integrated, and now they are part of the mainstream teaching of the Roman Church, at least implicitly. Here is how the Roman catholicity works: on the one hand, the traditional exclusivist and inclusivist positions are formally maintained, but on the other hand, they have developed in the "inclusive pluralism" or "pluralistic inclusivism" that Dupuis gave theological weight to in his work. There is no commitment to the ultimate authority of the Bible, and therefore the Roman Catholic system, can flex one way or the other away from gospel boundaries.

"Praedicate Evangelium"—Envisioning the Roman Catholic Church of the Future (July 1, 2022, Number 203)

The constitution of a country is a kind of identity card for the country itself. Its different components, its various articles, the procedures that are enacted . . . they all create a window into what the country stands for and what its rules are. Since a country's identity is reflected in every change of the constitution, any change signals a modification in the self-understanding of the entity.

The Roman Curia is governed by a kind of constitution that is issued by the Pope as the Head of the Church and Head of the State of the Vatican. It contains the rules that preside over the functioning of the Vatican departments and offices, which are at the service of the universal mission of the Roman Pontiff. It is the blueprint of the Vatican institution

---

94. Holy See, "Dominus Iesus."
95. Francis and Ahmad Al-Tayyeb, *Document on Human Fraternity*.

and is centered on the office of the Pope and practically implemented by the Roman Curia.

The recent promulgation of the Apostolic Constitution *Praedicate Evangelium* (PE)[96] on March 19, 2022, gives the opportunity to examine how the Roman Catholic Church understands and organizes her institutional life as far as the present and the future are concerned.[97] More importantly, PE shows the inherent connection between the theological vision and the institutional outlook of the Roman Church, at least from the viewpoint of the Curia. Prior to PE, the Roman Curia operated under the constitution *Pastor Bonus* issued by John Paul II in 1988, and so it is also interesting to notice the changes after twenty-five years. The constitution defines the Roman Curia as "the institution which the Roman Pontiff ordinarily makes use of in the exercise of his supreme pastoral office and his universal mission in the world." Furthermore, it states, "The Roman Curia is composed of the Secretariat of State, the Dicasteries and other bodies, all juridically equal to each other."

Of course, PE is a juridical document, and some interest and expertise in canon law is needed to come to terms with its contents.[98] The focus of this article will not so much be on the institutional rearrangement of the Roman Curia and its organizational structure but rather on the theological vision that sustains it and constitutes its framework. In what follows, I will try to look at PE from two different angles: the reordering of institutional priorities that it envisages and the significance of those priorities for the overall life of the Roman Catholic Church. Evangelicals are not always aware of the institutional picture and pay little attention to it. However, Rome is a big institution, and one cannot come to terms with it without considering it. Therefore, this will be an exercise of evangelical discernment applied to the changing structure of the Roman Curia.

The Reordering of Priorities

"Christ summons the Church as she goes her pilgrim way. . . to that continual reformation of which she always has need, insofar as she is a

---

96. Holy See, "Praedicate Evangelium."

97. So far, the text of PE is only available in Italian. This explains why the document has so far received less attention than what it would deserve.

98. An introductory presentation of PE can be found in Ghirlanda, "'Praedicate Evangelium,'" 41–56 and Maradiaga, *Praedicate Evangelium*.

human institution here on earth."[99] These words by Pope Francis, which are actually a quotation from Vatican II, reflect a deep conviction concerning the need for an ongoing reformation in the church.[100] What kind of reformation did he have in mind? In some sense, PE is the institutional answer to the question asked at the beginning of his pontificate. In a nutshell, Francis's own understanding of the reformation of his church has to do with the increase of "synodality," i.e., the involvement of many players in the decision-making process. The Pope wants to change the way the universal church is governed, in such a way that the local church—dioceses, bishops' conferences—plays a much larger role in the decisions that affect it, without questioning the universal ministry of the Pope. In short, Francis wishes to shorten the distance between Rome and the particular churches, to ensure that they act better together. According to him, reformation is therefore a participatory dynamic in the internal organization of the Roman church in a synodical outlook. PE spells out what it means for the Pope to think and act toward this kind of reformation.

In *The Joy of the Gospel*, the Pope wrote:

> I dream of a "missionary option," that is, a missionary impulse capable of transforming everything, so that the Church's customs, ways of doing things, times and schedules, language and structures can be suitably channeled for the evangelization of today's world rather than for her self-preservation. The renewal of structures demanded by pastoral conversion can only be understood in this light: as part of an effort to make them more mission-oriented, to make ordinary pastoral activity on every level more inclusive and open, to inspire in pastoral workers a constant desire to go forth and in this way to elicit a positive response from all those whom Jesus summons to friendship with himself.[101]

Now nine years after *The Joy of the Gospel*, PE is the tool by which the Pope wants mission to be at the center of the Vatican institutional life and not just a set of activities run by the Vatican institutions. It is a change of symbolic and conceptual significance.

PE attempts to make the Roman Curia at the service of mission. This concern is made clear by the prominence given to the Dicastery

---

99. Francis, "Evangelii Gaudium," 26.
100. Spadaro and Gali, *Riforma*.
101. Francis, "Evangelii Gaudium," 27.

for Evangelization, which is the first in order of the departments of the Curia.[102] The Dicastery for Evangelization (directly chaired by the Pope with two pro-prefects in the sections into which it is divided) is formed through the merger of the Pontifical Council for Promoting the New Evangelization[103] and the Congregation for the Evangelization of Peoples. The Pope himself takes full and direct responsibility to lead it. It has never happened before that the Pope would reclaim such a position and have such direct involvement.

In the list of PE, the Dicastery for Evangelization is followed by the Dicastery for the Doctrine of the Faith (which historically always had the first position among the old congregations). The reverse of the order between the two is significant. The latter dicastery is followed by the new Dicastery for the Service of Charity, which was previously a simple office, that of Apostolic Charity. The triadic order is, therefore, evangelization, doctrine, charity. The more prominent role of "charity" is signaled by the institutional upgrade from office to dicastery.

It is worth pausing for a moment and reflecting on the order that is envisioned by PE. Evangelization comes first and takes priority over doctrine. Evangelization is to become the first concern of the Roman Curia. Doctrine seems to be at the service of evangelization, no longer the other way around as has been the case for centuries. The Roman Curia is no longer supposed to be primarily a defensive structure guided by a body watching over doctrine but needs to become an outward vector at the service of the mission of the church. The shift is indicative of the new trajectory Pope Francis wants his church to move even beyond his time.

PE is not a detailed plan yet, but from the institutional perspective, it signals a significant change of priority. It is as if what was envisioned in *The Joy of the Gospel* has come to fruition. Through the restructuring of the Roman Curia, evangelization and mission are now at the institutional center of the Vatican. The legacy of Pope Francis is a subject open to

---

102. Here is the list of the dicasteries as they are arranged by PE: Dicastery for Evangelization; Dicastery for the Doctrine of the Faith; Dicastery for the Service of Charity (formerly the Office of Papal Charities); Dicastery for the Eastern Churches; Dicastery for Divine Worship and the Discipline of the Sacraments; Dicastery for the Causes of Saints; Dicastery for Bishops; Dicastery for the Clergy; Dicastery for Institutes of Consecrated Life and Societies of Apostolic Life; Dicastery for the Laity, Family and Life; Dicastery for Promoting Christian Unity; Dicastery for Interreligious Dialogue; Dicastery for Culture and Education; Dicastery for Promoting Integral Human Development; Dicastery for Legislative Texts; Dicastery for Communication.

103. The Council for Promoting the New Evangelization was created by Pope Benedict XVI in 2010. See: De Chirico, "Vatican File 1."

various interpretations. Doctrine has never received much attention by Pope Francis. Many of his critics have pointed out the doctrinal confusion if not failure in his leadership.[104] Other aspects of his reign are receiving some pushback. Whatever one thinks of him, PE is perhaps his most important and lasting contribution and something that all people inside and outside of the Roman Catholic Church will have to deal with.[105]

What Does Evangelization Mean?

Given the importance of evangelization and mission in the new outlook of the Roman Curia, it is important to grapple with the theology of evangelization that lies at the heart of PE. "Evangelization" seems to be a popular word in Catholic circles. Being traditionally part of the vocabulary used by evangelicals (and also referred to as "evangelism"), it has become increasingly used by Roman Catholics, too. It was Paul VI with his 1975 exhortation *Evangelii Nuntiandi* who introduced it in Catholic language.[106] It was Benedict XVI who launched in 2010 a new Vatican department to support efforts towards the "new evangelization." It is Pope Francis who regularly speaks about and practices forms of evangelization, making it a central task of the church, as attested in his 2013 exhortation *The Joy of the Gospel*. With PE, evangelization is given institutional importance.

"Evangelization" is a word that Rome has re-signified to suit its theological vision of embracing the world and in order to fulfill its calling to be, as Vatican II says, a "sign and instrument of the unity between God and mankind."[107] A similar genetic modification has occurred with other words that have historically belonged to the evangelical vocabulary, e.g., "conversion," "unity," and "mission." These words are some examples of the way in which Roman Catholicism can maintain the same spelling while giving these terms a distinct Roman Catholic meaning.[108]

104. De Chirico, "Vatican File 159." See also "Is the Pope Catholic?"

105. As an aside, another important nuance that PE introduced has to do with the possibility for a lay person to preside over a dicastery, and this by virtue of the principle that "the power of governance in the Church does not come from the sacrament of orders, but from the canonical mission" received by the Pope with the conferral of office.

106. Paul VI, "Evangelii Nuntiandi."

107. Second Vatican Council, "Lumen Gentium," 1.

108. De Chirico, *Same Words*. In this book, De Chirico explores words such are "generation," "justification," "cross," etc., showing that the way these words are understood by Rome is significantly different from their biblical meaning. On Rome's attempt at redefining biblical words, see also "Vatican File 56."

In *The Joy of the Gospel*, the "heart" of the gospel is summarized in this way: "the beauty of the saving love of God made manifest in Jesus Christ who died and rose from the dead."[109] In this apparently evangelical definition of the gospel, something is missing: while the objective good news of God is rightly related to the narrative of Jesus Christ, the subjective part of it (i.e., repentance from one's own sin and personal faith) is omitted. The tragedy of being lost without Jesus Christ is also downplayed. For this reason, nowhere in the document are unrepentant unbelievers called to repent and believe in Jesus Christ. Non-Catholic Christians are already united in baptism,[110] Jews don't need to convert,[111] and with believing Muslims, the way is "dialogue" because "together with us they adore the one and merciful God."[112] Other non-Christians are also "justified by the grace of God" and are associated to "the paschal mystery of Jesus Christ."[113] The gospel appears not to be a message of salvation from God's judgment but instead access to a fuller measure of a salvation that is already given to all mankind. According to Francis, therefore, evangelization and mission are the joyful willingness to extend the fullness of grace to the world that is already under grace.

The word "evangelization" is used here; the practice of it is apparently endorsed. Evangelicals, for whom the word strikes deep spiritual chords, may celebrate the emphasis that the Roman Catholic Church is putting on evangelization, now in an embedded form in the Roman Curia. Yet a careful and honest reading of the document shows that the kind of "evangelization" the Pope is advocating for here is something utterly distant from the biblical meaning of the word.

Apart from *Evangelii Gaudium*, the most recent encyclical *All Brothers*[114] is another window into Pope Francis's theology of evangelization. In this document, Francis pleads the cause of universal fraternity and social friendship. Although it does not directly deal with evangelization, it nonetheless shapes the missiological framework of Francis's theology of evangelization.

Among other issues, *All Brothers* raises a soteriological question. If we are all brothers as we are all children of God, does this mean that all

109. Francis, "Evangelii Gaudium," 36.
110. Francis, "Evangelii Gaudium," 244.
111. Francis, "Evangelii Gaudium," 247.
112. Francis, "Evangelii Gaudium," 252; quoting "Lumen Gentium," 16.
113. Francis, "Evangelii Gaudium," 254.
114. Francis, "Fratelli Tutti."

will be saved? The whole encyclical is pervaded by a powerful universalist inspiration that also includes atheists.[115] Religions in the broad sense are always presented in a positive sense, and there is no mention of a biblical criticism of religions nor of the need for repentance and faith in Jesus Christ as the key to receiving salvation.[116] Everything in the encyclical suggests that everyone, as brothers and sisters, will be saved. Evangelization is surely impacted by this assumption.

Then there is a christological issue. Even though Jesus Christ is referred to here and there, his exclusive and "offensive" claims are kept silent. Francis cleverly presents Jesus Christ not as the "cornerstone" on which the whole building of life stands or collapses but as the stone only for those who recognize him. Above Jesus Christ, according to the encyclical, there is a "God" who is the father of all. We are children of this "God" even without recognizing Jesus Christ as Lord and Savior. Jesus is thus reduced to the rank of the champion of Christians alone, while the other "brothers" are still children of the same "God," regardless of faith in Jesus Christ. Evangelization cannot escape from being shaped by this shallow Christology.

Thirdly, there is an ecclesiological issue. If we are all "brothers," there is a sense in which we are all part of the same church that gathers brothers and sisters together. The boundaries between humanity and church are so nonexistent that the two communities become coincident. Humanity is the church, and the church is humanity. This is in line with the sacramental vision of the Roman Catholic Church which, according to Vatican II, is understood as a "sign and instrument of the unity of the whole human race."[117] According to *All Brothers*, the whole of the human race belongs to the church not on the basis of faith in Jesus Christ but on the basis of a shared divine sonship and human fraternity.

After sampling the theology of evangelization in Francis's programmatic documents, it is useful to compare it with standard evangelical accounts of evangelization. According to the 1974 *Lausanne Covenant*, perhaps the most representative evangelical document of the 20th century, evangelism is "the proclamation of the historical, biblical Christ as Saviour and Lord, with a view to persuading people to come to him personally and so be reconciled to God."[118] Notice the different elements

---

115. Francis, "Fratelli Tutti," 281.
116. Francis, "Fratelli Tutti," 277–79.
117. Second Vatican Council, "Lumen Gentium," 1.
118. Lausanne Movement, "Lausanne Covenant."

of this neat and clear definition: "proclamation," "historical and biblical Christ," "persuasion," and the emphasis on one's personal reconciliation to God.

What "evangelization" is talked about in PE? The immediate answer is that of *The Joy of the Gospel* and *All Brothers*, and this is not really good news for evangelicals. The word is the same, but the meaning is far different.[119] In its understanding and practice of evangelization, the Roman Catholic Church legitimately brings in the whole of its theological system, which is based on a combination of the Bible and traditions, Christ and the saints, faith and folk piety, and so on. Its evangelization promotes and commends this kind of blurred and erroneous gospel. Before celebrating the fact that with PE the Roman Catholic Church has become seriously engaged in evangelization, one needs to understand what kind of evangelization Rome stands for: it is a flawed view of what "preach the Gospel" means according to the Bible.

The Biblical Jubilee and the Roman Catholic Holy Year: Twins or Strangers? (October 1, 2024, Number 233)

In the religious world and beyond, a mobilization is underway in preparation for the 2025 Jubilee called by Pope Francis with the bull *Spes non Confundit (Hope Does Not Disappoint)*.[120] The Roman Catholic Church has already been preparing for some time. Millions of people plan to make some kind of "pilgrimage" to Rome or the designated places, whether secular or religious.

One is inundated with news but struggles to understand what is happening. After all, most people know that the word "jubilee" comes from somewhere in the Bible. The book of Leviticus, chapter 25, says that every fifty years, a year was established to restore livable conditions for all. The three basic provisions of the jubilee year were the restitution of sold property, the freeing of slaves, and the resting of the land. Clearly, this was something disruptive. The question is, How is it that the Roman Catholic Church calls what is going to happen in 2025 a "jubilee"? Is

---

119. In *Same Words, Different Worlds*, De Chirico argues that while Rome uses the same words of the gospel, its account of the gospel is flawed because the Roman Catholic Church is not committed to Scripture alone as its foundational principle, and therefore its understanding of the Bible is determined by non-biblical sources.

120. Francis, "Spes Non Confundit."

there a difference between a jubilee and a holy year? The Roman Catholic Church tends to use the two terms interchangeably, but is it legitimate to confuse them?

The Tradition of the Holy Years

First of all, it should be pointed out that jubilees, from the Middle Ages onward, have also been referred to as holy years. In fact, in the medieval Catholic tradition, the idea of a "holy" year was placed side-by-side with that of jubilee, eventually becoming synonymous or at least an element of specification. The year in question was defined as "holy" insofar as it began, took place, and ended with sacred rites officiated by the Pope or ecclesiastical authorities; by extension, the entire period delimited by somewhat sacred ceremonies was called a holy year. Actually, the latter definition better suits the congruous number of such years called by various popes over the centuries. They retain the name of the biblical jubilee, even though the measures taken and the spirituality promoted under these circumstances are more related to medieval Catholicism than the biblical message.

From Boniface VIII to the Present Day

Pope Boniface VIII called the first holy year in history with the bull *Antiquorum habet fida relatio* of February 22, 1300. The immediate occasion for this initiative was the accreditation of the rumor that was circulating more and more insistently that, in the centennial year, those who—repentant and confessed—visited the basilicas of St. Peter and St. Paul would obtain a "most full remission of sins." The idea of redemption proper to the jubilee had morphed into that of an indulgence for the benefit of pilgrims. The influx to Rome was considerable, and the granting of the "remission" was extended until the end of the year to meet everyone's needs. The jubilee of Boniface VIII responded to popular religiosity's need to celebrate a great cathartic event of peace and forgiveness after the troubled era of the Crusades. Among the pilgrims of this first holy year is Dante Alighieri, who referred to it in some verses of the Divine Comedy, the XVIII canto of the Inferno, and the XXXI canto of Paradise. Two years after the jubilee, Boniface VIII promulgated the famous Bull *Unam Sanctam*, in which he affirmed the supremacy of the theocratic power of the church over any other earthly institution. In this way, the widespread sentiment was satisfied, and the authoritarian conception of the church was reaffirmed.

During the Avignonese parenthesis of the papacy (1305–77), the expiration of the holy year was no longer linked to the centenary but was provisionally established in the order of fifty years. Thus, the jubilee of 1350 was celebrated without the presence of the Pope (Clement VI) but with a strong involvement of the Roman population. But Pope Urban VI decided to set the deadline every thirty-three years, taking the years of Jesus' earthly life as the yardstick; therefore, he called the holy year in 1383. Outside of any precise scanning, Boniface IX celebrated a jubilee of his own in 1390, while the coming of the centenary and the unexpected influx of pilgrims to Rome led him to repeat it in 1400. Subsequent ones were called by Martin V (1425) and Nicholas V (1450). The twenty-five-year practice was made binding by a bull of Paul II (1470). Sixtus IV took advantage of the 1475 jubilee to beautify Rome with major works such as the Sistine Chapel and the Sixtus Bridge over the Tiber River. The greatest artists of the time worked in Rome in preparation for that event. The jubilee became an event to beautify the Pope's city and to provide it with accommodations for pilgrims. In the century of the Protestant Reformation, holy years were celebrated by Alexander VI (1500), Clement VII (1525), Julius III (1550), and Gregory XIII (1575). On the latter occasion, an estimated 300,000 pilgrims from all over Europe arrived in Rome. The tone of the celebrations ranged from the pursuit of a spiritual dimension to the ostentation of ceremonial pomp and ecclesiastical power. During the seventeenth and eighteenth centuries, ordinary holy years were called at regular intervals by Clement VIII (1600), Urban VIII (1625), Innocent X (1650), Clement X (1675), Innocent XII (1700), Benedict XIII (1725), Benedict XIV (1750), and Pius VI (1775). The difficult situation of the Catholic Church in the Napoleonic era prevented Pius VII from holding a jubilee in 1800.

However, the tradition resumed in 1825 with Leo XII, only to be interrupted again in 1850 due to the events of the Roman Republic and the temporary absence of Pius IX from the Vatican. The Pope himself was able to call the holy year in 1875; however, the occupation of Rome by the Italian army did not allow the celebration of public ceremonies or even the influx of crowds. The first jubilee of the 20th century was organized by Leo XIII (1900). It was followed by that of Pius XI (1925) and, in the aftermath of the end of World War II, by that of Pius XII (1950). During that year, the dogma of Mary's Assumption into heaven was proclaimed. The last ordinary jubilee was celebrated by John Paul II (2000). The one in 2025 called by Pope Francis is thus in a long Roman Catholic tradition.

In addition to these twenty-six jubilees called "ordinary" jubilees, because they are more or less tied to predefined deadlines, the Catholic Church has also promoted "extraordinary" holy years to celebrate certain worthy events deemed to be of a certain importance. The custom of proclaiming holy years of an extraordinary nature dates back to the 16th century, precisely in the wake of the Protestant Reformation, which had strongly denounced the scandal of indulgences. Instead of curbing and deeply revising the doctrine and practice in question, the Catholic Church reacted by increasing initiatives to distribute indulgences. For this reason, the ordinary jubilees were no longer deemed sufficient given the considerable time lag from one to the next, and there was therefore the additional holding of extraordinary years. In the 17th century alone, forty were organized! The last ones celebrated were those of Pius XI (1933) on the occasion of the 19th centenary of the Redemption, that of John Paul II (1983) to commemorate the 1950th anniversary of the same event, and the Jubilee of Mercy called by Pope Francis in 2015–16. Pope Wojtyla also convened a Marian year (1987), which is further evidence of the departure from the content and spirit of the biblical jubilee by the Catholic tradition of holy years, while Pope Ratzinger convened a "Pauline" one (2008–9) to commemorate the apostle Paul, and Pope Francis convened one dedicated to "St. Joseph" (2020). In general, it can be said that holy years are indicators that reflect the Catholic Church's emphases, practices, and journey over time but have a nonexistent relationship with the biblical jubilee.

The Issue of Indulgences

Beyond the historical sequence of the holy years and the names of the popes to whom they are linked, it is important to point out what were and what are still the qualifying moments planned for the celebration of these anniversaries. In this regard, it can be said that a set of religious practices typical of medieval Catholicism were associated with the jubilee, with the result that they ended up taking precedence over the demands posed by the jubilee itself. The holy year is more a product of Roman Catholic spirituality than of biblical jubilee. The hallmark of the holy year is medieval religiosity later elaborated over the following centuries but not faith based on Scripture.

Thus, the Roman Catholic jubilee is characterized primarily by a pilgrimage to Rome, with an associated visit to its major basilicas and an offer of "general forgiveness" in relation to the system of ecclesiastical indulgences. At this point in the discussion, it should become clear that both prescriptions are clearly foreign to the biblical jubilee. The latter, in fact, did not involve a pilgrimage to Jerusalem or any other place. In this regard, it should be recalled that the theme of pilgrimage is a rich biblical metaphor for the Christian life, but the practice of pilgrimage to a particular place is not prescribed either for the jubilee or other circumstances. As for forgiveness connected with jubilee, it clashes with the finality of Christ's work. By his incarnation, death, and resurrection, Jesus accomplished all that was necessary for man to receive true forgiveness. His jubilee consists of the gift of forgiveness to those who believe in him. Because of the jubilee of the Lord Jesus, offers of forgiveness related to the ecclesiastical apparatus are useless, wrong, and anachronistic.

The issue of indulgences is reminiscent of the violent controversy that arose during the Protestant Reformation when not only the excesses but the very institution of indulgences was radically challenged. To the distracted eyes of most, indulgences may appear a somewhat cumbersome legacy of medieval Catholicism but deprived of legitimacy in the practice of the contemporary Roman Catholic Church. Today, one hears that indulgences are no longer offered, as they have been more or less tacitly abolished. Yet, the opposite is true. In fact, the institution of indulgences is certainly one of the typical aspects of the jubilee and, as John Paul II notes in the Bull *Aperite portas Redemptoris* of January 6, 1983, the gift of indulgences is "proper and characteristic of the Holy Year." It consists of the remission before God of the temporal penalty for sins granted by the church. In the Catholic view, just as Christ's sacrifice must be "re-presented" at the Mass, so the forgiveness of the sins of the faithful must be administered periodically by the church that participates in that sacrifice. The Catholic Church, far from abolishing this much-contested practice, has instead further specified and regulated it without affecting its essential features in the least.

To this end, after discussions on the matter by the Second Vatican Council, Paul VI promulgated the constitution *Indulgentiarum*

Doctrina[121] and later published *the Enchiridion indulgentiarum*[122] to regulate the whole issue. The latter document was updated again in 1986. In addition, the two greatest doctrinal texts of Catholicism, the 1983 *Code of Canon Law* and the 1992 *Catechism of the Catholic Church*, contain doctrinal definitions and pastoral provisions on the subject, testifying to the extreme vitality of the doctrine and practice of indulgences, even in view of the Holy Year of 2025.[123]

Pope Francis's Holy Year

As already noted, Pope Francis, prior to the one in 2025, had already proclaimed the Holy Year of Mercy in 2015. The bull calling that jubilee is titled *Misericordiae Vultus* (*The Face of Mercy*). The Pope addresses the topic of indulgences using language that is much more personal and relational than juridical and traditional while maintaining the substance of the theology and practice of indulgences.[124]

Now, in anticipation of the Jubilee of 2025, the May 9, 2024, Bull of Indiction, *Spes non Confundit* (*Hope Does Not Disappoint*), recalls the biblical text of Rom 5:5 and the theme of hope found in the New Testament.[125] However, in addition to the formal reference, the Pope hooks the Catholic event to the medieval tradition of holy years that drew inspiration from sources other than biblical ones. He speaks of a "grace event," but this is a conception of grace that is mediated through the ecclesiastical institution that opens its "treasury" and is "merited" by pilgrims in various ancient and updated ways. The "Norms Concerning the Granting of Indulgences" issued on May 13, 2024, specify that the grace of forgiveness can be acquired through a series of devotional practices such as the traditional crossing of "holy doors" and visiting the designated churches but also by those who "recite in their own home or there where the impediment holds them back (e.g., in the chapel of the monastery, hospital, nursing home, prison) the Lord's Prayer, the Profession of Faith in any legitimate form and other prayers in conformity with the purposes of the

---

121. Paul VI, "Indulgentiarum Doctrina."

122. Paul VI, "Indulgentiarum Doctrina."

123. *Code of Canon Law*, canons 992–97; *Catechism of the Catholic Church*, § 1471–79.

124. Francis, "Misericordiae Vultus," 21–22.

125. Francis, "Spes Non Confundit."

holy year, offering up their sufferings or hardships in their own lives."[126] Given that we are in a digital age, the norms for the granting of indulgences have also been adapted by providing that the latter is obtainable "by abstaining, in a spirit of penance, at least during one day from futile distractions, real but also virtual, induced for example by the media and social networks, and from superfluous consumption."[127]

Now, out of ecumenical modesty, a wise communication strategy, or both, indulgences are mentioned only fleetingly in the official publications of the Catholic Church. Little is said about the exercise of this practice other than a reference to tradition; just as it is not emphasized, so it is not denied. The whole theological framework of indulgences outlined by the recent magisterium remains firmly in place and constitutes what is not said explicitly but reiterated implicitly in the Papal letter. The Jubilee of 2025 will still be a year in which the opening of the holy door of St. Peter's will sanction the beginning of the Catholic Church's bestowal of the remission of sins on the millions of pilgrims who will flock *in urbe* (in the city) but also *extra urbem* (outside of the city).

Which Connection Then?

By contrast, the Jubilee of Jesus Christ, foreshadowed by the prophets and fulfilled by the Messiah, made ultimate forgiveness possible for believers. The Son of God paid the penalty and guilt of sins, and those who believed in him were set free. Just as his sacrifice was unique, unique also is his forgiveness. Jesus himself gives this forgiveness and does not give it to others to manage. The whole message of the Christian jubilee revolves around the person and work of Christ—the executor and guarantor of the jubilee—without providing for ecclesiastical involvements, mediations, and administrations in remitting sins that only God can forgive. Instead, the holy year called by the Vatican has the Roman Catholic Church at its center in the role of dispenser of indulgences. The Bible says that Christ's sacrifice was unique and final for the salvation of those who believe, and so the practice of indulgences questions, and indeed denies, the perfect efficacy of Jesus' work. Instead of bringing one closer, indulgences distance one from the jubilee of the Lord Jesus.

---

126. Holy See, "Decree on the Granting," sec. 2, para. 5.
127. Holy See, "Decree on the Granting," sec. 3, para. 5.

While it is true that jubilee was brought about by the Lord Jesus (e.g., Isa 61:1–3 and Luke 4:16–21), the church can only proclaim and practice it but not administer it, let alone make money from it. The year 2025 will certainly be a holy year of religious tradition, but it cannot be called a jubilee in the biblical sense.

This is an excerpt from my booklet *Il Giubileo. Molto più e molto meglio di un anno santo*.[128]

More Than the Heart of Jesus, the Heart of Roman Catholicism. On the Latest Encyclical of Pope Francis (December 1, 2024, Number 235)

Dilexit Nos (DN, "He loved us," a quotation from Rom 8:37) is the fourth encyclical of Francis's pontificate signed on October 24.[129] After 2013's *Lumen Fidei* (*The Light of Faith*, although written by Benedict XVI and thus not his brainchild),[130] 2015's *Laudato Si'* (*Praise Be to You*)[131] on environmental issues, and 2020's *All Brothers* on universal fraternity,[132] DN takes its cue from the Roman Catholic devotion to the Sacred Heart of Jesus to elaborate a more general reflection on the heart, affections, and compassion in a world full of evils.

The encyclical consists of five chapters, which are made up of 220 paragraphs, and it comes out while the celebration of the 350th anniversary of the first manifestation of the Sacred Heart of Jesus to St. Margaret Mary Alacoque is still underway. Not surprisingly, the text mentions Jesus' apparitions in Paray-le-Monial (France) between late December 1673 and June 1675. Francis also names some mystics particularly connected to this devotion: Therese of Lisieux (1873–97) and Faustina Kowalska (1905–38). The encyclical stitches together biblical reflections, patristic quotations, historical examples, and devotional practices that all converge at times on the human heart, other times on the heart of Christ, and always on the devotion of the "sacred heart."

---

128. De Chirico, *Jubilee*.
129. Francis, "Dilexit Nos."
130. De Chirico, "Vatican File 61."
131. De Chirico, "Vatican File 110."
132. De Chirico, "Vatican File 181."

Devotion to the Sacred Heart is pervasive in Roman Catholic spirituality. Images of the bleeding heart, dedicated processions, mystical writings, collective imagery, and iconography in churches are all spaces imbued with this relatively modern tradition. Even the prestigious Catholic University of Milan is named after the Sacred Heart. This is to say that DN grafts onto very fertile ground for Roman Catholicism, which the Pope evidently wants to enhance further.

In DN, the whole movement of Roman Catholicism can be seen in the watermark: there is some biblical quotation that is then elaborated in practices that take leave from the Bible as they go to focus on images and devotions that seek to "actualize" the biblical message. Through recourse, further revelations shift attention away from the biblical Christ and onto the Christ imagined by the church and mediated by it.

In DN, the biblical starting point flows into popular piety. The message of Scripture is blurred to make room for the world of devotions. Moreover, for the Pope, popular piety is the "immune system of the church," instead of being considered an excrescence to be always kept in check and treated with biblical antidotes.[133]

St. Margaret Mary Alacoque herself, who initiated the devotion of the Sacred Heart, tells of revelations that led her to corporal mortifications (self-flagellation, sticking needles, ingesting other people's vomit, etc.), encouragement to devote herself to the cult of Our Lady, and even to the heart of Mary.[134] Well, Pope Francis recalls with approval that Pius XII in 1956 stated that "the worship of the Sacred Heart expresses in an excellent way, as a sublime synthesis, our worship of Jesus Christ"[135] and that it is even "a synthesis of the Gospel."[136] Perhaps it is a synthesis of the Roman Catholic gospel but certainly not the biblical gospel! Indeed, DN gives voice to the Roman Catholic account of the "Sacred Heart," not Jesus' heart as the Bible presents it to us.

This brief introduction to DN is worth concluding with a reference to a work almost contemporaneous with the Catholic apparitions of the Sacred Heart and the beginning of its devotion. The work is entitled *The Heart of Christ in Heaven Toward Sinners on Earth* and was first published

---

133. Francis, "Pope Francis to Chorus."
134. Francis, "Dilexit Nos," 176.
135. Francis, "Dilexit Nos," 79.
136. Francis, "Dilexit Nos," 83.

in 1651. It became the most popular work of the Puritan Thomas Goodwin (1600–80).[137]

Here, we find an excellent example of what it means to meditate on the heart of Christ biblically without giving room for spurious and misguided devotions. In the book, Goodwin sets out to show from the Scriptures that, in all his heavenly majesty, Christ is not now detached from believers and indifferent but has a very strong affection for them. Goodwin begins with the beautiful assurances given by Christ to his disciples, taking as an example of this love the washing of Christ's feet (John 13). The heart of his argument, however, lies in the exposition of Heb 4:15, in which Goodwin shows that, in all his glorious holiness in heaven, Christ is not unkind toward his people; if anything, his heart beats stronger than ever with tender love for them.

Instead of the "sacred heart" of *Dilexit Nos*, so hopelessly steeped in traditions and practices that are contrary to the gospel, we need to know and experience the heart of Jesus as the Bible (*sola Scriptura!*) presents it.

---

137. Goodwin, *Heart of Christ*.

3

General Themes

"The Word of God Precedes and Exceeds the Bible." (April 15, 2013, Number 57)

Pope Francis on Scripture and the Church

AFTER A MONTH OF sparking events surrounding the Vatican, the time has come to shift into a more routine mood. Pope Francis has attracted a lot of attention from the media and has sent various messages of change and renewal. After the initial surprise, the various Vatican departments are coming to terms with a less pompous papacy, and the Pope himself is beginning to shape his own views on a number of open issues that are on the Vatican agenda.

After the first weeks, marked by what seemed new and extraordinary, Pope Francis has now begun to do what a Pope in Rome normally does, e.g., preside over different liturgical events, receive international delegations, meet with bishops from around the world, speak at various occasions, etc. The normal pace of the papacy is beginning to emerge. After using more "pastoral" language in his first homilies that almost everybody seemed to like, the more theological bent of Francis's thought is coming through as he has more opportunities to deliver speeches of various forms. One of his first opportunities was a speech he gave on April 12 to the members of the Pontifical Biblical Commission convened in the Vatican to discuss the theme "The Inspiration and the Truth of the Bible." Here is a summary of Francis's address and a few remarks on this very important subject for all Christians in general, and for evangelicals in particular.

The Non-Identity Thesis

After commending the commission for the choice of the topic, the Pope highlighted the nature of Scripture and its relationship to the Word of God. The Bible, according to Francis, is "the testimony in written form to the Word of God." Scripture is not associated with the Word of God on a one-to-one basis but is rather perceived as a witness to something co-inherent yet different. Following this comment, the Pope adds that "the Word of God precedes and exceeds the Bible." In other words, the Pope does not endorse an identity view between Scripture and the Word but supports a dynamic view of the relationship between the Word of God and the Bible whereby Scripture witnesses to a Word that is before and beyond the Bible. The Word is present in the Bible but not confined to it. The Word is spoken and told by the Bible but the two do not coincide, being that the Bible is only a (partial) witness to the (fuller) Word. According to this view, what the Bible says is what the Word says, but what the Word says is not necessarily what the Bible says.

Francis rightly recognizes that the center of the Christian faith is a "person" and not a book, i.e., the person of Jesus Christ, the incarnate Word of God. Yet the inference is that "the horizon of the divine Word (i.e., Jesus Christ) embraces Scripture and extends over it."[1] In rather technical language, Francis goes on to say that the Bible is the "canonical memorial that attests the event of Revelation."[2] The sentence needs some theological unpacking, but it is clear that the "memorial" language coupled with the notion of "attestation" support the view that there is a gap between the Bible and the Word of God. There is nothing original in this account; it has been the theological standard of the Word advocated by the Catholic Church since Vatican II.

---

1. Francis, "Address (Pontifical Biblical Commission)," para. 2.
2. Francis, "Address (Pontifical Biblical Commission)," para. 2.

Scripture is Subject to the Church

Once the identity between the Word and the Bible is refused and substituted with the dynamism of a "living" revelation that exceeds the Bible, there stems the need for an arbiter that is able to recognize the living Word in and beyond the Bible. While Protestant Liberalism submits the Bible to the final judgment of conscience or reason, Roman Catholicism believes that the magisterium of the church has ultimate authority over Scripture. This is what Pope Francis believes as well. In quoting Vatican II (which is actually a quotation of Vatican I), he says that "all of what has been said about the way of interpreting Scripture is subject finally to the judgment of the church, which carries out the divine commission and ministry of guarding and interpreting the word of God."[3] Of course, here Francis is recalling the Roman Catholic view that there is a profound unity between Scripture, tradition, and the magisterium of the church to the extent that one cannot be pitted against the other two and vice versa. The critical point here is that the magisterium represents the only "living" voice of the Word, and its interpretation of Scripture is what really matters and what finally counts. So, instead of letting Scripture speak to the church and over the church by the Spirit, the church is the only authorized voice of the Word which is witnessed in Scripture and which also extends beyond it. Again, the Pope quotes Vatican II (which in turn quotes the Council of Trent) when he says that "it is not from Sacred Scripture alone that the church draws her certainty about everything which has been revealed. Therefore, both sacred tradition and Sacred Scripture are to be accepted and venerated with the same sense of loyalty and reverence."[4]

There will be other times when Pope Francis will address theological issues to express his views. However, this speech to the Pontifical Biblical Commission is an indication of the fact that the Pope will presumably not bring change to basic doctrinal issues and that he is rather conservative in his Roman Catholic theological outlook. Actually, the emphasis and tone of the speech seem to be willing to draw a line between what the Roman Catholic Church believes and the "Scripture alone" principle of the Protestant faith.

---

3. Second Vatican Council, "Dei Verbum," 12; quoting Pius IX, "On Revelation."
4. Second Vatican Council, "Dei Verbum," 9.

The Pope Francis's Dogma: "God is Present in Every Person's Life" (September 20, 2013, Number 65)

Previous popes communicated on the printed page through encyclicals and official speeches only. One of the major changes that Pope Francis is introducing is that he is reversing the balance. He speaks more through newspapers. Last week, his reply to the editor of the Italian daily newspaper *La Repubblica* and his interview with different Jesuit journals demonstrated this trend, and the interest is evident by the broadcast media coverage generated.

The more Pope Francis speaks, the more his theology is becoming clearer. He has always said that the traditional dogmas and the Catechism are in the background of what he affirms and that nothing of substance changes in his remarks on God's infinite mercy and the goodness within every human being. This is true only in part. Different Roman Catholic interpreters have always played with the task of putting different accents on the same sheet music and Francis is deliberately putting his preferred accent—*fortissimo*—on another key dogma. In light of his Marianism and mission-minded approach already elaborated, the last two written outputs and interviews have shed further light on his basic view of the relationship between nature and grace.

"A Dogmatic Certainty"

Talking to his fellow Jesuit journalists from across the world (Sept 19), Pope Francis said many things, and these comments are attracting lots of positive reviews. Here we will focus on this particular one:

> "I have a dogmatic certainty: God is in every person's life. God is in everyone's life. Even if the life of a person has been a disaster, even if it is destroyed by vices, drugs or anything else—God is in this person's life. You can, you must try to seek God in every human life. Although the life of a person is a land full of thorns and weeds, there is always a space in which the good seed can grow."[5]

This Pope is not someone who likes to use dogmatic language, at least on the surface. Yet, here he is using the strongest language possible. He really wants to mean what he is saying. God is in everyone's life. This unqualified statement raises questions about what the Pope thinks of the nature

---

5. Spadaro, "Big Heart," para. 82.

of sin in human life and the reality of us "falling short" of God in our sin (e.g., Rom 3:23). While teaching that those who believe in him shall be saved, the Bible is clear in saying that we are enemies of God because we are sinners and are therefore under his judgment. The Pope, instead, wants to affirm the dogma that God is present because there is always some residual "good" in man.

"Obeying One's Conscience"

One further comment by Pope Francis reinforces his dogmatic view on man's inherent openness to God's presence. Responding to the editor of *La Repubblica* (September 11), he writes the following:

> "You ask me if the God of Christians forgives one who doesn't believe and doesn't seek the faith. Premise that—and it's the fundamental thing—the mercy of God has no limits if one turns to him with a sincere and contrite heart; the question for one who doesn't believe in God lies in obeying one's conscience. Sin, also for those who don't have faith, exists when one goes against one's conscience. To listen to and to obey it means, in fact, to decide in face of what is perceived as good or evil."[6]

Put simply: obeying one's conscience is what God will take account of in granting forgiveness. Notice that the Pope here is not speaking of those who have never heard the gospel but of those who don't believe it while knowing what they are doing. Apparently, to go against one's conscience counts more than going against God's revelation. Although the Bible teaches there is no excuse before God's righteous judgment (e.g., Rom 2:1), Francis here says that that the conscience is the final judge to whom God will submit himself. The human conscience is the determinative factor for God's forgiveness.

The "Grace-Within-Nature" Scheme

These two statements, i.e., God is in every person and obeying one's conscience is what really matters, are thus part of a coherent "dogma" of human goodness and universal salvation.

What is important to observe is not so much the details of each statement but rather the general theological vision that lies at its core.

6. Francis, "Letter to a Non-Believer," para. 20.

Traditionally, Roman Catholicism has worked within the nature-grace scheme largely dependent on its pontifically ratified Thomistic tradition. According to this theological metanarrative, nature, although partially flawed by sin, is elevated by grace to its supernatural end and the sacramental system of the church is the way in which grace operates this elevation.

Moreover, in the 20th century, this scheme was significantly modified and received an important endorsement at Vatican II. Whereas the old scheme implied that grace needed to be "added" to nature, the new version claims that grace is already part of nature and works within itself, not as something extrinsic but rather intrinsic to it. Grace is inherent to nature and through the sacramental system of the church, which unfolds itself more and more.

One advocate of a "grace-within-nature" framework was Karl Rahner (1904–84), himself a Jesuit as well. His view of the "anonymous Christian" stated that each human being, for its being a human being, is already graced and therefore a Christian, even though he is not aware of it or does not want to be such.

While not using the Rahnerian language, Pope Francis works within a similar "dogmatic" framework. God is present in everyone, and one's conscience is what will ultimately count. In spite of all its missional allure and merciful attitude, what Francis is saying is not good news for gospel-centered people.

Liberation Theology, the Prodigal Daughter (February 28, 2014, Number 75)

There was a time, only a few years ago, when the simple reference to "liberation theology" would cause many eyebrows to raise in the Vatican. Those times are now over. What was perceived and even publicly denounced as one of the most dangerous threats confronting the Roman Catholic Church is now seen as a legitimate, if not necessary, stream of its ever-expanding life.

Liberation Theology As It Was Then

Liberation Theology was the title of a seminal book published in 1973 by Peruvian theologian Gustavo Gutiérrez in which he advocated the idea that theology should be at the service of "integral" liberation, i.e., spiritual and economic freedom resulting in social justice. It was a new way of doing theology that would prioritize the people's cries "from below" rather than the expectations of the ecclesiastical intellectual hierarchy "from above." It would work its way bottom-up rather than top-down and would consider the poor as the major theological player rather than the receiving end of decisions made by the rich and would denounce as oppressive the capitalistic *status quo* that the Catholic Church would have instead assumed in Latin America. Other noted exponents are Leonardo and Clodoveo Boff of Brazil, Jon Sobrino of Spain, and Juan Luis Segundo of Uruguay.

Its critics associated liberation theology with Marxist ideology, materialistic anthropology, and revolutionary politics that would turn the traditional teaching and practice of the church upside down. The Catholic Church strongly reacted against it. John Paul II, while paying lip service to some of the concerns expressed by liberation theology, was active in trying to silence it as much as he could. In the mid-eighties, his theological watchdog, Cardinal Ratzinger, then heading the Congregation for Sacred Doctrine, worked hard to limit its influence. Those days are now over. Why? *Mutatis mutandis*, has liberation theology changed its basic message or has the church modified its stance? The latter seems to be the case.

Liberation Theology As It Is Now

Two substantial changes have made this shift possible. One, of course, is that since 2013 the Pope is Latin American. While it is not possible to classify Francis as a liberationist, he nonetheless shares a concern for the poor, an interest in the margins of the world and an appreciation of folk Catholicism. He simply does not seem to see Marxist categories working in and through what liberation theology tried to articulate. The "soft gospel" of the Pope puts less emphasis on theological and ideological issues, and in so doing he has significantly softened the controversy. The other change is that the present head of the Congregation for Sacred Doctrine is Cardinal Gerhard Ludwig Müller (since 2012), a German like Ratzinger, but, unlike his predecessor, a disciple and admirer of Gustavo Gutiérrez. Rome is now in the position of reassessing liberation theology, even beyond past critical evaluations and disciplinary measures.

Two recent books by Müller illustrate how the Vatican now views liberation theology from a completely different perspective. *An der Seite der Armen: Theologie der Befreiung* (*On the Side of the Poor: Liberation Theology*) is a 2004 German title that the Cardinal wrote with Gutiérrez himself. *Povera per i poveri: La missione della chiesa* (*Poor for the Poor: The Mission of the Church*) is a 2014 title that has just been published by the Vatican Press.

In these highly sophisticated books, Müller argues that liberation theology is a "regional" theology that finds her home in the "catholicity" of the Roman Church and stands in continuity with the classical theology of the church. It was preceded by the *Nouvelle Théologie* (*New Theology*), which predated Vatican II and was subsequently prepared by the theology of Karl Rahner. From Henri De Lubac, liberation theology learned that grace works within nature and not from outside of it. From Rahner it embraced the idea that grace is already in nature and not something foreign to it. In Müller's view, liberation theology is a regional application of what mainstream Catholic theology had already affirmed before and after Vatican II.

Liberation theology is no longer viewed as being a pseudo-theology soaked in Marxist ideology but is instead a fully recognized daughter of the church which took seriously the re-orientation that Vatican II gave to Catholic theology and implemented it into the particular context of Latin America. This is the latest exercise of Roman catholicity, whereby something that is in apparent conflict is instead seen as a part of the whole, i.e., the Roman Catholic synthesis.

"Not a School of Samba." Francis and the Catholic Charismatic Movement (June 9, 2014, Number 81)

It was an impressive picture. During the first weekend of June, fifty-thousand people gathered together in the Olympic Stadium of Rome, not for a football match but instead to see Pope Francis as he joined the Catholic Charismatic movements for their annual celebration. In his speech the Pope gave a bit of an autobiographical story of his encounter with these Renewal movements. Today, one Catholic out of ten claims to be charismatic (120 million people on the whole), and most of non-Western Roman Catholicism is heavily influenced by Charismatic spirituality.

From Skepticism to Full Endorsement

In his speech, Francis candidly recalled that his first impressions of the movement were rather mixed. The charismatic way of singing and worshipping seemed to him more of a "school of samba" than a properly defined Catholic liturgy. His reservations, however, were overcome as he better understood the movement. From a skeptical observer, Bergoglio became a staunch supporter of it.

Bergoglio's personal change of mind over time reflects the journey that the Catholic Church as a whole made in its evaluation of the movement. From an initial puzzlement over what appeared to resemble the manners of evangelical Pentecostalism, the Catholic Church worked hard to create a space for Charismatics within the wide fold of Roman Catholicism. The attempt went in a twofold direction. First, it made sure that the Charismatic experience was grafted into the sacramental system of the Catholic Church. Speaking in tongues and the other supernatural events were then considered as subsequent realizations of the already-received sacraments administered by the church. It was not something different or new or disruptive but something that was grounded in the traditional sacramental theology and actually reinforced it, although in its own unique way.

Once the theology was safeguarded, a second move was necessary, i.e., strictly connecting the movement to the hierarchical structure of the Roman Church. Pentecostalism was a child of the "free church" or even "parachurch" mentality, based on the spontaneity of the group and the prominence of the experience of the individual, which is far from the ordinary Catholic sense of belonging to the mother church. Paul VI and John Paul II suggested an institutional framework for the Catholic Charismatics whereby the first article of their statutes would insist that the movement was part of the Roman Catholic Church under the leadership of its bishops and ultimately under the authority of the Roman Pontiff.

In so doing, both the theology and the institution of the church were preserved, and the Charismatic movement became all-in-all a "child" of the Catholic Church. From being a potential threat, it became a powerful arm of the present-day Roman Church and one of its main hopes for the future. In the early seventies the initial turning point of the Catholic approach occurred at the Gregorian University of Rome (the flagship Jesuit academic institution), and now the Jesuit Pope fully confirms the extremely positive attitude of the church as a whole toward the Catholic Charismatics.

The Role of Renewal Movements Within the System

The Catholic Charismatic movement is just of the many contemporary renewal movements that operate within the Roman Catholic Church. This institution, beside its hierarchical apparatus, is innervated by different movements, each one bringing its own "gift" (singular) to the church, which in turn holds all the "gifts" (plural). Renewal movements have always been in and around the church with their specific vocation. The Roman Church as a system has fought those movements that would not integrate themselves into the sacramental theology and hierarchical structure of the church but has welcomed those that were willing to become an organic part of it. The Protestant Reformation is an example of the former, the Franciscan movement an example of the latter. These integrated renewal movements have become a means to stretch the catholicity of the system without changing its core.

The same thing happened with the Catholic Charismatic Renewal. Once appeased by the Roman sacraments and the Papal structure, the system has been able to fully metabolize it. As other renewal movements in the course of history, the Charismatic Renewal is a means for the expansion of the system that adds to it and solidifies it, without purifying and changing it.

Is Scripture True Only in a "Limited" Way? The Truth of the Bible According to the Pontifical Biblical Commission (August 28, 2014, Number 88)

The "Biblical Renewal" is one of the most significant movements that has both preceded and followed the Second Vatican Council (1962–65). After centuries of prohibiting the circulation of the Bible in the vernacular languages and forbidding access to it, the Roman Catholic Church has been working hard to reconnect with the Scriptures. Leo XIII's encyclical *Providentissmus Deus* defended a high view of the inspiration of the Bible while Pius XII's encyclical *Divino Afflante Spiritu* welcomed historical-critical methods into Catholic exegesis. These two magisterial statements are the tracks within which the present-day Roman Catholic approach to the Bible can be found. A traditional appreciation of the Bible as an inspired book, on the one hand, and a critical reading of it which questions the clarity and finality of Scripture, on the other, are the two poles that open the door for the intervention of the magisterium for the interpretation of Scripture.

Vatican II's Dogmatic Constitution *Dei Verbum* is the highest authoritative statement on the Bible which combines the two emphases within the framework of a triangular dialectics between tradition, Scripture, and the magisterium. A summary of *Dei Verbum* was offered by Pope Benedict XVI in his letter *Verbum Domini*, in which he writes that the Word of God "precedes and exceeds sacred Scripture, nonetheless Scripture, as inspired by God, contains the divine word."[7] Here we find the classic reference to inspiration but also the preceding existence of tradition that envelops the Bible and speaks through the church's magisterium. According to Catholic teaching the Bible only "contains" the Word and this difference between Scripture and the Word allows for both critical readings of the Bible and the need for a human authority to discern what it contains and what it doesn't.

The most recent pronouncement on this doctrine is an extended document released by the Pontifical Biblical Commission (February 22, 2014), which is the Vatican's official study group on biblical issues. The title well captures the discussed topic: "The Inspiration and the Truth of Sacred Scripture." This 250-page text is basically an elaboration of what *Dei Verbum* had argued as far as the scope of biblical inerrancy is concerned, i.e., that the Bible "teaches, without error that truth which God wanted put into the sacred writings for the sake of our salvation."[8] What, though, is the significance of relating inerrancy to "the sake of our salvation"? Is it then a kind of inerrancy that is limited only to the message of salvation? What about the rest of the Bible? Is it without error? And how can that which is related to salvation be distinguished from the rest? And who can discern what is without error, and what is instead disputable? Roman Catholic theology has been discussing these issues since Vatican II and the Pontifical Biblical Commission has now entered this very important debate.

The document attempts to reaffirm and expand on what *Dei Verbum* highlights. The truth of the Bible is affirmed but is related to the "project of salvation,"[9] the "salvific plan,"[10] and "our salvation."[11] The detailed bib-

7. Benedict XVI, "Verbum Domini," 17.
8. Pontifical Biblical Commission, *Inspiration and Truth*, 11.
9. Pontifical Biblical Commission, *Inspiration and Truth*, 3.
10. Pontifical Biblical Commission, *Inspiration and Truth*, 4.
11. Pontifical Biblical Commission, *Inspiration and Truth*, 63.

lical overview on the truth of Scripture is understood as limiting the inerrancy of the text to its soteriological purpose. As for the rest, "in the Bible we encounter contradictions, historical inaccuracies, unlikely accounts, and in the Old Testament there are precepts and commands that are in conflict with the teaching of Jesus."[12] More specifically, the Abrahamic narratives are considered more as interpretations than historical facts,[13] the crossing the Red Sea is more interested in actualizing the Exodus than reporting its original events,[14] most of the book of Joshua has little historical value,[15] and Jonah's story is an imaginary account.[16] In the New Testament, the reference to the earthquake in the passion's narratives is a "literary motif" rather than a historical report.[17] More generally, the Gospels have a normative value in affirming Jesus' identity, but their historical references have a "subordinate function": in other words, the theology of the Gospels is valid, but their historical reliability is less important.[18] How the two aspects can be neatly distinguished is not explained. In the end the truth of the Bible is "restricted" to what it says about salvation.[19]

Another section of the document deals with the "ethical and social issues" raised by the alleged truth of the Bible, e.g., the theme of violence and the place of women. The hard and "offensive" texts of Scripture (e.g., the conquest narratives and the imprecatory psalms) are not read in Catholic services due to "pastoral sensitivity."[20] According to the document, how they can be the Word of God is difficult to say. Again, the standard criterion to discern the inerrancy of the text is to "look at what it says about God and men's salvation,"[21] leaving the rest to the historical-critical readings and cultural sensibilities of the time. In a telling final statement, the document says that "the goal of the truth of Scripture is the salvation of believers."[22] The implication is that what the Bible says

---

12. Pontifical Biblical Commission, *Inspiration and Truth*, 104.
13. Pontifical Biblical Commission, *Inspiration and Truth*, 107.
14. Pontifical Biblical Commission, *Inspiration and Truth*, 108.
15. Pontifical Biblical Commission, *Inspiration and Truth*, 127.
16. Pontifical Biblical Commission, *Inspiration and Truth*, 110.
17. Pontifical Biblical Commission, *Inspiration and Truth*, 120.
18. Pontifical Biblical Commission, *Inspiration and Truth*, 123.
19. Pontifical Biblical Commission, *Inspiration and Truth*, 105.
20. Pontifical Biblical Commission, *Inspiration and Truth*, 125.
21. Pontifical Biblical Commission, *Inspiration and Truth*, 136.
22. Pontifical Biblical Commission, *Inspiration and Truth*, 144.

beyond salvation (however defined) is not to be taken as necessarily true in the same sense.

What about the role of the church in this matter? Since the truth of the Bible is not plenary but needs to be discerned according to its salvific purpose, it is the church that mediates the acceptance and the proclamation of the truth of sacred Scripture.[23] It is the church (the Roman Catholic Church) that selects and limits what the truth of Scripture is. According to the document, then, the Bible is true as far as its message of salvation is concerned and as far as higher criticism dictates. Ultimately, it is the church that defines the truth of Scripture and rules over it.

The Pontifical Biblical Commission's document *The Inspiration and the Truth of Sacred Scripture* argues for a "limited inerrancy" of Scripture (limited to the message of salvation) and reiterates historical-critical views about the unreliability of the historical accounts of both the Old and the New Testament. It is a Roman Catholic blend of traditional and critical views of the Bible which finally exalts the role of the church. While rejoicing for some fruits of the "biblical renewal" that is taking place in Roman Catholicism, especially as far as the encouragement to all to read the Scriptures is concerned, the battle for the truth of Scripture still rages. In no way has Rome come closer to *sola Scriptura*, i.e., the obedience to the self-attesting Word of God written that truly witnesses to the person and work of Jesus Christ. Roman Catholicism has nuanced its position and has relaxed the sharp edges of its opposition, but it still maintains the prominence of the church over the Bible.

How Does the Catholic Church Rejuvenate? (September 1, 2016, Number 128)

Hierarchical. Institutional. Sacramental. Traditional. This set of markers defines the essence of the Roman Catholic Church as a permanent, conservative, top-down religious organization. This is only one side of the coin, however. Rome is also home to movements and groups that express a different sociological outlook. Especially after the Second Vatican Council, many new forms of community have blossomed in the Catholic world: think of the Charismatic Renewal movement, the Focolare movement, the Neocatechumenal way, Communion and Liberation, and Cursillos de Cristanidad, just to name a few of the most known Catholic

---

23. Pontifical Biblical Commission, *Inspiration and Truth*, 149.

groups that involve millions of people around the world. Today, these movements attract growing numbers of people and are the means by which the Roman Catholic Church, particularly in the West, counters the decline. While the traditional parish model hobbles, these movements generally flourish. Serving the "missionary" input encouraged by Pope Francis, they are able to attract new people or to reengage disconnected Catholics.

The relationship of these two components of the Catholic Church has not always been easy. The territorial dimension of the hierarchical church, centered on the authority of the bishop, has found it difficult to come to terms with the charismatic energy of the movements, more inclined to follow their own lay leaders than the local bishops. The well-established patterns of the former have at times clashed with the innovative ways of the latter. The remoteness of much nominal Catholic practice appears to be very different from the intensity offered by the movements. Tensions were experienced to the point of undermining the unity of the Roman Church.

Iuvenescit Ecclesia

After years of gradual and progressive integration of the movements in the sacramental and institutional structure of the Roman Church, it is no surprise to find that the Congregation for the Doctrine of the Faith (the highest authoritative Vatican voice in matters of doctrine) recently came out with a document addressing this very topic (May 15, 2016). *Iuvenescit Ecclesia* (*The Church Rejuvenates*) is a detailed study on how the hierarchical and charismatic gifts need to match in the life of the church. The whole point is to show the necessity and compatibility of both. According to the document, the church is hierarchical in its nature. It is in and through the hierarchy that the church is also sacramental, i.e., the church dispenses God's grace through the sacraments, the Eucharist being the most important one, and lives out its peculiar form of communion, i.e., the church being *cum Petro* (with Peter, with the Pope) and *sub Petro* (under Peter, under the Pope). Quoting Vatican II but failing to support it biblically, the Vatican Congregation argues that "Jesus Christ himself willed that there be hierarchical gifts in order to ensure the continuing presence of his unique salvific mediation."[24] What that means is

---

24. Congregation for the Doctrine of the Faith, *Iuvenescit Ecclesia*, 14.

that Christ's mediation is made present in the hierarchical structure of the Roman Church.

While reaffirming the absolute necessity of the hierarchical nature of the Roman Catholic Church, the document also speaks of "coessentiality"[25] in introducing the charismatic gifts. Both the hierarchical and the charismatic dimensions are essential for the church to be such. Applying this theological point to the issue at stake the document argues that the present-day ecclesial movements are legitimate expressions of the charismatic dimension of the church. They are corporate manifestations of the inner vitality of the hierarchical church. The only way to secure the "harmonic connection"[26] is to serve the hierarchical and sacramental structure of the church centered on the Pope and the bishops. If this point is preserved, the movements have freedom to exist within the Roman Catholic Church.

Both-And

Following Vatican II, the documents apply the integration process that has been characterizing Roman Catholic theology and practice since its beginnings. The system opens itself up to the point of integrating the new point, the new emphasis, the new movement, making sure that it does not harm its stability but serves its expansion. Each movement captures a new form of spirituality, a specific devotional emphasis, a distinct way of living out the Roman Catholic faith, and inserts it into the wider synthesis held together by the hierarchical church. The stability of the institution is matched with the dynamism of the ecclesial movements. The vertical and hierarchical structure of the former is countered by the horizontal breadth of the latter. The absorption of these movements is the last instance of the catholicity of Rome expanding its platform without renewing its core.

The current flurry of activity within Roman Catholic movements does not indicate, in and of itself, that there is hope for a biblical reformation within the Roman Catholic Church in an evangelical sense. It will only be as these movements make changes in the structural elements underlying the nature of Roman Catholicism, not expanding it further but purifying it in the light of God's Word, that they can have a truly

---

25. Congregation for the Doctrine of the Faith, *Iuvenescit Ecclesia*, 10.
26. Congregation for the Doctrine of the Faith, *Iuvenescit Ecclesia*, 7.

reforming function according to the gospel. In today's scenario, these movements, although interesting, seem to promote the Roman Catholic project of integration rather than that of biblical reformation. As the document makes it clear, these movements are meant to rejuvenate Rome, not to reform it biblically.

The "Uncertain Teaching" of Pope Francis (March 1, 2017, Number 134)

Yes or no. This is the only way a Pope (or the Congregation for the Doctrine of the Faith, the Vatican office responsible for Catholic doctrine) can answer a question posed by a cardinal or group of cardinals if and when they inquire about the correct interpretation or application of Catholic teaching. "Yes or no" was the expected answer that never came to a letter written to the Pope by four cardinals[27] in September 2016, pleading with him for clarity regarding the apostolic exhortation *Amoris Lætitia*. The letter asked the Pope five short questions about the exact meaning of some statements contained in the document on whether or not divorced individuals living in new relationships can have access to the Eucharist. Given that different bishops around the world are giving different answers (some saying yes, others no), the four cardinals addressed the Pope himself hoping to receive an authoritative and univocal interpretation of the matter.

So far, no answer has come, and the Pope has made it known that no answer will ever come. The Pope's silence is causing perplexity and some worries in many Catholic circles. Is Catholic teaching becoming subject to many shades of grey? The incident also gives an opportunity to reflect on the Pope's whole approach to the stability of doctrine. Is this absence of yes or no only to be limited to this specific case, or is it a feature of an overall theological vision that lacks rigid reference points?

Magisterium on the Move

This is not an obnoxious issue. One of the most respected Roman Catholic theologians in Italy, Severino Dianich, asked the very question in his recent book *Magistero in Movimento* (*Magisterium on the Move*). There are times in the Catholic Church that its teaching seems to be moving

---

27. LifeSiteNews, "Full Text of 4 Cardinals' Letter to Pope."

from well-established traditional patterns. The last season of movement was Vatican II when, for example, the church changed its mind on religious freedom (which had previously been strongly opposed) and the non-Christian religions (which had previously been given only negative assessments). Now, under the reign of Francis, Dianich argues that we are witnessing another phase of doctrinal movement. Moreover, echoing the title of a book published in the 1980s, Dianich asks whether we are witnessing an "uncertain magisterium"?

To answer the question, Dianich examines the "classical" theological structure based on the argumentative patterns and thought-forms derived from the Graeco-Roman culture. This theological model was based on univocal and fixed meanings and conveyed in juridical language. This structure has been paramount and unchallenged for centuries. Now, more than 50 years after Vatican II (1962–65), the theological structure that Francis is giving voice to appears to be the result of multiple different languages and contaminations of various genres. Dianich identifies a number of reasons that have accelerated the change:

1. The outgoing church that Francis has in mind needs to use simple language and popular media;
2. The attention given by him to people's hearts rather than their minds or reason makes communication more "emotional" than "cognitive";
3. His interest in the "theology of the people" makes him interested in the feelings and aspirations of the ordinary faithful rather than the intellectuals.

All this makes his teaching less definitive, more evocative, less permanent, more hospitable, less rigid, and more dynamic.[28]

Evolving Teaching in Terms of Both-And

Together with other observers, Dianich also argues that Francis's teaching is more "pastoral" than "doctrinal." He is not interested in questioning traditional doctrine as such, although the style and content of his ministry are very different from the "doctrinal magisterium" of his predecessors, i.e., John Paul II and Benedict XVI. He seems to be interested in

---

28. Dianich, *Magistero in Movimento*.

moving in terms of making it become more "merciful" and open-ended. Programmatically, Francis said at the Conference of the Italian Catholic Church in 2015 that Christian doctrine "has no hard face; its body moves and grows, it has tender meat: Christian doctrine is called Jesus Christ."[29] Tender rather than hard meat. A person rather than a body of beliefs. This appears to be the meaning of doctrine according to the Pope. In light of these remarks, it is possible to argue that *Amoris Lætitia* applied this "pastoral" model to the issue of admission of the Eucharist to divorced persons. The Pope here does not formally deny any traditional teachings of the church (how could he possibly do so?) but makes them evolve pastorally towards more inclusive forms of access to the sacraments.

According to Dianich, the Pope is implementing "the most decisive consequences of the teaching of Vatican II." The "pastoral" Pope is applying the "pastoral" council. The outcome is that the teaching is moving on towards more embracing and "catholic" outlooks. The traditional theological structure was geared to give yes or no answers. The post-Vatican II structure is more inclined to suggest both-and types of answer on all kinds of issues. Pope Francis is embodying this new "pastoral" approach and this is the reason why he will not answer the five questions that were asked of him. The Roman Catholic Church used to be thought of as a bulwark of clear and definitive teaching, thus attracting many people looking for a safe haven in the turmoil of the modern world. Vatican II "updated" all this. Pope Francis is now showing what it means for the present-day Roman Church to live with a teaching that is "tender" and elusive.

Pope Francis's Re-Interpretation and Actualization of Gnosticism and Pelagianism: A Plausible Suggestion? (June 1, 2018, Number 150)

Pope Francis is hardly known for his interest in historical theology. Unlike his predecessor, Benedict XVI, Francis's speeches and writings usually contain no reference to patristic, medieval, or modern sources. The texts he consistently quotes are his own. His "down-to-earth" communication style is aimed at simplicity and immediacy, with little or no concession to theological erudition. There is one exception, though. Since his programmatic apostolic exhortation *Evangelii Gaudium* (*The Joy of the Gospel*),

---

29. Francis, "Discorso."

he has often referred to the dangers of "gnosticism" and "pelagianism" as present-day threats for the church.

Here are the somewhat cryptic concerns of the Pope:

> One is the attraction of gnosticism, a purely subjective faith whose only interest is a certain experience or a set of ideas and bits of information which are meant to console and enlighten, but which ultimately keep one imprisoned in his or her own thoughts and feelings. The other is the self-absorbed promethean neopelagianism of those who ultimately trust only in their own powers and feel superior to others because they observe certain rules or remain intransigently faithful to a particular Catholic style from the past. A supposed soundness of doctrine or discipline leads instead to a narcissistic and authoritarian elitism, whereby instead of evangelizing, one analyzes and classifies others, and instead of opening the door to grace, one exhausts his or her energies in inspecting and verifying. In neither case is one really concerned about Jesus Christ or others. These are manifestations of an anthropocentric immanentism. It is impossible to think that a genuine evangelizing thrust could emerge from these adulterated forms of Christianity.[30]

A Warning Against "Subjective" and "Traditionalist" Deviations

Gnosticism and pelagianism were two ancient currents of religious and theological thought that the church had to deal with in the first centuries of its life. Gnosticism is the belief that the material world is created by an emanation of the highest God, trapping the divine spark within the human body. This divine spark could be liberated by "gnosis," i.e., a direct participation in the divine. Gnosticism was mainly countered by church fathers like Ireneus of Lyon (130–202 AD), who insisted on the goodness of creation, the reality of sin, and the embodied Son of God who saves us entirely by way of his death and resurrection.

Pelagianism is the belief that original sin did not taint human nature and that the will is still capable of choosing good or evil without special divine aid. It was mainly fought against by Augustine of Hippo (354–430

---

30. Francis, "Evangelii Gaudium," 94. Other references to gnosticism and pelagianism can be found in his encyclical *Lumen Fidei*, fn67, and in his "Message to Participants."

AD), who underlined the transmission of original sin to all mankind and the utter inability of sinful man to change his destiny without the intervention of divine grace.

What About Francis's Interpretation of Gnosticism and Pelagianism?

From the outset, it seems that the Pope is actually referring to movements and trends within Roman Catholicism that he labels as gnosticism and pelagianism. He opposes these trends and warns Catholics about being trapped by them. For Francis, neo-gnosticism is a "subjective faith": the implicit concern is that it lacks the sacramental, institutional, Marian, and hierarchical outlook of the Roman Catholic faith. Is he here warning against the danger of absorbing too many doses of the "evangelical" faith, which is often caricatured as "subjective" because it focuses on personal faith and witness? Is he admitting that he is concerned with the spreading of "evangelical spirituality" around the world and trying to counter its success by derogatorily labeling it as the latest form of gnosticism? Moreover, is he also referring to the danger of a cafeteria Catholicism where people subjectively pick and choose what they want to believe and practice?

As far as pelagianism is concerned, the Pope seems to address another critical front. Neo-pelagians "trust only in their own powers and feel superior to others because they observe certain rules or remain intransigently faithful to a particular Catholic style from the past."[31] It is clear that he is pointing to traditionalist sectors of the Church of Rome, which dislike that his more casual style and pastoral "reforms" run contrary to well-established patterns. By warning against the latest forms of gnosticism and pelagianism, he is criticizing what he perceives as deviances on both the right front (the traditionalist) and the left front (the evangelical and the secular).

A Two-Edged Sword

Gnosticism and pelagianism provided alternative accounts to biblical Christianity. That is why they have always been perceived as lethal, and that is the reason why the Pope refers to them in very negative and critical terms. However, Francis does not present a historically accurate or

---

31. Francis, "Evangelii Gaudium," 94.

theologically comprehensive assessment of gnosticism and pelagianism.[32] He uses (and perhaps abuses) them to fight his own battles. He is more interested in warning against vague present-day forms of these trends—to the point of disregarding their established meaning—than talking as a church historian about what happened in the past and gathering lessons for today's church.

This "creative" way of redefining historical heresies for the sake of present-day quarrels could also be used against Francis. From a "traditionalist" point of view, he too seems to endorse a "subjective" form of Catholicism whereby people are told to follow their consciences and to gather in the church (the "field-hospital" that includes all) with no personal cost of repentance and faith.[33] Is this not also a form of gnosticism whereby you are expected to follow the "spark" that is in you? On the other hand, secular voices and evangelicals could take issue with Francis for maintaining an ecclesiastical and magisterial apparatus which is grounded on medieval canon law, a monarchical and absolutist political state (i.e., the Vatican), the Vatican bank, a complex combination of works and religious practices, etc. Is this not a form of pelagianism, i.e., a work-based system which obscures the primacy of grace?

Playing with historical theology and re-engineering its vocabulary for present-day purposes is never a neutral business. The denounced abuse can be easily turned back on the denouncer. The task of defending God's church from threats and dangers needs clearer and more accurate tools.

---

32. The lack of Francis's historical and theological accuracy is perhaps one reason behind the recent document by the Congregation for the Doctrine of the Faith, *Placuit Deo* (February 22, 2018), in which both modern versions of gnosticism and pelagianism are treated in more historically informed ways and seen as dangers in "certain aspects of Christian salvation." It is interesting to note that the two applications by Pope Francis are not really followed through.

33. De Chirico, "Vatican File 72."

4

Big Picture
The Theology of Pope Francis

Is the Pope Catholic?[1]

ON MARCH 13, 2013, Jorge Mario Bergoglio became Pope Francis, marking a significant transition in the Roman Catholic Church. What he has been saying and doing since being elected—for instance, his affirming attitudes toward all, his noisy silence over traditional doctrine, his ambiguous language, his thoroughgoing Marianism, and his lack of clarity on several key issues—has caused many to wonder where his thought came from. Some have acclaimed him as the "great reformer";[2] others have argued that he is bringing about a "revolution of tenderness and love."[3] Yet others too have found it difficult to square his words and actions into the established patterns of traditional Roman Catholicism.

There is a general perception that Pope Francis's pontificate has entered an irreversibly declining phase, a sort of late autumn that is a prelude to the end of a season. It is not just a question of age: Yes, Pope Francis is elderly and in poor health. But aging aside, the pontificate finds itself navigating a descending parabola. It started with the language of "mission" and "reform." Francis's tenure, now more than ten years old, was immediately engulfed in a thousand difficulties, particularly within

---

1. For original publishing information, see De Chirico, "Is the Pope Catholic?"
2. Ivereigh, *Great Reformer*.
3. Kasper, *Pope Francis' Revolution*.

the Catholic Church. Many of these problems were caused by the ambiguities of Francis himself, to the point that the push envisaged at the beginning turned out to be broken, if not wholly inconclusive.

In this article, after surveying his intellectual journey prior to becoming Pope, we will pause on some questions that have been asked in relation to him. They provide a variety of interpretative keys to coming to terms with the complexity of Francis's papacy, both inside and outside of the Roman camp. The final section will suggest a hermeneutic of Pope Francis within the dialectics of the "Roman" and the "catholic" dimensions of Roman Catholicism.

I. Who Is Pope Francis?

If you want to get to know a person, ask questions about where he comes from. Massimo Borghesi's recent intellectual biography looks at the life of Jorge Mario Bergoglio (Pope Francis) from a particular angle.[4] Borghesi focuses on the intellectual influences (e.g., books, journals, authors, friendships, networks) that have shaped Bergoglio's thought. In so doing, he provides a fruitful perspective on the genesis and development of the vision that Bergoglio embodies and promotes as Pope. In addition to surveying all the relevant literature, Borghesi has also worked on a questionnaire that Pope Francis responded to, giving further details and filling in the blanks of previous attempts. According to this well-researched analysis, Bergoglio's intellectual biography seems to be marked by three main influences: Jesuit sources, Latin American sources, and Vatican II.

Bergoglio's formative years as a student in philosophy and theology were profoundly impacted by his reading of French Jesuit intellectuals like Henri de Lubac, Gaston Fessard, and Michel de Certeau. They introduced the young Bergoglio to the Catholic dialectical thought, which shies away from rigid Thomism and toward the dynamic synthesis of embracing opposites and enlarging the overall vision. In this Jesuit school of thought—which, by the way, became the matrix of the theology of the Second Vatican Council (1962–65)—what are perceived as oppositions become "tensions," at times painfully disruptive but also potentially creative and always to be maintained as such. Bergoglio became persuaded that human thought is always "in tension," never fixed or stable. He

---

4. Borghesi, *Bergoglio*.

distanced himself from abstract definitions and propositions. He learned always to think in programmatically "open" and "loose" thought-forms.

Intertwined with this dialectical tendency was Bergoglio's early exposure to liberation theology. Since his first attempts to come to terms with its growing popularity in Latin America, Bergoglio has not been interested in the Marxist ideological and political framework of much of the liberation theology of those years. However, he was definitely attracted to the "theology of the people," which is a side aspect of liberation theology. According to this particular way of theologizing, the people's concerns, preoccupations, and aspirations need to be theology's starting point. Rather than considering folk devotions and beliefs as a premodern stage that will be overcome by political liberation, the "theology of the people" assumes them as vital and central. Marian devotions and practices become the most appreciated expressions of the people's hearts, even if they are contrary to Scripture. Theology and pastoral practice must therefore be developed only in a bottom-up way. In this view, the Bible can in no sense be the supreme norm for faith and life. In Borghesi's terms, the future Pope embraced "a liberation theology without Marxism."[5] This is the context of Bergoglio's important emphasis on "the people" as the principal subject of theology and church life.

Bergoglio's early fascination with French Jesuit thought was further consolidated by his reading of the lay Uruguayan Catholic philosopher Alberto Methol Ferré (1929–2009). From Ferré he learned that human thought is always unstable, mobile, and ever-renewing. This was yet another injection of Catholic dialecticism that moved Bergoglio further away from static and traditional Thomism.

Ferré suggested that with Vatican II, the Roman Catholic Church had finally overcome both the Protestant Reformation and the Enlightenment. After fiercely fighting them up front (from the sixteenth century to the nineteenth century), Rome eventually came to terms with its ability to assimilate and absorb the Reformation and the Enlightenment rather than opposing them. At Vatican II, the Catholic Church took the "best" of both and launched a "new" Reformation and a "new" Enlightenment. They were no longer adversaries but contributed positively to the "catholic" accomplishment. In short, after Vatican II, the Reformation as such is over and has been absorbed within the ongoing renewal of the Church of Rome.

---

5. Borghesi, *Bergoglio*, 71.

Building on his early Jesuit influence and Ferré's thought, Bergoglio grew in his conviction that the Catholic Church was the "*complexio oppositorum*" (the whole that makes room for the opposites). His study of German theologian Romano Guardini (1885–1968) corroborated the Catholic dialectical dimension of his thought. Guardini argued that Roman Catholicism is a *Weltanschauung*, an all-embracing worldview, the only one capable of handling multiple tensions between diverging poles and bringing them to a "catholic" unity. From Guardini, Bergoglio developed his idea of unity as a "polyhedron," a geometric figure with different angles and lines, all of which have their own peculiarity. It is a figure that brings together unity and diversity, and Roman Catholicism is the home of unity as a polyhedron. This explains Francis's commitment to ecumenical and interreligious unity, which downplays differences and concentrates on generic commonalities. In this view, unity is governed not by biblical truth and biblical love but by the embracing view of Rome that holds together all angles and lines of life.

Borghesi's intellectual biography makes it clear that Francis's pontificate comes from afar. It is the result of a long series of developments within Catholic thought, from Jesuit sources to Latin American influences up to the Vatican II matrix of contemporary Rome—and all without the correction of the Word of God. One needs to immerse oneself in what happened at the Second Vatican Council to begin to make sense of what Francis is saying and doing now. All analyses of Francis being an "evangelical" or a "kerygmatic" Pope are simplistic and shortsighted. He is much more than that in ways that are dialectical, open-ended, and at the service of the Catholic vision to embrace the whole world.

II. A Hugging Pope?

Many Roman Catholics (and also many non-Catholic observers), accustomed to associating the Papal magisterium with an authoritative, coherent, and stable form of doctrinal teaching, are perplexed if not dismayed by a Pope who seems both to say and not say, to argue for something and to undermine it, to state one position and then contradict it the next breath. As a Jesuit, Pope Francis tends to use an equivocal style, a dubitative and incomplete form of argumentation, an "open" logic, a colloquial, if not casual, tone, and a pastoral style that often lacks clarity and coherence. Officially, the Pope's teachings are set in the context of the historical traditions of the church. In this sense, nothing changes. In reality, however, Francis is accentuating the developmental and inclusive dynamic of Roman Catholicism as it emerged from Vatican II. According to this trend, while there is a sense in which nothing changes, everything is nonetheless rethought, re-expressed, and updated. The "Roman" side of the teaching does not change, while the "catholic" side does change.

A book by the Sicilian Roman Catholic theologian Massimo Naro is a helpful guide in the theological universe of Pope Francis.[6] From the outset, Naro readily acknowledges that the theology of Pope Francis is "an innovative proposal," even when compared with the updating trends of Vatican II. Above all, the Pope's vocabulary needs to be taken into consideration. If you want to try to enter the world of Francis, here are his central words: "mother church," "faithful people of God," "popular spirituality," "mercy," "synodality," "polyhedric ecclesiology," "processes to initiate," "existential peripheries," "humanism of solidarity," "ecological conversion," "dialogue," and "fraternity and brotherhood."[7] Not all are new words; some of them are terms that have already been used in Roman Catholic teaching; however, Francis now gives them a new nuance or a distinct significance.

Naro further suggests that there are two theological frameworks that give meaning to his words: the "theology of the people" and the "theology of mercy." For Francis, theology begins not with biblical revelation or the abstract principles of the official church's teaching but with the common and daily stories of men and women who must be welcomed and affirmed in their particular contexts and life journeys. This attention to the "inside" of the world and to the level where "the people" live pushes him to elevate forms of popular spirituality as authentic religious experiences. He is not scandalized by the "irregular" situations of life in which people find themselves, such as divorce, cohabitation, or same-sex relationships. Instead of teaching an external standard (in theology or morality), the Pope begins where people are, assuming that where they are, there is something good that needs to be affirmed.

According to Francis, "the people" are not the passive and obedient recipients of a top-down ecclesiastical magisterium but active subjects whose religious experiences are true and real (even though not squared

---

6. Naro, *Protagonista è l'abbraccio*.

7. Naro, *Protagonista è l'abbraccio*, 19. For recent attempts at coming to terms with Francis's theology, see Dianich, *Magistero in movimento*; Lafont, *Pape François*; and De Chirico, "Theological Vision of Pope Francis."

with traditional patterns), and they therefore need to be part of the teaching itself. "The people" make the teaching as much as the ecclesiastical authorities of the Roman Church promulgate it.

This version of the "theology of the people" is far from the evangelical belief that Scripture, as the inspired Word of God, is the source by which God teaches, rebukes, corrects, and trains (cf., 2 Tim 3:16). And whom does he train? Not those who want to affirm their own experiences and lifestyles but those who wish to repent from sin and reform their lives following the path indicated by the Bible. From a biblical perspective, Francis's "theology of the people" does not have the external criterion of the Word of God, which questions hearts, practices, and sinful habits and forges a new humanity that is always open to renewal in a process of ongoing sanctification.

Mercy is another keyword in the Pope's magisterium. In his way of putting it, mercy is "the bridge that connects God and man, opening our hearts to the hope of being loved forever despite the limits of our sins."[8] In this dense sentence, there is a strategic theological point. Among other things, as Cardinal Matteo Zuppi writes in the introduction, the Pope means that "at the center of the biblical message is not sin, but mercy."[9] In Naro's words, Christian theology must be freed from "hamartiocentrism,"[10] that is, from the centrality of sin. Sin must be replaced by the pervasiveness of God's mercy, which "can help us to break free from hamartiocentrism and to rediscover the tenderness of God."[11] In his view, Pope Francis has replaced sin with mercy at the center of his message.

In the Pope's theology, sin is at most "the human limit"[12] but not the breaking of the covenant, the rebellion against God, the disobedience to his commandments, or the subversion of divine authority that results in God's righteous and holy judgment. If sin is a "human limit," then the cross of Christ did not atone for sin but only manifested God's

---

8. Francis, "Misericordiae Vultus," 2.

[The English translation of the Papal text on the Vatican website is blurred and incorrect. It says ". . . the bridge that connects God and man, opening our hearts to the hope of being loved forever *despite our sinfulness*" (italics added). However, the Latin official text says "praeter nostri peccati fines," which needs to be translated as "despite the limits or bounds of our sins" as the Italian, French and Spanish versions rightly translate.]

9. Naro, *Protagonista è l'abbraccio*, 16.
10. Naro, *Protagonista è l'abbraccio*, 93.
11. Naro, *Protagonista è l'abbraccio*, 114.
12. Naro, *Protagonista è l'abbraccio*, 91.

mercy in an exemplary way. The words used by the Pope are the same as those of the evangelical faith (e.g., mercy, sin, grace, gospel) but are given a different meaning than in the gospel.[13] Francis sees everything from the perspective of a metaphysic of mercy that swallows sin without passing through propitiation, expiation, or reconciliation, which the cross of Jesus Christ wrought to give salvation to those who believe in him. If everything is mercy and sin is only a limit, the "popular" and "merciful" account of the gospel taught by Pope Francis is another "catholic" variant of the deviation on which the Church of Rome was established and on which, sadly, it continues to move forward.

III. A Protestant Pope?

"Here I stand": these are the famous words spoken by Martin Luther in front of the Diet of Worms in 1521. Questioned about his convictions as they had been outlined a few years before in the Ninety-Five Theses, Luther stood firm on the truth of the Bible and its good news: sinners can be justified by Christ alone through faith alone. It was clear to all what he believed. The Council of Trent (1545–62) was the official response of the Roman Catholic Church to the issues raised by the Protestant Reformation. By rejecting the tenets of the Protestant understanding of the gospel and declaring its proponents anathema, Trent endorsed the view that sinners could not be justified by faith alone; instead, Catholicism insisted on an ongoing journey of good works, punctuated by the sacraments administered by the church. Where Trent stood was and is crystal-clear.[14]

In recent decades, though, the situation has become blurred. The 1999 Joint Declaration on the Doctrine of Justification[15]—signed by mainstream Lutherans and the Church of Rome—introduced ambiguities in language, juxtapositions of terms, and theological nuances that make it difficult to understand where the signatories stand in comparison to Luther's and Trent's viewpoints. After the declaration, Rome's position on justification is harder to ascertain.[16] This ambiguous context is Pope Francis's framework when he speaks on the topic.

13. For an exploration of this theme, see De Chirico, *Same Words*.

14. It is no surprise that justification was dealt with during the first session of the council. The session lasted seven months (from June 21, 1546, to January 13, 1547), and it was the most intense topic that the council addressed. See O'Malley, *Trent*.

15. Lutheran World Federation, "Joint Declaration."

16. See De Chirico, "Not By Faith Alone?"

In the ecumenical ceremony that commemorated the Reformation in Lund (Sweden) in 2016, Pope Francis made a perfunctory reference to the doctrine of justification.[17] In a generally positive comment on Luther, the Pope argued that "the doctrine of justification expresses the essence of human existence before God," thus seeming to be in accord with what evangelicals might say about the doctrine. Recognizing justification as something essential is surely a pointer toward its primary importance for the Christian life. But notice that the Pope speaks of the essential role of justification in "human existence" in general, not just in the Christian life. The context of this statement does not restrict it to Christians, believers in Christ, or disciples of Jesus. The Pope is not referring to the essence of the Christian life but to human existence as a whole

Here is the ambiguity. Does this mean that justification is essential for all human beings, regardless of whether or not they are Christians? Does it mean that justification is a constitutive component of life in general, a defining mark of the existence of all men and women? Does it mean that all those living a "human existence" are essentially justified? Certainly, this is not the meaning that either Luther or the Council of Trent gave to justification. For Luther, there was a sense in which justification could be defined as "the essence of human existence before God," with the caveat that this would refer only to those who have received the grace of God by faith alone. In other words, justification is the essence of the *Christian life*, not of human life in general.

On the surface, then, the Pope's comment on justification seems to be very biblical and indeed very Protestant. A closer look reveals, though, that things are not as clear as they appear. While affirming the importance of justification, Pope Francis seems to confuse it with a universal property that all human beings share. If this is what the Pope meant, he is very far from what either Luther or Trent stood for. Indeed, he is very close to a universalist, all-embracing, humanistic "gospel" that betrays the biblical gospel of salvation in Christ alone by faith alone for those who repent and believe.

Arguably, what Pope Francis said in Lund on justification is generic and can be interpreted in different ways. It is not possible to say for sure that this is what he had in mind. Therefore, one needs to look for other references to justification elsewhere in his writings or speeches.

---

17. Francis, "Homily (Lund)."

Another quotation is worth pondering. In his widely acclaimed 2013 exhortation, *The Joy of the Gospel*,[18] the programmatic document of his pontificate, Francis writes, "Non-Christians, by God's gracious initiative, when they are faithful to their own consciences, can live justified by the grace of God."[19] This section of the exhortation deals with ecumenical and interreligious dialogue in the context of mission. According to Pope Francis, non-Catholic Christians are already united in baptism,[20] Jews do not need to convert,[21] and with believing Muslims, the way is "dialogue" because "together with us they adore the one and merciful God."[22] Other non-Christians are also "justified by the grace of God" and are linked to "the paschal mystery of Jesus Christ."[23]

Justification, according to the Pope, seems to be the outcome of following one's own conscience. It is still "by God's gracious initiative" (although not necessarily by his grace alone), but it is no longer by faith—let alone by faith alone. It is through the conscience that men and women are linked to the paschal mystery of Jesus Christ—that is, the work of Christ as it is reenacted at the Eucharist, the chief sacrament of the church. Faith in Jesus Christ is gone. The gospel appears to be not a message of salvation from God's judgment but instead a vehicle to access a fuller measure of a salvation that is already given to all humankind through the conscience. What about faith in Jesus Christ? What about his justice being credited to the sinner? Are, therefore, all human beings justified ultimately by following their consciences? By grace but not by faith?

At this point, it becomes clear that the Lund reference to justification being "the essence of human existence" was purposefully and intentionally designed to mean that justification defines everyone's life, not only that of the believing Christian. This reference in *The Joy of the Gospel* makes it abundantly clear that the Pope, while using the language of justification, has radically altered its meaning and made it synonymous with a universal existence embracing the whole of humanity. He is using the word in an ambiguous way, but a closer inspection reveals its non-biblical content.

18. Francis, "Evangelii Gaudium,"
19. Francis, "Evangelii Gaudium," 254.
20. Francis, "Evangelii Gaudium," 244.
21. Francis, "Evangelii Gaudium," 247
22. Francis, "Evangelii Gaudium," 252; quotation of Holy See, "Lumen Gentium," 16.
23. Francis, "Evangelii Gaudium," 254.

Is Pope Francis's justification what Luther stood for? And, more decidedly, is this what the Bible teaches about justification? The Pope is saying radically different things. Therefore, before listing Pope Francis as a friend of the evangelical faith, we must understand what he is saying on his own terms. Beyond commonalities in the use of words, he belongs to a different world.

IV. A Heretical Pope?

Roman Catholics as individuals and groups may have different opinions about the Pope. After all, the Church of Rome is not a monolith, and even Catholic people are polarized by their views of the Pope. But what happens when negative voices become more frequent, more outspoken, and more radical in their criticism, as seems to be the case in recent months? While public opinion is still heavily influenced by the overall positive image that Francis has and continues to consider him a kind of hero, within Catholic circles, the "wait-and-see" approach toward some awkward aspects of his teaching is coming to an end. Groups of intellectuals, priests, and even cardinals are voicing their growing embarrassment and are doing it publicly and with a severe tone. In raising their concerns, they point not to peripheral elements but to crucial matters of doctrine. The irony is that the one who is supposed to guard the Roman Catholic deposit of faith is charged with allegations of introducing confusion, if not heresy.

At least three criticisms of Pope Francis are worth considering. Let us briefly look at them chronologically.

In September 2016, four cardinals (three of whom have recently died) sent to the Pope five questions (in Latin, *dubia*, doubts)[24] concerning the interpretation of key parts of his 2016 post-synodal exhortation on the family, *Amoris Lætitia*.[25] In the explanatory note, they give voice to the "grave disorientation and great confusion" that exist in the Catholic community. According to the cardinals, the contrasting interpretations of the Papal text arise from its ambiguity and the apparent contradictions with previous official teaching on the readmission of divorced people to the Eucharist. Although they asked the Pope to clear any ambiguity, Francis never responded and perhaps will never do so. Their doubts will remain unanswered.

24. Pentin, "Full Text and Explanatory Notes."
25. Francis, "Amoris Lætitia."

In July 2017, more than two hundred Catholic priests and intellectuals from around the world wrote "a filial correction concerning the propagation of heresies" to the Pope,[26] thus elevating the tone of the criticism to the denouncing of doctrinal deviations. Their observations were no longer questions but real corrections made to the Pope's teaching. The word "heresy" was evoked in looking at the demise of the traditional teaching on marriage and the sacraments, as they see happening and severely threatening the future credibility of their church.

Finally, at the end of July 2017, Father Thomas Weinandy, a Capuchin priest, a former chief of staff for the United States Bishops Committee on Doctrine, and a current member of the Vatican's International Theological Commission, made public a letter sent to the Pope.[27] In it, he argues that "a chronic confusion seems to mark your pontificate obscured by the ambiguity of your words and actions. This fosters within the faithful a growing unease. It compromises their capacity for love, joy and peace." Moreover, Weinandy charges Francis with "demeaning" the importance of doctrine, appointing bishops who "scandalize" believers with dubious "teaching and pastoral practice," giving prelates who object the impression they will be "marginalized or worse" if they speak out, and causing faithful Catholics to "lose confidence in their supreme shepherd." This is hard language coming from a mainstream Roman Catholic theologian who has spent his whole life in the service of his church and the Vatican. These three criticisms are extremely serious and perhaps a tipping point in Catholic circles as far as the uneasiness toward Pope Francis is concerned.

V. An Interfaith Pope?

The 2020 encyclical *All Brothers* has been rightly called the "political manifesto" of Pope Francis's pontificate. In fact, there is much politics and much sociology in *All Brothers*,[28] a very long document (130 pages) that looks more like a book than a letter. Francis wants to plead the cause of universal fraternity and social friendship. To do this, he speaks of borders to be broken down, of waste to be avoided, of human rights that are not sufficiently universal, of unjust globalization, of burdensome pandemics,

---

26. Correctio Filialis, "Correctio Filialis."
27. Weinandy, "Critical Letter."
28. Francis, "Fratelli Tutti."

of migrants to be welcomed, of open societies, of solidarity, of peoples' rights, of local and global exchanges, of the limits of the liberal political vision, of world governance, of political love, of the recognition of the other, of the injustice of any war, and of the abolition of the death penalty.

Pope Francis has disseminated these themes in many speeches and in his other encyclical, *Laudato Si'*,[29] on care for the environment. Not surprisingly, he himself is by far the most cited author in the work (about 180 times), which evidences the circular trend of his thinking (the need to be self-strengthening) and the "novelty" of his teaching with respect to the traditional themes of the social doctrine of the Roman Catholic Church.

Only in the eighth (last) chapter of the encyclical does the Pope deal with the theme of fraternity with religions, and here the document becomes more "theological." This section can be considered an interpretation of the Document on Human Fraternity for World Peace and Living Together that Francis himself signed in Abu Dhabi with the Grand Imam of Al-Azhar, Ahmad Al-Tayyeb, in 2019.[30] More than just a reflection, this section is a jumble of quotations (better: self-quotations) that, by overlapping plans and juxtaposing issues, ends up confusing rather than clarifying. Despite this, its basic message is sufficiently clear: we are all brothers as children of the same God. This is Pope Francis's theological truth.

When *All Brothers* talks about God, it does so in general terms that can fit Muslim, Hindu, and other religions' accounts of God or gods, as well as the Masonic reference to the Watchmaker. To further confirm this, *All Brothers* ends with a "Prayer to the Creator" that could be used both in a mosque and in a Masonic temple. Having removed the "stumbling block" of Jesus Christ, everyone can turn to an unspecified divinity to experiment with what it means to be "brothers"—brothers in a divinity made in the image and likeness of humanity, not brothers and sisters on the basis of the work of Jesus Christ who has died and risen for sinners. *All Brothers* genetically modified the biblically understood meaning of fraternity by transferring it to common humanity. In doing so, it has lost the biblical boundaries of the word and replaced them with pan-religious traits and contents. Is this a service to the gospel of Jesus Christ?

Many people, the vast majority of people, will not read Pope Francis's long encyclical *All Brothers*. They will only hear a few sentences or lines repeated here and there as slogans. However, what everyone will retain

---

29. Francis, "Laudato Si'."
30. Francis and Al-Tayyeb, "Document on Human Fraternity."

lies in the effective opening of the document: "'All brothers.'" After quoting this famous greeting of Francis of Assisi, the Pope goes on to fill the words with his own meaning: we are all brothers (and sisters). It is a very powerful universalist and inclusive message that communicates the idea that the lines of demarcation between believers and nonbelievers, atheists and agnostics, Muslims and Christians, and evangelicals and Catholics are all so fluid and relative that they do not undermine the bonds of fraternity that they all share. The French Revolution had already launched "fraternity" as a secular belonging to human citizenship (together with "freedom" and "equality"), but now the Pope defines it in a theological sense. We are "brothers"—not because we are citizens but because we are children of the same God. According to Pope Francis, we are all children of God and therefore brothers and sisters of all those among us.

In *All Brothers*, there is the understandable anxiety aimed at dissolving conflicts, overcoming injustices, and stopping wars. This concern is commendable, even if the analyses and proposals are political and therefore can be legitimately discussed. What is problematic is the theological key chosen to overcome divisions: the declaration of human fraternity in the name of the divine sonship of all humanity. The Pope uses a theological category ("all brothers as all children of God") to create the conditions for a better world.

What are the theological implications of such a statement? Here are a few: first, *All Brothers* raises a soteriological question: if we are all brothers because we are all children of God, does this mean that all will be saved? The entire encyclical is pervaded by a powerful universalist inspiration that also includes atheists.[31] Religions, in the broad sense, are always presented in a positive sense,[32] and there is mention neither of a biblical criticism of religions nor of the need for repentance and faith in Jesus Christ as the key to receiving salvation. Everything in the encyclical suggests that everyone, as brothers and sisters, will be saved.

Second, there is a christological issue. Even though Jesus Christ is referred to here and there, his exclusive and offensive claims are kept silent. Francis cleverly presents Jesus Christ not as the cornerstone on which the whole building of life stands or collapses but as the stone only for those who recognize him. Above Jesus Christ, according to the encyclical, there is a "God" who is the father of all. We are children of this

---

31. Francis, Fratelli Tutti, 281.
32. Francis, Fratelli Tutti, 277–79.

"God," even without recognizing Jesus Christ as Lord and Savior. Jesus is thus reduced to the rank of the champion of Christians alone, while the other "brothers" are still children of the same "God," regardless of faith in Jesus Christ.

Third, there is an ecclesiological issue. If we are all "brothers," there is a sense in which we are all part of the same church that gathers brothers and sisters together. The boundaries between humanity and church are so ill-defined that the two communities become coincident. Humanity is the church, and the church is humanity. This is in line with the sacramental vision of the Roman Catholic Church, which, according to Vatican II, is understood as a "sign and instrument of the unity of the whole human race."[33] According to the encyclical, the whole of the human race belongs to the church, not on the basis of faith in Jesus Christ but on the basis of a shared divine sonship and human fraternity.

After the Council of Trent (1545–63) and up to Vatican II (1962–65), Roman Catholicism related to the "others" (be they Protestants, other religions, or different cultural and social movements) through its "Roman" claims and called them to return to the fold. The "brothers" were only Roman Catholics in communion with the Roman Pope. The others were "pagans," "heretics," and "schismatics," excluded from sacramental grace, which is accessible only through the hierarchical system of the Roman Catholic Church. With Vatican II, it was Rome's "catholicity" that prevailed over its "Roman" centeredness. Protestants have become "separated brothers," other religions have been viewed positively, and people in general have been approached as "anonymous Christians." Now, according to Francis's encyclical, we are "all brothers." The expansion of catholicity has been further stretched. From being excluded from the "Roman" side of Rome, we are now all included by the "catholic" side of Rome.

VI. A Liquid Pope?

Since sociologist Zygmunt Bauman coined the expression "liquid modernity," the adjective "liquid" has been applied to almost all phenomena: liquid society, liquid family, and liquid love. In our world, liquidity seems to describe well the vacillating, uncertain, fluid, and volatile features of contemporary life. Everything is mobile, plastic, and soft; nothing can be put into solid, stable, and lasting casts.

33. Second Vatican Council, "Lumen Gentium," 1.

To the already-wide range of associations, liquidity has been added as a descriptor for a specific religious tradition—in this case, liquid Roman Catholicism. In an article in *First Things*, George Weigel, a conservative American intellectual, writes about it in a worried tone.[34] For some time, Weigel and other exponents of Roman Catholic traditionalism in the United States have expressed their frustration (to put it mildly) at the massive injection of liquidity into Roman Catholicism by Pope Francis, which includes the uncertain teaching on doctrinal and moral subjects of primary importance, a kind of intolerance toward the pre-conciliar liturgy, the constant pickaxing of the Roman Catholic institution with repeated criticism of clericalism, the ways the Pope acts outside the box and so destabilizes customs, and the welcoming and merciful message at the expense of the doctrinal and moral requirements of the *Catechism of the Catholic Church*. All of these make Francis a "liquid" Pope who is liquifying an institution that has made its rocky and immutable structure a distinctive identity trait.

In addition to Francis, Weigel sees the Roman Catholic Church troubled by other sources of liquidity. Weigel's article indicates his alarm at the requests that are emerging from the so-called Synodal Path of the German Catholic Church, including a series of conferences of the Catholic Church in Germany to discuss a range of contemporary theological and organizational questions. Supported by the majority of German bishops, these requests include celibacy becoming optional for clergy (married life being the other option), opening ministries to women (the diaconate first, then one day the priesthood perhaps), and recognition (with ecclesiastical blessing) of homosexual unions. These are just some of the controversial proposals that are about to arrive at the Vatican. There are growing concerns all over the Roman Catholic world about the German Synodal Path. In this regard, Francis's liquidity is just a pale version of the turbo-liquidity coming out of Catholic Germany.

Weigel and the circles of Catholic traditionalism in the United States witness these processes of liquefaction horrified. For them, Roman Catholicism is a canonically compact religion, sacramentally coherent, institutionally stable, and doctrinally integrated. They have in mind a Roman Catholicism that is more "Roman" than "Catholic," anchored to its unchangeable dogmas, tied to its consolidated tradition, characterized by fidelity and obedience on the part of the faithful, and centered

---

34. Weigel, "Liquid Catholicism."

on its ecclesiastical hierarchies. Liquid Roman Catholicism, for them, is a pathology of catholicity that runs the risk of protestantizing Rome and dispersing its uniqueness in the bewildering contemporary age.

It is interesting to observe these internal conflict dynamics in Roman Catholicism from the outside. Often, in the past, Roman Catholic apologetics contrasted evangelical fragmentation with Roman Catholic solidity, denigrating the former and exalting the latter. It was not a credible argument in the past, but it is even less so today. Roman Catholicism is as divided internally as any other religious movement of global reach. Moreover, traditional Roman Catholic apologetics contrasted the stability of Rome with the volatility of the Reformation. This argument too was superficial and one-sided, and it is even more so now. Roman Catholicism is undergoing significant transformation processes. The fact that Rome is deemed to be *semper eadem* (always the same) needs to be seen in light of its ongoing updating and development.

The key elements to come to terms within this issue are twofold. First, one needs to consider the dual nature of Roman Catholicism, which is, at the same time, "catholic" (liquid) and "Roman" (solid). Its genius has always been to combine the two faces in order to make them coexist and reinforce each other. Today, it is its liquidity that seems to be prevalent, but its solidity will not fail, as Roman Catholicism comprises both. The second key element is the interpretation of the Second Vatican Council (1962–65), which fostered change.[35] Vatican II has given Roman Catholicism such an injection of liquidity that today it is impacting the solid structures of Rome as never before. Will the long-term outcomes of Vatican II be able to liquefy them completely? Unlikely.

Rome will remain liquid and solid, perhaps in a different arrangement than it combines them today, but it is still "catholic" and, at the same time, "Roman." Weigel and other Roman Catholic traditionalists dream of a return to a more "Roman" Catholicism, but have they not yet understood that their religion is also increasingly "catholic" at the same time?

VII. A More "Catholic" Than "Roman" Pope

After celebrating the five hundred years of the Protestant Reformation, with its call to the church to submit to the authority of Scripture and its

---

35. As Shaun Blanchard has reminded us in a recent article; see Blanchard, "Reform Was Real."

recovery of the good news that we are saved by Christ alone through faith alone, it is appropriate to ask whether Rome is still grappling with the same issues that gave rise to it. Luther took issue with the Pope and his theology and practice of dispensing God's pardon through indulgences. Luther's standard was the biblical gospel, and he challenged the Catholic Church to embrace afresh the gospel. Rome responded by absorbing some of Luther's concerns about grace and faith within the sacramental system largely shaped around Roman elements and within its synergistic theology significantly marked by Catholic components, thus reinforcing the overall Roman Catholic synthesis rather than reforming it according to the Word of God.

Ever since, the Roman Catholic system has been swinging and bending one way or another to accommodate either progressive or traditional trends, either reiterating Roman emphases or introducing Catholic ones and then rebalancing the whole. However, the church was not reformed because it did not recognize the external and supreme authority of Scripture and the gospel of salvation by faith alone. As it stands, it will never be renewed according to the Word of God. It will certainly accommodate "Catholic" movements like the Charismatic renewal and "Roman" movements like the Marian groups and then refix the overall synthesis. It will even accommodate an emphasis on biblical literacy while commending unbiblical devotions and beliefs: both—and, Roman and Catholic!

Roman Catholicism is what it is because it inherently combines the "Roman" element with the "catholic" one. Both are essential components of the synthesis offered by the Roman Catholic system. The genius of Roman Catholicism is its being at the same time Roman and catholic, one *and* the other, one never *at the expense of* the other.

It is "Roman" in the sense that it is organically attached to the city and the Church of Rome and, by extension, to the institutions, canon laws, dogmas, hierarchy, and political outlook associated with it. Much of this derives from a complex history marked by an imperial ideology.

It is "catholic" in the sense of being inclusive, global, embracing, and open to different movements, trends, and trajectories. The Roman elements provide stability and continuity, while the Catholic element fosters development and renewal. Roman Catholicism is able to hold the tension deriving from its dual identity and maintain it at a manageable balance.

What is happening with Pope Francis is to be understood against the background of the tensions between the Roman and Catholic poles within Roman Catholicism. Francis is strongly pushing Rome's "catholic" agenda, embracing all, affirming all, expanding the boundaries of the church, and expanding its traditional boundaries.

Some traditionalist circles are reacting strongly because they see the danger of losing the Roman elements represented by the well-established teachings and practices of the church. They see the Catholic swallowing the Roman. They see the risk of the Catholic taking precedence over the Roman and therefore severing the dynamic link that has characterized Roman Catholicism for centuries. Whereas with the previous Pope (Benedict XVI), the overall balance was more in favor of the Roman than the Catholic, with Francis the Roman Catholic pendulum is swinging toward the catholicity of Rome. Francis's critics believe that he has gone too far and want the pendulum to reverse toward more reassuring Roman elements.

What is happening now with the criticism of Pope Francis is business as usual in the Roman Catholic Church: at times, the pendulum swings one way before readdressing the overall balance. It could be argued that the Second Vatican Council was a great push toward the Catholic element, and the reigns of John Paul II and Benedict XVI were subsequent attempts to moderate it in terms of reinforcing the Roman elements. With Francis, the Catholic is again winning the day. These tensions will continue as long as Roman Catholicism exists. They are inner movements within the system. Pope Francis is the living embodiment of this tension.

Nothing is going to break abruptly, and more importantly, no biblical reformation is possible under these conditions. Roman Catholicism will be stretched and go through a stress test but will be able to handle both Francis's catholicity and his critics' insistence on the Roman component. The synthesis will be expanded, but the gospel will not be allowed to change Rome. This is why the Reformation is not over.

A Window into the Theological Vision of Pope Francis[36]

Synopsis[37]

Pope Francis seems to be an easy character to come to terms with. Frugal, transparent, and down-to-earth, he is one of the most popular

36. For original publishing information, see DeChirico, "Window into the Theological Vision."

37. When Cardinal Jorge Mario Bergoglio was elected as Pope Francis on March 13,

public figures around the globe. What about the theological vision that permeates his papacy? In order to have a glimpse of Francis's spiritual horizon, one needs to take his Jesuit identity into account. Despite the kind manners of the man, a certain anti-Protestant attitude lingers in the Pope's mind and heart. Although he does not seem to be pushing a Roman Catholic outlook as dogmatic as his predecessor's, he nonetheless has his own "dogmatic certainties," and they are not what one may expect them to be. Furthermore, his insistence on "mission" needs to be grasped within the whole of his theological framework. The use of the same word by other Christians does not necessarily imply the same meaning. Mission is the outworking of Francis's program and fits his own personal interpretation of the papacy. This theological portrait of the Pope will indicate the particular blend of catholicity he is embodying and advocating. Since catholicity is what Roman Catholicism stems from, Francis's version of catholicity is perhaps the most significant mark of his papacy.

Jesuit Anti-Protestantism?

Friendly. Appreciative. Always wanting to stress commonalities and to lay aside differences. This has been the popular image of Pope Francis in his dealings with non-Catholics thus far. This may have been the rule, but now there is an exception that sheds light on a less-known aspect of his thought. The recent republication of a lecture on the history of the Jesuits that Archbishop Bergoglio gave in Argentina in 1985 indicates the kind of harsh assessment that he gave of the Protestant Reformation in general and of John Calvin in particular. The lecture was republished in Spain in 2013 and then translated into Italian in book form.[38]

In examining the history of the Jesuits, Bergoglio gives special attention to their interactions with the Reformation and their role in the Latin American missions. According to him, the inevitable consequences

---

2013, the first question that many Vatican experts asked was, What did he write? What books did he publish? The answer was simple and straightforward: none. Contrary to his predecessor, Benedict XIV, who had been a major theologian in the post-Vatican II Roman Catholic Church, Bergoglio was not a scholar. So, are we left completely without open windows onto his thought prior to the beginning of his papacy? Not necessarily. There is at least one hint that helps us to appreciate the theological worldview Bergoglio is coming from. It is not the only element that defines his background but still a significant one, and it will prove an intriguing entry point into the unfolding theological vision of his papacy.

38. Francis, *Chi sono i gesuiti*.

of the Reformation are the annihilation of man in his anxiety (resulting in existential atheism) and a leap in the dark by a type of superman (as envisaged by Nietzsche). Both outcomes lead to "the death of God" and a kind of paganism that manifests itself as Marxism and Nazism—all this originating from the "Lutheran position"! Bergoglio argues that the Reformation is the root of all the tragedies of the modern West, from secularization to the death of God, from totalitarian regimes to ideological suicides.

There is nothing new under the sun. This disparaging and appalling view of the Reformation had been the common reading of modern European history by scores of Counter Reformation Catholic polemists until recent decades. Bergoglio did not invent it. He rather reaffirms it as if more thorough historical research and theological and cultural analyses never took place after the Council of Trent. What can we make of his friendly tones toward Protestants if he really thinks that the "Lutheran position" is to be blamed for all the evils of Western civilization?

There is more. Bergoglio makes a distinction between Martin Luther the "heretic" and John Calvin the "heretic" and "schismatic." The Lutheran heresy is "a good idea gone foolish," but Calvin is even worse because he also tore apart man, society, and the church. As for man, Bergoglio's Calvin split reason from the heart, thus producing the "Calvinist squalor." In society, Calvin pitted the bourgeoisie against the other working classes, thus becoming "the father of liberalism." The worst schism happened in the church, however. There, Calvin "beheaded the people of God from being united with the Father." He beheaded the people of God from its patron saints. He also beheaded them from the mass, that is, the mediation of the "really present" Christ. In summary, Calvin was an executioner that destroyed man, poisoned society, and ruined the church.

Despite the much-applauded yet inconsequential "words of apology" recently extended to Pentecostals and Waldensians, Pope Francis still demonstrates he has mixed feelings about the whole of the Protestant Reformation.

A Dogmatic Certainty

The more Pope Francis speaks, the clearer his theology becomes. He has always said that the traditional dogmas and the catechism are in the background of what he affirms and that nothing of substance changes in his remarks on God's infinite mercy and the goodness within every human being. This is true only in part. Different Roman Catholic interpreters have always played with the task of putting different accents on the same sheet music, and Francis is deliberately putting his preferred accent—*fortissimo*—on another key dogma.

Talking to Jesuit journalists from across the world, Pope Francis said many things, and these comments attracted lots of positive reviews. Here we will focus on this particular one: "I have a dogmatic certainty: God is in every person's life. God is in everyone's life. Even if the life of a person has been a disaster, even if it is destroyed by vices, drugs, or anything else—God is in this person's life. You can, you must, try to seek God in every human life. Although the life of a person is a land full of thorns and weeds, there is always a space in which the good seed can grow."[39]

This Pope is not someone who likes to use dogmatic language, at least on the surface. Yet, here he is using the strongest language possible. He really wants to mean what he is saying. God is in everyone's life. This unqualified statement raises questions about what the Pope thinks of the nature of sin in human life and the reality that we all "fall short" of God because of our sin (e.g., Rom 3:23). While teaching that those who believe in Christ shall be saved, the Bible is clear in saying that humans universally are sinners and therefore are enemies of God and under his judgment. The Pope, instead, wants to affirm the dogma that God is present because there is always some residual "good" in man.

One further comment by Pope Francis reinforces his dogmatic view on man's inherent openness to God's presence. Responding to the editor of *La Repubblica* (September 11), he wrote the following:

> You ask me if the God of Christians forgives one who doesn't believe and doesn't seek the faith. Premise that—and it's the fundamental thing—the mercy of God has no limits if one turns to him with a sincere and contrite heart; the question for one who doesn't believe in God lies in obeying one's conscience. Sin, also for those who don't have faith, exists when one goes against one's conscience. To listen to and to obey it means, in fact, to decide in face of what is perceived as good or evil.[40]

Put simply: obeying one's conscience is what God will take account of in granting forgiveness. Notice that the Pope here is not speaking of

---

39. Francis, "Interview with Pope Francis."
40. Francis, "Open Dialogue."

those who have never heard the gospel but of those who don't believe it, knowing what they are doing. Apparently, to go against one's conscience counts more than going against God's revelation. Although the Bible teaches there is no excuse before God's righteous judgment (e.g., Rom 2:1), Francis here says that the conscience is the final judge to whom God will submit himself. The human conscience is the determinative factor for God's forgiveness.

These two statements—God is in every person, and obeying one's conscience is what really matters—are thus part of a coherent "dogma" of human goodness and the consequential hope for universal salvation. What is important to observe is not so much the details of each statement but rather the general theological vision that lies at its core. Traditionally, Roman Catholicism has worked within the nature-grace scheme largely dependent on its pontifically ratified Thomistic tradition. According to this theological metanarrative, nature, although partially flawed by sin, is elevated by grace to its supernatural end, and the sacramental system of the church is the way in which grace effects this elevation.

Moreover, in the twentieth century, this scheme was significantly modified and received an important endorsement at Vatican II. Whereas the old scheme implied that grace needed to be "added" to nature, the new version claims that grace is already part of nature and works, not as something extrinsic, but intrinsic, to it. Grace is inherent to nature and through the sacramental system of the church it unfolds itself more and more.

One advocate of a "grace within nature" framework was Karl Rahner (1904–1984), himself a Jesuit like Pope Francis. His view of the "anonymous Christian" stated that each human being is already inherently graced and therefore a Christian, even though he is not aware of it or does not want to be such. While not using the Rahnerian language, Pope Francis works within a similar "dogmatic" framework. God is present in everyone, and one's conscience is what will ultimately count. Despite all its missional allure and merciful attitude, what Francis is saying is not good news for gospel-centered people.

What About Mission?

Together with the dogmatic certainty about human conscience, mission is another defining word. Pope Francis wrote the apostolic letter titled *The Joy of the Gospel* (*Evangelii Gaudium*), the second magisterial document of his pontificate (the previous being the encyclical *Light of Faith* and the most recent one being *Laudato Si'* on ecological concerns).[41] It is the first, however, to come entirely from his own pen (and was originally written in Spanish). In 2010, Benedict XVI launched the idea of the "new evangelization," and in 2012, he convened a Synod of Bishops to discuss it. Now we have Francis's interpretation of the new evangelization in an authoritative statement, which is also a compendium to interpret most of what the Pope has been saying and doing so far.

Although *Evangelii Gaudium* comes one year after the synod and is quoted twenty-seven times, Francis's whole approach to the topic is more dependent on the 2007 Latin American document of Aparecida.[42] More than the "new evangelization," this Pope loves to speak about "mission." The former attempts at reaching the non-practicing Catholics, the latter is a style of the whole church going in all directions. The former is particularly relevant for the ever-more-secular West; the latter is a "catholic" agenda for the world. The vision of Pope Francis is an outward one, and "mission" (whatever it may mean) is at the center of it. His church will not be on the defensive but will be engaged proactively in promoting its vision.

The word "joy" is repeated fifty-nine times and is the common theme of the document. The Pope wants to give a joyful flavor to mission. The gospel is also part of the title but has a lesser role in it. The "heart" of the gospel is summarized in this way: "The beauty of the saving love of God made manifest in Jesus Christ who died and rose from the dead."[43] In this apparently evangelical definition of the gospel, something is missing: while the objective good news of God is rightly related to the narrative of Jesus Christ, the subjective part of it (i.e., personal faith and repentance from one's own sin) is omitted.

The tragedy of being lost without Jesus Christ is also downplayed. For this reason, nowhere in the document are unrepentant unbelievers called to repent and believe in Jesus Christ. Non-Catholic Christians are

---

41. Francis, "Evangelii Gaudium."

42. In May 2007, the bishops of Latin America and the Caribbean met at the shrine of the Virgin of Aparecida in Brazil for their fifth general conference. The final draft of the document was edited by a committee presided over by the future Pope Francis and contains many elements that can be found in his teaching and attitude. See CELAM, "Concluding Document."

43. Francis, "Evangelii Gaudium," 36.

already united in baptism,[44] Jews don't need to convert,[45] and with believing Muslims, the way is "dialogue" because "together with us they adore the one and merciful God."[46] Other non-Christians are also "justified by the grace of God" and are associated to "the paschal mystery of Jesus Christ."[47] The gospel appears not to be a message of salvation from God's judgment but instead is a vehicle to access a fuller measure of a salvation that is already given to all mankind. According to Francis, therefore, mission is the joyful willingness to extend the fullness of grace to a world that is already under grace. Is this the mission that the Bible calls us to?

The Catholicity of Pope Francis

What has been the "Francis effect" on the church? The simplest answer is that he is envisaging a different kind of catholicity. Both his insistence on the human conscience and mission stem out of his catholicity. In the Roman Catholic understanding, catholicity has to do simultaneously with unity and totality. The basic premise is that multiplicity should be brought into a unity. The church is seen as an expression, a guarantor, and a promoter of true unity between God and humanity and within humanity itself. In Vatican II terms, the church is a "sacrament of unity." As long as the institutional structure that preserves this unity remains intact (i.e., the Roman element), everything can and must find its home somewhere within its realm (i.e., the catholic element).

The Catholic mindset is characterized by an attitude of overall openness without losing touch with its Roman center. It is inherently dynamic and comprehensive, capable of holding together doctrines, ideas, and practices that in other Christian traditions are thought of as being mutually exclusive. By way of its inclusive *et-et* (both-and) epistemology, in a catholic system, two apparently contradicting elements can be reconciled into a synthesis that entails both. In principle, the system is wide enough to welcome everything and everyone. The defining term is not the Word of God written (*sola Scriptura*) but the Roman Church itself. From a Catholic point of view then, affirming something does not

---

44. Francis, "Evangelii Gaudium," 244.
45. Francis, "Evangelii Gaudium," 247.
46. Francis, "Evangelii Gaudium," 252; quotation from Holy See, "Lumen Gentium," 16.
47. Francis, "Evangelii Gaudium," 254.

necessarily mean denying something else but enlarging one's own perspective of the whole truth. In this respect, what is perceived as being important is the integration of the part into the Catholic whole by way of relating the thing that is newly affirmed to what already exists.

Catholicity allows doctrinal development without a radical breach from the past and also allows different kinds of catholicity to coexist. Each Pope has his own catholicity project. John Paul II (the former Archbishop of Krakow, Poland, Karol Józef Wojtyła) pushed for the church to become a global player, thus expanding geographical catholicity and its profile with the media. Benedict XVI (the former Prefect of the Congregation for the Doctrine of the Faith, Joseph Ratzinger) tried to define catholicity in terms of its adherence to universal "reason," thus trying to reconnect the chasm between faith and reason that the Western Enlightenment had introduced. These catholicity projects are not mutually exclusive, but they all contribute to the overall dynamic catholicity of the church.

After more than two years of his pontificate, it is becoming apparent what kind of catholicity Francis has in mind. He wants to build on John Paul II's global catholicity while shifting emphases from Wojtyła's doctrinal rigidity to more inclusive patterns. He pays lip service to Ratzinger's rational catholicity but wants to move the agenda from Western ideological battles to "human" issues that find appeal across the global spectrum. If Ratzinger wanted to mark the difference between the church and the world, Francis tries to make them overlap. In shaping the new catholicity, he seems closer to the pastoral tone of John XXIII, who was canonized (i.e., declared a saint) in 2014. So, there is continuity and development. This is the gist of catholicity.

Francis has little time for nonnegotiable truths and gives more attention to the variety of people's consciences. He is more interested in warmth than light, in empathy than judgment. He focuses on attitude rather than identity and on embracing rather than teaching. He underlines the relational over the doctrinal. For him, proximity is more important than integrity. Belonging together has priority over believing differently.

Of course, all these marks are not pitted against each other, but their relationship is worked out within a new balance whereby the first one determines the overall orientation. Roman catholicity works this way: never abandoning the past, always enlarging the synthesis by repositioning the elements around the Roman center. Francis calls this catholicity "mission," and this word lies at the heart of his theological vision. The word is familiar and intriguing for Bible-believing Christians, yet one needs to understand what he means by it beyond what it appears to mean on the surface.

What Do You Think About Pope Francis? (September 24, 2015, Number 113)[48]

Pope Francis in one of the most liked leaders in today's world. In 2014 *Time Magazine* voted him "Man of the Year," and his popularity is on the increase, especially outside of the Catholic Church. In secular circles, including left-wing thinkers and LGBT movements, many seem to resonate with his apparent approachability and simplicity. With his insistence on mercy, love and tenderness, Francis likes to make his message simple, inclusive, and non-judgmental.

Evangelicals are not immune to Francis's charm and kindness: many are attracted by his seemingly biblical language (e.g., conversion, mission, personal relationship with Jesus) and his less formal type of spirituality. This is just one side of the coin, however. Other descriptions of Francis depict him as a "chess player" due to his Jesuit ability to maneuver in unpredictable ways after establishing a personal relationship with people. Others still consider him a "liberal" due to his apparently universalistic views of salvation for all men in spite of their religion or lack of it. Still others think he is an "anti-capitalist" due to his harsh comments on free-market economies. The overall picture is therefore one of complexity. Wherever you land in your opinion of him, here are five traits essential to understanding Pope Francis.

Francis Is a Very Gifted Politician

A priest does not climb up the ladder of the Roman Catholic hierarchy and become Pope without having profound political gifts. Francis shares uncanny similarities to President Obama, another extraordinarily talented politician. Obama and Francis both emerged onto the public stage with charm and an amazing ability to communicate. They understand

---

48. By Leonardo De Chirico and Greg Pritchard. Gregory A. Pritchard, PhD Northwestern University, is President of the Forum of Christian Leaders, Director of the European Leadership Forum, author of *Willow Creek Seeker Service*.

their respective audiences and winsomely communicate their message. They both exude a star power that is magnetic and draws people to them.

There are two important aspects of their common political gift: empathetic listening and reflective communication.

We see Obama's ability to sympathetically listen to those of vastly different opinions when he was elected President of the Harvard Law Review. In a revealing article by Jodi Kantor in the New York Times, before he became a candidate for the US presidency, Obama's relational political style was described in some detail. The context is important: Harvard Law School at that time was a hotbed of political conflict. Bradford Berenson, a future associate White House counsel in the Bush administration and classmate of Obama explained, "I have worked in the Supreme Court and the White House and I never saw politics as bitter as at Harvard Law Review in the early '90s."[49]

Kantor talked to dozens of Obama's classmates and summarized that they "could not remember his specific views" and that even his closest friends didn't "know exactly where he stood." What everyone did remember was Obama's extraordinary ability to listen to them and make them feel understood. "Obama cast himself as an eager listener, sometimes giving warring classmates the impression that he agreed with all of them at once." Obama had a surprising ability to connect to the belligerent factions at Harvard Law School and not show his own cards: "People had a way of hearing what they wanted in Obama's words." In the midst of one political dustup, Obama calmed the waters and "students on each side of the debate thought he was endorsing their side." One classmate remembering the incident commented: "Everyone was nodding, Oh he agrees with me."[50]

Today many evangelicals are experiencing Pope Francis in a similar way: "Oh, he agrees with me." Hundreds of evangelical leaders are coming to Rome on a pilgrimage to meet this highly relational Pope. They experience a Pope who is listening to them and who sounds like them. One Pentecostal evangelist gave the Pope a "high five." After talking to Francis, one major evangelical theologian was naive enough to question whether Francis even believed in the category of a Roman Catholic Pope. Evangelical leaders are experiencing the magnetic presence and listening

---

49. Kantor, "Obama Found Political Voice," para. 23.
50. Kantor, "Obama Found Political Voice," para. 28.

ear of a relationally warm but giving and canny politician who appears to agree with all of them.

We see the second element of Obama's and Francis's political gift in their common style of communicating; they identify with their audience and therein cause their audience to identify with them. Obama, in the prologue to his autobiography, explains the result of this style: "I serve as a blank screen on which people of vastly different political stripes project their own views."[51] When Obama was emerging as a national candidate, this skill served him well. When he was considering becoming a candidate for the presidency, his closest advisors recommended that he run before he had a detailed Senate voting track record while he could most profitably use his blank screen magnetism.[52] At this moment the same can be said of Francis: he is charming, deflects old ways of thinking, and like the most gifted of politicians, has created "a blank screen on which people of vastly different political stripes project their own views."

Francis is a Jesuit with an Anti-Protestant Slant

Francis is the first Jesuit Pope in history. It is sort of an irony to think that a Pope who appears to be close to evangelicals actually belongs to the religious order that was founded to fight Protestantism. The former soldier Ignatius of Loyola (1491–1566) gathered a group of friends who called themselves The Society of Jesus (*Societas Jesu*), and eventually they were commissioned by the Pope to stop the spread of Protestantism. Their task was to imitate the strengths of Protestantism, i.e., spiritual depth and intellectual brightness, but to use them as catholic weapons against it. The Jesuit order provided the "alternative" catholic way to the Protestant faith. It comes as no surprise then that the first saint that Pope Francis proclaimed in 2013 was Pierre Favre (1506–46), a French first-generation Jesuit with a "smiling face" who, more than others, tried to look like a Protestant in order to drive people back to the Roman Church.

Furthermore, the Jesuit side of Pope Francis is clear enough, given his published (and never retracted) opinion that Luther and Calvin destroyed man, poisoned society, and ruined the church! In his 1985 lecture on the history of the Jesuit order, he gave severe evaluations of Luther (a "heretic"), and especially of Calvin (a "heretic" and "schismatic"),

---

51. Obama, *Audacity*, 11.
52. Zernike and Zeleny, "Obama in Senate."

bringing about the "Calvinist squalor" in society, in the church, and in man's heart. According to that lecture, Protestantism lies at the root of all evils in the modern West. The fact that this lecture was republished unchanged in 2013 in Spanish and translated in 2014 into Italian with his permission, but without a mitigating word of explanation, indicates that this assessment still lingers in the Pope's heart and mind. He recently added a harsh comment on the Puritans, falsely associating them with a bigoted and merciless form of Christianity. This friendly Pope to evangelicals is a Jesuit whose entire mission of order is to defend the Roman Church against Protestantism. Certainly, Francis is a smiling Jesuit, but the anti-Protestant still beats in his heart.

Francis Is Selectively Radical

The third trait addresses Francis's radicalism. In a recent book, *Pope Francis' Revolution of Tenderness and Love*, Cardinal Walter Kasper argues that Francis is not a liberal but a radical in the etymological sense of the Latin word "radix," meaning root or originating principle.[53] According to Kasper, the Pope is challenging the church to be radical in the sense of rediscovering the roots of the gospel, which are joy, mission, frugality, solidarity with the poor, freedom from legalism, and collegiality.

Kasper's reading of Francis is clever and insightful. It encourages us to move beyond the usual polarizations between "liberals" and "conservatives" within the church by introducing a third category, that of "radicals."

Francis appears to be radical on certain issues but much less so with others. He is radical on poverty but silent on the massive financial power of his church. He seems to be radical on mercy but never mentions original sin and divine judgment over all sinners outside of Christ. He is radical in advocating for simplicity but keeps the expansive apparatus of an empire of which he is the head. He is radical in denouncing the tragedies of unethical capitalism but seems to be much less outspoken towards the immoral deviations of one's personal sexual life. In other words, his radicalism is somewhat selective. Radical in one area, much less so in another.

In a certain sense, "liberals" are radical on social issues, while "conservatives" are radical on doctrinal issues. Everyone is radical in some sense. There are different shades of radicalism. Francis's radicalism is

---

53. See Kasper, *Pope Francis' Revolution*.

much closer to the liberal version than the conservative one. Therefore, playing a bit with words, the question is whether or not his radicalism is radically different from a more liberal tendency. Historically speaking, the root of theological liberalism lies in the preference given to religious feelings over doctrinal expressions. And this is exactly what the Pope seems also fond of doing. If mercy and tenderness describe the overall message of Francis, they sound more like liberal catchwords than traditional ones.

Francis Is a Latin American

Francis comes from Latin America, where over the course of the 20th century, Roman Catholicism lost its religious monopoly, and a full 19 percent of the continent is now Protestant. The traditional Latin American Roman Catholic response to the numerical growth of evangelicals has been labeling them as "sects" and "cults," but this derogatory approach did not stop millions of people from leaving the Catholic Church to join various evangelical churches. The risk of losing the region has caused the Catholic Church to do something it has never done before: to choose a non-European as Pope, to choose a Latin American as Pope.

Now the Pope himself is directly involved in rescuing the continent, strengthening the Roman Catholic Church and reaching out to evangelicals from the Vatican. His visits to Brazil, Ecuador, Bolivia and Paraguay within the first two years of his papacy are an indication of the importance of this task in his agenda.

Secondly the influence of Latin America on Francis is visible in his focus on the poor. Latin American was the home of liberation theology, with its Marxist categories and condemnation of capitalism. Yet even those Latin American Christian leaders who rejected the Marxist analysis, which is embedded in a full-blown liberation theology, still have often prioritized the poor in their theological thinking and emphasized those passages of Scripture which reflect this concern. Francis's condemnation of capitalism's evils has surprised many in the West but shouldn't if one understands Francis's cultural roots.

Francis Is an Ecumenical Leader

Francis is the most ecumenical Pope ever. Francis, before his election to the papacy, built relationships with evangelical leaders, attended evangelical conferences in his home country, and regularly visited a Youth with a Mission prayer center for personal prayer. Since he became Pope, Francis has gone to an Italian Pentecostal church and apologized for how Roman Catholics have persecuted Pentecostals and welcomed hundreds upon hundreds of evangelical leaders to the Vatican. What is behind Francis's extraordinary openness and warmth toward evangelicals?

We find the answer in a fascinating article in the Catholic Herald: "The Pope's Great Evangelical Gamble."

> Somewhere in Pope Francis's office is a document that could alter the course of Christian history. It declares an end to hostilities between Catholics and Evangelicals and says the two traditions are now "united in mission because we are declaring the same Gospel." The Holy Father is thinking of signing the text in 2017, the 500th anniversary of the Reformation, alongside Evangelical leaders.[54]

The author explains that the Pope believes that "the Reformation is already over" because the Lutheran World Federation and Vatican's "Joint Declaration on the Doctrine of Justification" was signed in 1999.

What is going on here?

The last two popes, John Paul and Benedict, in response to the 1999 statement, did not announce that the Reformation is over. Benedict, while still leading the Congregation of the Doctrine of the Faith, issued a second official Vatican statement which explained that the joint statement was inadequate and listed a number of serious differences between the historic Lutheran position and the Roman Catholic position. In short, Benedict explained that the Council of Trent, which condemned Protestant/evangelical central convictions as anathema, was still in force.

But Francis is a different kind of Pope. He is not a high-powered theologian confronting relativism or clarifying doctrine like a Benedict or a philosopher theologian like John Paul II, whose Vatican produced the Roman Catholic Catechism. Francis is sincere, kind, and loving. But

---

54. Coppen, "Pope's Great Evangelical Gamble."

he is a committed Roman Catholic ecumenical leader, and most importantly, he is doing evangelism in the same way Roman Catholics have evangelized throughout their history. Roman Catholics have extended their influence by absorbing movements, converting kings, and using physical force. This last method is no longer a widespread strategy of the Roman Catholic Church. In fact, Francis has apologized for how Roman Catholics have persecuted Pentecostals, indigenous native groups, Waldensians, etc.

But the Roman Catholic evangelistic methods of absorbing movements and converting kings are both being actively used by Francis in his present PR campaign toward evangelicals. For example, Roman Catholicism did not reject the Charismatic movement but absorbed it and a new sort of Catholic was created, a "charismatic Catholic." The Roman Catholic method of absorption is now focused on evangelicalism, seeking to dismiss the differences and emphasize the shared beliefs. Or, as the Catholic Herald describes it, "the Pope's great evangelical gamble" is Francis's attempt to "declare an end to hostilities between Catholics and evangelicals." Francis is seeking to establish a new sort of Catholic, an "evangelical Catholic."

The first step toward this broader absorption is the conversion of kings. Over the previous two millennia, the Catholic Church has historically extended its influence by means of converting the kings and queens of political power, and within a generation or two, their kingdoms. This same method is being used today to convert kings of influence. Although a flood of Roman Catholics are becoming evangelicals, there is a trickle of evangelical leaders (kings of influence) converting to Roman Catholicism.

The importance of this should not be underestimated. Evangelicalism is easily the fastest-growing Christian movement in the last century. According to Oxford Press's World Christian Encyclopedia, the Roman Catholic Church stagnated with only 6 percent growth over a century, while evangelicalism grew twenty times as fast, with 122 percent growth as a percentage of the world's population. The Roman Catholic leaders are aware that millions of Roman Catholics each year are converting to evangelical churches all across the world. When Benedict was still Pope, he gave a lecture in his home country of Germany and expressed confusion of how to respond to the enormous growth of the global evangelical church.

> The geography of Christianity has changed dramatically in recent times, and is in the process of changing further. Faced with a new form of Christianity, which is spreading with

overpowering missionary dynamism, sometimes in frightening ways, the mainstream Christian denominations often seem at a loss . . . This worldwide phenomenon—that bishops from all over the world are constantly telling me about—poses a question to us all: what is this new form of Christianity saying to us, for better and for worse?[55]

But while Benedict seemed confused, Francis is bringing evangelicals close and saying we are the same and the Reformation is over. Francis is not confused or "at a loss" but knows exactly what he is about.

The Siren Call of Unity

In our fragmented and violent world, unity is one of the catchwords that many people are attracted to. Francis is strongly advocating for Christian unity and ultimately the unity of mankind. His passion for unity makes many evangelicals think that he is the person who may achieve it. Francis developed his idea of ecumenism as a polyhedron. The polyhedron is a geometric figure with different angles and lines. All different parts have their own peculiarity. It's a figure that brings together unity and diversity.

Where does this view of unity come from? In pre-Vatican II Roman Catholic ecumenism, other Christians were drastically invited to "come back" into the Catholic fold and to conform to its doctrines and practices under the rule of the Pope. With Vatican II (1962–65), Roman Catholicism updated its ecumenical project and embraced a concentric circle type of unity in which the one and only church "subsists in" the Roman Catholic Church and other churches and communities gravitate around this center according to their degree of nearness or distance from it. According to Vatican II and subsequent magisterial teachings, Christian unity is threefold:

1. Professing the same faith,
2. Celebrating the same Eucharist (i.e., the Roman Catholic way), and
3. Being united under the same sacramental ministry in apostolic succession (i.e., under the Pope).

How does the polyhedron kind of unity as advocated by Pope Francis fit with this post Vatican II view of unity? For example, as far as the

---

55. Benedict XVI, "Address of His Holiness."

second mark of unity is concerned, is the Pope saying that the sacrificial understanding of the Eucharist and the theology of transubstantiation belong at the center of Christian unity, or are they particulars that can accommodate differences? Or is the Pope saying that apostolic succession, which is the basis of the hierarchical structure of the Roman Catholic Church, is still part of the center, or is it a variable that is secondary to Christian unity?

Polyhedrons are fascinating figures, and Francis's use of the image of a polyhedron is thought-provoking. However, the problem for Christian unity does not primarily lie in the metaphors used but in the theological vision that nurtures it. If the Catholic Eucharist and the Catholic sacramental system are part of the center of Christian unity, one can make reference to spheres or polyhedrons all he likes, but the substance of the problem still remains. The unity proposed by Francis still gravitates around the Roman Catholic Church and its distinct outlook and not around the biblical gospel that calls all Christians to conform to the mind of Christ.

Conclusion: How Should Evangelicals Respond to Francis?

An increasing number of evangelicals say, "I like this Pope; he talks about Jesus a lot . . ." True, Francis knows the language that evangelicals use (e.g., "conversion," "mission," "personal relationship with Jesus") and is able to articulate it in a winsome way.

The basic rules of interpretation, however, tell us that using the same words does not necessarily mean saying the same things. It is important to understand what Francis means by the words he uses. As already pointed out, in order to understand Francis's vocabulary one needs to come to terms with Vatican II. This important council fudged the theological meaning of important key words in order for the Catholic project to be implemented. In his language, for instance, conversion does not mean (what evangelicals mean) turning away from sin to grace, from judgment to pardon, from a state of reprobation to being saved. For Francis, conversion means coming closer to Christ on the assumption that everyone is already in the sphere of his saving grace, though at different distances.

In Francis's view, all those who follow their consciences are right with God. They may want to convert, i.e., come closer and experience a deeper measure of grace. Moreover, Francis believes that Muslims are brothers and sisters who pray to the same God as Christians do. For them conversion may mean getting deeper in their religious commitments but not necessarily turning away from Islam and embracing faith in Jesus Christ alone. The word "conversion" is the same, but the theological meaning is hugely different.

Take "mission" as another example. In Francis's vocabulary, "mission" does not mean going out in the world to proclaim the gospel of salvation in Jesus. It rather means calling people to come closer to the salvation that all people already are part of by being human though in different degrees. For Francis there is no "in or out" sense in this understanding of mission. The whole of humankind is already "in" a state of grace: mission is the task of calling people to engage it deeper, not to call them "in." They are already "in." Here again, words are the same, but their meaning is vastly different.

Evangelicals have to do their homework in order to go beyond the surface of mere phonetics in order to grasp the profoundly different theological vision underpinning Francis's language. They may find it surprising how far Francis is from the standard evangelical understanding of the biblical gospel.

Moreover, in talking about unity, Francis is open to all, be they Christians or non-Christians, religious or secular people. He calls Muslims brothers and sisters. He prays with them, saying that they are praying to the same God. To secular people, he says to follow their conscience and they will be fine. Evangelicals are just one piece in his vision. Unity like a polyhedron means that according to Francis, there are different ways to relate to the Catholic Church, but Rome maintains central stage.

Francis may use similar language, be a nice person, and be passionate about unity. But he is still the Pope of the Roman Catholic Church. The Roman Church, while not being static, nor a monolithic reality, does not really change in its fundamental commitments. It expands itself but does not purify itself. It embraces new trends and practices but does not expel unbiblical ones. It grows but it does not reform itself according to gospel standards.

"What do you think about Pope Francis?" is a pointed question for evangelicals especially. They seem to be the target of Pope Francis's efforts towards friendship, reconciliation, and unity. Befriending evangelicals by talking and behaving like them may be a Jesuit way to convert evangelical kings of influence and absorb the evangelical movement, the fastest growing portion of the Christian world. This is why it is vitally important for evangelicals to know who Pope Francis really is.

The (Not So) Puzzling Theology of Pope Francis (February 1, 2022, Number 198)

Among the many puzzling things introduced by Pope Francis, his teaching (magisterium) is perhaps the level that was most impacted by the Argentinian Pontiff. The contents of his encyclicals, apostolic exhortations, bulls, speeches, occasional interviews, etc., have been described as "uncertain," "in motion," "ambiguous," "nuanced," at times even "heretical"—and by Roman Catholics![56]

Many Roman Catholics (and also many non-Catholic observers), accustomed to associating the Papal magisterium with an authoritative, coherent, and stable form of doctrinal teaching, are perplexed if not dismayed by a Pope who seems both to say and not say, to argue for something and to undermine it, to state one position and then contradict it the next breath. As a Jesuit, Pope Francis tends to use an equivocal style, a dubitative and incomplete form of argumentation, an "open" logic, a colloquial if not casual tone, and a pastoral trait which often lacks clarity and coherence. Officially, the Pope's teaching is set in the context of the historical traditions of the church. In this sense, nothing changes. In reality, however, Francis is accentuating the developmental and inclusive dynamic of Roman Catholicism as it emerged from Vatican II (1962–65). According to this trend, while there is a sense in which nothing changes, everything is nonetheless re-thought, re-expressed, and updated. The "Roman" side of the teaching does not change, while the "catholic" side does change.

A recent book by the Sicilian Roman Catholic theologian Massimo Naro, *Protagonista è l'abbraccio* is a helpful guide in the theological universe of Pope Francis.[57] From the outset, Naro readily acknowledges that the theology of Pope Francis is "an innovative proposal" even when compared with the updating trends of the Second Vatican Council.

Above all, the Pope's vocabulary needs to be taken into consideration. If you want to try to enter the world of Francis, here are his central words: "mother church," "faithful people of God," "popular spirituality,"

---

56. De Chirico, "Vatican File 134," and "Vatican File 144."
57. See, Naro, *Protagonista è l'abbraccio*.

"mercy," "synodality," "polyedric ecclesiology," "processes to initiate," "existential peripheries," "humanism of solidarity," "ecological conversion," "dialogue," "fraternity and brotherhood."[58] Not all are new words; some of them are terms that have been already used in Roman Catholic teaching but are now given a new nuance or a distinct significance by Francis.

Naro further suggests that there are two theological frameworks that give meaning to his words, i.e., the "theology of the people" and the "theology of mercy." For Francis, theology does not begin with biblical revelation nor from the abstract principles of the official teaching of the church but from the common and daily stories of men and women who must be welcomed and affirmed in their particular contexts and life journeys. This attention to the "inside" of the world and to the level where the "people" live pushes him to elevate forms of popular spirituality as authentic religious experiences. He is not scandalized by the "irregular" situations of life in which people find themselves, e.g., divorce, cohabitation, or same-sex relationships. Instead of teaching an external standard (in theology or in morality), the Pope begins where people are assuming that where they are, there is something good that needs to be affirmed.

According to Francis, the "people" are not the passive and obedient recipients of a top-down ecclesiastical magisterium but active subjects whose religious experiences are true and real (even though not squared with traditional patterns) and therefore need to be part of the teaching itself. The "people" make the teaching as much as the ecclesiastical authorities of the Roman Church promulgate it.

You don't need to be a trained theologian to catch how this version of the "theology of the people" is far from the evangelical belief that Scripture, as the inspired Word of God, is the source by which God teaches, rebukes, corrects, and trains. And who does he train? Not those who want to affirm their own experiences and lifestyles but those who wish to repent from sin and reform their lives following the path indicated by the Bible. From a biblical perspective, Francis's "theology of the people" does not have the external criterion of the Word of God, which questions hearts, practices, sinful habits, etc., and forges a new humanity that is always open to renewal in a process of ongoing sanctification.

Mercy is another keyword in the Pope's magisterium. In his way of putting it, mercy is "the bridge that connects God and man, opening our

---

58. Naro, *Protagonista è l'abbraccio*, 19.

hearts to the hope of being loved forever despite the limits of our sins."[59] In this dense sentence there is a strategic theological point. Among other things, as Cardinal Matteo Zuppi writes in the introduction, the Pope means that "at the center of the biblical message is not sin, but mercy."[60] In Naro's words, Christian theology must be freed from "hamartiocentrism,"[61] i.e., from the centrality of sin. Sin must be replaced by the pervasiveness of God's mercy, which "can help us to break free from hamartiocentrism and to rediscover the tenderness of God."[62] In his view, Pope Francis has replaced sin with mercy at the center of his message.

In the Pope's theology, sin is at most "the human limit"[63] but not the breaking of the covenant, the rebellion against God, the disobedience to his commandments, or the subversion of divine authority that results in the righteous and holy judgment of God. If sin is a "human limit," then the cross of Christ did not atone for sin but only manifested God's mercy in an exemplary way. The words used by the Pope are the same as those of the evangelical faith (e.g., mercy, sin, grace, gospel), but they are given a different meaning than the gospel.[64]

Francis sees everything from the perspective of a metaphysic of mercy that swallows sin without passing through propitiation, expiation, or reconciliation, which the cross of Jesus Christ wrought to give salvation to those who believe in him. If everything is mercy and sin is only a limit, the resulting message is fundamentally *different* from the biblical gospel.

The traditional Roman Catholic teaching (from the Council of Trent to the 1992 *Catechism of the Catholic Church*) conflicts at crucial points with the evangelical faith summarized in the Reformation slogans "Christ Alone," "Scripture alone," and "faith alone." The "popular" and "merciful" account of the gospel taught by Pope Francis is another "catholic" variant

---

59. Francis, *Bull of Indiction*, 2.

[The English translation of the Papal text on the Vatican website is blurred and incorrect. It says ". . . the bridge that connects God and man, opening our hearts to the hope of being loved forever *despite our sinfulness*" (italics added). However, the Latin official text says "praeter nostri peccati fines," which needs to be translated as "despite the limits or bounds of our sins" as the Italian, French and Spanish versions rightly translate.]

60. Naro, *Protagonista è l'abbraccio*, 16

61. Naro, *Protagonista è l'abbraccio*, 93.

62. Naro, *Protagonista è l'abbraccio*, 114.

63. Naro, *Protagonista è l'abbraccio*, 91.

64. De Chirico, *Same Words*.

of the deviation on which the church of Rome was established and on which, sadly, it continues to move forward.

From "Metaphysical" to "Popular": A Window on the Roman Catholic Theology of the Future? (December 1, 2023, Number 222)

In the beginning was Roman Catholic metaphysics: Aristotelian in outline, revisited and improved by Thomas Aquinas, capable of integrating some biblical and Augustinian insights, elastic to the point of metabolizing mystical and rationalistic streams, open to updating with respect to modernity while maintaining its solid structures. Metaphysics was taught in Roman Catholic seminaries (two years of metaphysics preceded the study of theology in the training of priests). It was at the heart of catechesis, the watermark of the church's documents, and the imprint of its public morality and theology. In short, it was the recognizable mark of the Roman Catholic Church. Metaphysics started from "first principles" and, in the light of reason as helped by revelation (coming from tradition and the Bible), by deductive means and procedures, arrived at every nook and detail of human life. With this metaphysics, Rome fought against the Protestant Reformation, the Enlightenment, and modernism.

Then came Vatican II (1962–65), and that solid framework was stress-tested. It went through a season of development and updating, introducing a new set of emphases. The "pastoral" tone was preferred to the "doctrinal" one. The top-down structure made room for more bottom-up processes. The season of "genitive" theologies (of demythologization, enculturation, hope, liberation, post-colonialism, ecumenism, interreligious dialogue, etc.) battered classical metaphysics. In the name of "renewal," there was a certain theological restlessness and an eagerness to change the paradigm.

Then there was Pope Francis (2013–25). Of eclectic and unfinished theological training, Argentine and non-academic, the Pope immediately showed his frustration with the schematism of metaphysics, denouncing its abstract and "clerical" character, in his view far away from people's problems and offering answers to questions of the past that nobody is asking. In their own way, the "outgoing" trajectory of which he became an interpreter and the "synodality" he championed are formulas that apply to theology as well.⁶⁵ In concrete terms, in 2018, with the Constitution Veritatis Gaudium, the Pope sent signals to the ecclesiastical universities, preparing them for a new season. After the death of Benedict XVI, Francis changed the leadership of the Congregation for the Doctrine of the Faith, giving it to a "non-metaphysical" theologian like Víctor Manuel Fernández.⁶⁶ Now, with the document *Ad theologiam promuovendam* (*Promoting Theology*),⁶⁷ he changed the statute of the Pontifical Academy of Theology, which is a Vatican institution at the service of the Pope's theological ministry. In this text, Pope Francis envisages his way of doing theology.

In imagining the academy of the future, Francis hopes that theology will experience an "epistemological and methodological rethinking," a "turning point," a "paradigm shift," a "courageous cultural revolution." In the background is dissatisfaction with traditional metaphysics and its theological methods. According to Francis, theology must be "fundamentally contextual" and no longer start from "first principles." It must translate into a "culture of dialogue" with all and no longer think of itself as only lecturing to the world, religions, and others. It must be "transdisciplinary" and no longer prioritize philosophy over the other disciplines. It must be "spiritual" and not abstract and ideological, "popular" and not detached from people's common sense, "inductive" and not deductive.

In so doing, the Pope distances himself from the legacy of metaphysical theology that has been the paradigm of Roman Catholicism throughout the ages. Is his way of looking at theology something that Thomas Aquinas, Robert Bellarmine, Leo XIII, John Paul II, Joseph Ratzinger-Benedict XVI, etc., would recognize as being in line with the tradition of Rome? Not really. Perhaps Karl Rahner, some liberation theologians, and their disciples would.

"Promoting theology" seems to be a manifesto of an account of Roman Catholic theology that, without naming traditional metaphysics, distances itself from it in significant ways. It does not appear to abolish metaphysics by decree but subjects it to accelerated "updating" and "development" such that its connotations are changed. In a nutshell, the Roman Catholic theology of the future will be done differently.

As noted at the outset, traditional metaphysics has absorbed all the orientations that have emerged, even those that initially seemed contrary

---

65. Karr, "Synodality."
66. De Chirico, "Vatican File 218."
67. *Pillar*, "'Ad Theologiam Promovendam.'" Italian text: Francis, "Ad Theologiam Promovendam."

to its arrangement. It has demonstrated great adaptability at the service of Roman catholicity, i.e., the ability to integrate new ideas and methods without changing the fundamental commitments of the Roman Catholic Church. The question is, Is the direction Francis wants theology to take compatible with its well-established patterns? Is it a radical change with unpredictable consequences? For sure, in the wake of Vatican II as interpreted by Francis, Roman Catholic theology will be increasingly different not only in emphasis but also in language, style, themes, and content. Those who think of Rome as the home of stability have yet another indication that Rome does develop and change. Tradition is an evolving process.

It is feasible to say that the Roman Catholic theology of the future will be *et-et*, both-and: both the one established over the centuries and the one Pope Francis desires. Both approaches to theology are not committed to Scripture as the supreme authority. The former reflects a philosophical system rather than the Bible; the latter mirrors the context more than the Word of God. In both cases, theology is hardly evangelical but rather two ways of voicing Roman Catholic theology: one more "Roman" (metaphysical), the other more "catholic" (contextual).

5

The Tridentine Paradigm

Between Trent and Aparecida. The Trajectory of Pope Francis (August 26, 2013, Number 64)

SINCE HIS ELECTION, POPE Francis has been impressing the public opinion with his extrovert attitudes, simple habits, and charming language. The recent World Youth Day (WYD) in Brazil confirmed each of these attributes. Most people seem to admire the new "Franciscan" style of the Papacy, i.e., a blend of frugal manners, emphasis on mercy, and apparent approachability. Few, however, have taken the time to deal with Francis's theological vision that is inspiring his papacy.

The Tridentine Background . . .

An initial step to embarking on such a task is reading his first encyclical *Lumen Fidei*,[1] in which Francis (with Benedict XVI, who is the main drafter of the document), among other things, updates the theology of the Council of Trent. In this highly authoritative document he reiterates the doctrine of salvation by faith through sacraments and works, thus renewing the Catholic rejection of the Protestant *Sola Fide*, i.e., the good news that we are saved by grace alone through faith alone. The attachment to Trent and the Counter-Reformation may seem remote if not

1. Francis, "Lumen Fidei."

alien to Francis (although we should never forget that he belongs to the Jesuit order), but the hard theological evidence says the contrary. In the foundational doctrine of salvation, Trent is still alive and well, perhaps in the friendlier tone of Pope Bergoglio, but it is there, untouched as ever. While the outlook of the Papacy is showing signs of change, the doctrinal core of the Church of Rome has been confirmed without significant developments.

. . . and The Vision of Aparecida

The WYD provided another important reference point that is at the heart of Francis's program and therefore must be considered. From Trent, in the middle of the Italian Alps, we journey to Aparecida (Brazil), "on the other side of the world," as Francis would put it. In 2007 the Latin American Bishops met in Aparecida for their Fifth General Conference, where the then Cardinal Bergoglio was one of the main inspirers of the final document.[2] It is a 165-page text that aptly defines Francis in terms of his theological language, pastoral emphases, and missionary agenda. Aparecida accurately depicts the theological vision of the Pope. Because of its importance we shall look at it more carefully in a future Vatican File.

For Francis, though, Aparecida is not only a foundational document, it is first and foremost a Marian shrine which was built to keep a statue of Mary that according to tradition was found in 1717 by a group of three fishermen. Since 2011, it has become the greatest Marian pilgrimage destination in the world. During the WYD week, in his speech to the Brazilian Bishops on July 27, Francis said that "Aparecida is the interpretative key for the Church's mission."[3] There is something important to be found there, something that helps in understanding what the church is all about in terms of its mission.

In explaining the intent of his comment, the Pope went on to say that "in Aparecida God offered Brazil his own mother" and revealed "his own DNA."[4] The gospel, though, is about God giving his Son to the world, but Francis here speaks of God offering his mother. This not merely a matter of theological minutiae!

---

2. See CELAM, "Concluding Document."
3. Francis, "Address (Rio de Janeiro)," 1.
4. Francis, "Address (Rio de Janeiro)," 1.

According to the Pope, the lesson of Aparecida has to do with the humility of the fishermen and their zeal to tell others about their discovery. This is the "interpretative key for the Church's mission": humility and mission. Notice, however, that we are talking about the recovery of a statue of Mary which has become a world-famous attraction for millions of people. The gospel is about a group of humble fishermen being called by Jesus to follow him and to tell others about him. Francis is here talking about people who found Mary and became missionaries for her. Again, this is no small difference!

Territorial Marianism

Aparecida is the national Shrine of Our Lady of Aparecida, a Marian center which is very dear to Pope Bergoglio. Prior to WYD, in his speech there on July 24, Francis said, "What joy I feel as I come to the house of the Mother of every Brazilian, the Shrine of our Lady of Aparecida! The day after my election as Bishop of Rome, I visited the Basilica of Saint Mary Major in Rome, in order to entrust my ministry as the Successor of Peter to Our Lady. Today I have come here to ask Mary our Mother for the success of World Youth Day and to place at her feet the life of the people of Latin America."[5]

Here we find some common threads of Francis's Marianism:

- The priority of his Marian devotion
- His first act as Pope was a Marian act
- His belief that the Papal office should be entrusted to Mary
- His prayer to Mary for the success of WYD
- His dedicating to Mary the people of Latin America.

This sentence summarizes the core of Francis's Marianism. What is even more striking, though, is his "territorial" understanding of Aparecida. When he says that Mary is the Mother of "every Brazilian," he is applying a "territorial" understanding of his religion, as if every Brazilian, in spite of religious pluralism that marks Brazil, is nonetheless a child of Mary. This attitude reflects how it is difficult for a Roman Catholic majority culture to accept the fact that Mary may be the mother of the Roman

---

5. Francis, "Homily (Basilica of the Shrine)."

Catholic Brazilians but not of those who may have a high respect for the biblical Mary without turning it into someone to be venerated.

When Pope Francis speaks extensively of "mission," "outreach," and "encounter with Christ"—a language that seems very evangelical—one should be aware that the background of it all lies between Trent and Aparecida. He stands between the Counter-Reformation emphasis on a synergistic gospel and the "missional" attitude that can be found in his thoroughgoing Marianism.

Trent, 450 Years Later (December 16, 2013, Number 70)

This year marks the 450th anniversary of the closing of the Council of Trent (1545–63), the most important event of the Roman Catholic Church in the modern era. A special commemorative event took place in the city of Trent with the presence of an official representative of Pope Francis.

Trent in a Nutshell

The Council of Trent was the official response of the Catholic Church to the 16th-century Protestant Reformation. The issues of the Reformation (grace alone, faith alone, Christ alone) were rejected as they were affirmed by the Reformers (mainly Luther) and recast in a sacramental framework that highlighted the contribution of human works and the mediating agency of the church. Actually, Trent declared the incompatibility of the Reformation with what became then the official doctrine of the Church of Rome and the unwillingness of Rome to undertake a process of radical revision in biblical perspective. In order to do that, Trent solidified the theology of the sacraments, hitting with a series of "anathema" those who held Protestant beliefs. Trent intervened in clarifying the Roman position (through decrees and canons) and in launching a series of changes that would impact the life of the church.

Trent was not an isolated event. The post-Trent phase of the church was marked by a staunch polemical attitude, first against Protestantism and then against modernity. If Trent was the Roman response to the Reformation, the season of the Marian dogmas (1854—immaculate conception of Mary; 1950—bodily assumption of Mary) and Papal infallibility (1870) were responses to the ideological challenges of modernity.

Trent's Heritage

Five centuries later, the Roman Catholic Church has definitely adopted a different pastoral and ecclesial "style" than that of Trent, but it has not substantially changed it nor denied it in whole or in part. There is no point in which Vatican II moves away from the dogmatic teaching of the Council of Trent. At Vatican II, Trent was kept in the background and remained within the framework of Roman Catholicism. The "Tridentine paradigm" was put, so to speak, in historical perspective, but not forsaken nor forgotten. Vatican II has metabolized Trent but in no way abandoned it.

With the 1999 Joint Declaration on the Doctrine of Justification between the Roman Catholic Church and the World Lutheran Federation, Trent was updated in its language and emphases but reiterated in its substance. The two positions were juxtaposed and held compatible, thus working with a "both-and" scheme that is quintessentially the Roman Catholic way of developing its doctrinal system. The Tridentine "anathemas" were lifted for those who hold the doctrines of the Reformation if reinterpreted ecumenically, but the theological core of contemporary Catholicism is still steeped in its Tridentine content: it is the institutional church that mediates the grace of God through its sacramental system. Grace alone was and is still rejected. A clear indication of this is the case is that nothing has changed in important areas like indulgences, purgatory, the sacramental prerogatives of the church, the cult of the saints, etc.

Pope Francis on Trent

On the occasion of the official celebration in Trent, Pope Francis sent a special envoy to Trent together with a letter.[6] In it he says that the anniversary "behooves the Church to recall with more prompt and attentive eagerness the most fruitful doctrine which came out of that council. Certainly not without cause, the Church has for a long time already accorded so much care to the Decrees and Canons of that Council that are to be recalled and observed."[7] "No doubt," the letter continues, "with the Holy Ghost inspiring and suggesting, it especially concerned the Fathers not only to guard the sacred deposit of Christian doctrine, but also to more clearly enlighten mankind." The same Spirit, according to the Pope,

---

6. Francis, "Epistula Data Valthero."
7. Francis, "Epistula Data Valthero," 1.

now guides the church "to restore and meditate upon the most abundant doctrine of Trent."[8]

Quoting Benedict XVI, Francis ends the letter by saying that "[the church] is a subject which increases in time and develops, yet always remains the same, the one subject of the journeying People of God."[9] It is the Pope that affirms the continuity between Trent and the present-day Roman Catholic Church. It is not a static continuity in that the church "develops" over time, but is a continuity in which the church changes, while always remaining the same. Both-and, again!

The "Catholic" Month of Pope Francis (November 30, 2014, Number 96)

"Marriage is between a man and a woman." "Unborn life is as precious and unique as any life." "Euthanasia is an unwarranted abuse of human freedom." "Adoptive children have the right to have a father and a mother." These are standard Roman Catholic positions on various hotly debated moral issues of our generation. So, what's the fuss about it? They were spoken and argued for by Pope Francis in two different speeches over the last few weeks.[10] After months of confusing messages sent by him about homosexuality ("Who am I to judge?"), the good in every "loving relationship" be it married or not, the need for the church to stay away from the heat of present-day ethical debates, his uneasiness towards anything "non-negotiable," Pope Francis has finally said things "Catholic." While he has always aligned himself to traditional Roman Catholic moral theology (he is the Pope, after all!), he has never gone public on these issues in such a clear-cut way and in such a short period of time.

The Aftermath of the Synod

This "Catholic" month by the Pope comes after the Synod on the family where the Catholic Church experienced a turbulent time of controversy among high-rank cardinals and bishops. Some progressive voices pushed for an update of the church's moral stance on human sexuality and human relationships. Strongly supported by secular public opinion, all

---

8. Francis, "Letter to Brandmüller," 2.
9. Francis, "Letter to Brandmüller," 2.
10. Francis, "All'Associazione"; Francis, "Al Colloquio."

applauding this "revolutionary" Pope, sectors of the church thought that the gap between the church and the Western masses could be bridged by the church adopting a more relaxed, less confrontational approach to these issues. The 2014 Synod witnessed a clash between these voices and more traditional ones, resulting in a temporary standstill waiting for next year's Synod, which will be re-convened on the same topic.

Where does Pope Francis stand in all this? In the months preceding the Synod, he repeatedly advocated for a "outward-looking" church, i.e., a church less concerned with dogmas and moral principles and more interested in getting closer to people, irrespective of their individual choices and deliberately abstaining from passing moral judgments on their moral lives. This consistent stream of messages seemed to create a sort of momentum and to form the background for significant changes in the church that the Synod was meant to introduce. Things went differently, however. In the meantime, significant criticism by important circles of the Catholic Church became outspoken and hit the Pope himself for his wavering and blurred words. This "Catholic" month by Francis can be thought of as a reassurance that he stands for the traditional moral teaching of the church and has in no way changed his mind. After months of pushing a seemingly progressive agenda, the Catholic pendulum is swinging the opposite way in order to regain stability until the next move.

Where Does He Stand?

A standing question remains though. Where does the Pope really stand on these issues? How do we account for this apparent U-turn? Who is able to grapple with what he has in mind? And, more generally, do we really know where he stands on a number of key doctrinal and pastoral points? So far, he has been keen to build bridges with all kinds of people, movements, and networks. A growing number of people around the globe call the Pope "a friend." Many evangelical leaders are in their midst. They have the impression that the Pope is very approachable and a transparent person, easy to become familiar with and quick to tune in. He seems to speak their language and to understand their hearts. He appears to be close to everyone. The evidence, however, is more complex. He is certainly capable of getting close to all, calling anyone "brother" and "sister," but how many people know what lies in his heart? He is certainly able to combine evangelical language, Marian devotions, and "politically correct" concerns while retaining a fully orbed Roman Catholic outlook. Do we really know Pope Francis? How much of this complexity is the result of him being a Jesuit? How much do we know about the depth of his theology and the all-embracing nature of his agenda?

The Bible wants our communication not to be trapped in a "yes" and "no" type of language at the same time (2 Cor 1:18–20) but to speak plainly about what we have in our hearts. Pope Francis's language tends to say "yes, yes" and "no, no" with the same breadth. The Word of God also urges us "to speak truthfully" (Eph 4:25) and to avoid "twisted words" (Prov 4:24). No one can throw a stone here because in this matter we are all sinners. Yet what the Pope has been saying so far did send contradictory messages. This "Catholic" month has shown an important side of Pope Francis, but the full picture is still a work in progress. The impression is that so far we have been collecting only superficial sketches of the Pope and that the real work is still to be done.

One Roman (Vatican) Stop After a Catholic (German) Push (September 1, 2022, Number 205)

Roman Catholicism is, by definition, Catholic (inclusive, welcoming, absorbing) and Roman (centralized, hierarchical, institutional) at the same time. The former characteristic gives it its fluidity, the latter its rigidity. It is soft like velvet and abrasive like sandpaper. Certainly, there are historical phases in which the Catholic prevailed over the Roman and vice versa. There are different combinations in the way the two qualifications are intertwined with each other.

For example, on the one hand, the Council of Trent (16th century) was very Roman, with its dogmatic definitions and its excommunications of those who upheld Protestant convictions on the supreme authority of Scripture and salvation by faith alone. On the other, the Second Vatican Council (20th century) was very Catholic, with its ecumenism towards non-Catholics and its embrace of the modern world. Pius IX (1792–1878) was a Roman Pope who rejected religious freedom and freedom of conscience; Francis is a Catholic Pope with his insistence on the fact that we are "all brothers" (Christians, Muslims, Buddhists, atheists, etc.) regardless faith in Christ. We could go on with other examples.

The point is that Roman Catholicism is always in a tense balance between its two sides: Catholic and Roman. Rome is not only

Catholic—otherwise it would dilute and disperse its institutional project centered on its hierarchical structures. It is not only Roman—otherwise it would become hardened in a closed system. It is both at the same time. An example of the Catholic and Roman dynamic is precisely at work these days and has as protagonists the "Synodal Path" of the German Catholic Church and the Vatican, the Holy See.

For some years now a Catholic initiative, the "Synodal Path," has been underway in Germany involving bishops, laypeople, and religious associations.[11] This series of meetings, discussions, and papers has gathered many critical voices within Roman Catholicism and has proposed innovations and changes to some consolidated Roman Catholic doctrines and practices: the German "Synodal Path" has approved the female diaconate (in view of the ordination of women to the priesthood), the official recognition of homosexual couples, the relaxation of admission to the Eucharist to all those who come forward, etc. These are all very Catholic measures, i.e., inclusive and progressive, broadening the traditional stance of the Roman Church.

Important sectors of German (e.g., Cardinal Walter Kasper) and international (e.g., conservative circles in the US) Roman Catholicism have expressed growing concerns over the disruptive turn of the "Synodal Path" and the "liquid" Roman Catholicism it endorses.[12] To try to restore order, in 2019 Pope Francis wrote a letter to German Catholics whose essence can be summarized in this way: "The German Synod is fine, changes are fine to some extent, but always stay within the Roman structures and remain united to the whole ecclesiastical institution."[13] In spite of the Papal message, this reminder went virtually unnoticed and the German "Synodal Path" continued undaunted with its very Catholic resolutions, challenging the Roman status quo.

On July 21 the news came out that, fearing a rupture of the balance between the Catholic and the Roman, the Vatican issued a "Declaration of the Holy See" in German and Italian.[14] The declaration essentially says two things: first, that the "Synodal Path" is all right insofar as it does not change the well-established beliefs and practices of the whole universal church; and second, if anything, its requests and recommendations can and should be brought to the broader Synod of Bishops on synodality

---

11. Pongratz-Lippitt, "Germany's 'Synodal Path.'"
12. De Chirico, "Vatican File 200."
13. Hagenskord, "Pope Urges German Church."
14. See Holy See, "Erklärung des Heiligen Stuhls"; "Dichiarazione della Santa Sede."

that will take place in Rome in 2023. This is the translation from the ecclesiastical jargon: "Dear German Catholics, you have pulled the rope too hard. Now the Roman structures of the church are calling you back in order to make your journey flow back into the Roman Catholic synthesis." In even fewer words: "Catholicity is fine but not at the expense of the Roman identity." Roman Catholicism is both Catholic and Roman.

The Vatican believed that the time had come to strike a Roman blow to the Catholic trajectory of the "Synodal Path." Rome feared that the pendulum of Catholicity ran the risk of breaking the framework of Romanism.

This Roman initiative by the Holy See is just the latest in a series of continuous adjustments that keep the system in a dynamic equilibrium. Compared to theological liberalism which, from Friedrich Schleiermacher onwards, pushes the accelerator of the historical Protestant churches on the reinvention of Christianity to adapt it to the dominant culture, Roman Catholicism is open to "development" and "updating" without losing its dogmatic commitments and institutional structure. The Catholic expansion must serve the purpose of reinforcing the Roman system; otherwise, it is not different from the liberal agenda.

For this reason, Roman Catholicism is not interested in a "reformation" according to the gospel. Rome wants to incorporate new and different emphases (e.g., evangelical, charismatic, traditionalist, liberal) without changing its sacramental and hierarchical self-understanding. Rome says it wants the gospel, but Rome also wants Mariology, the papacy, the sacraments—traditions and devotions that are contrary to the gospel—without obliterating its view that the Roman Church as it stands is a *de iure divino* institution, i.e., by divine law and therefore unchanging and unchangeable. If the tension between the Catholic and the Roman of Roman Catholicism is not broken and reformed by the truth of the gospel and by the power of the Holy Spirit, Rome will never really change: it will shift from here to there, always moving within the boundaries of its Catholic and Roman sides but without getting closer to Jesus Christ.

The End of the Tridentine Paradigm (or Where Is the Roman Catholic Church Going)? (December 1, 2022 Number 208)

It was the historian Paolo Prodi (1932-2016) who coined the expression "Tridentine paradigm" to indicate the set of identity markers that emerged from the Council of Trent (1545-63) and which shaped the Catholic Church for centuries, at least until the second half of the 20th century. In one of his most famous books, *Il paradigma tridentino*, Prodi explored the self-understanding of the institutional church of Rome which, in the wake of and in response to the "threat" of the Protestant Reformation, closed hierarchical and pyramidal ranks up to the primacy of the Pope.[15] The church consolidated its sacramental system, regimented the church in rigorous canonical forms and parochial territories, and disciplined folk devotions and the control of consciences. It relaunched its mission to counter the spread of the Reformation and to anticipate the Protestant states in an attempt to arrive first in countries not yet "evangelized." It promoted models of holiness to involve the laity emotionally and inspired artists to celebrate the new vitality of the church of Rome in a memorable form.

The Tridentine paradigm produced the *Roman Catechism* of Pius V (1566) as a dogmatic synthesis of the Catholic faith to which Catholics scrupulously had to abide, the controversial theology of Robert Bellarmine to support anti-Protestant apologetic action, and the great baroque creations by Gian Lorenzo Bernini (like the majestic colonnade of St. Peter's) to represent the church as the winner over its adversaries and new patron of artists and intellectuals.[16]

The Tridentine paradigm has withstood the challenge of the Protestant Reformation and more. With the same paradigm, Rome also faced a second push coming from the modern world: that of the Enlightenment (on the cultural side) and the French Revolution (on the political side) between the eighteenth and nineteenth centuries. With the same set of institutional, sacramental, and hierarchical markers that emerged from the Council of Trent, Rome defended itself from the attack of modernity and counterattacked. With the dogmas of the immaculate conception of Mary (1854) and Papal infallibility (1870), which are children of the Tridentine paradigm, Rome elevated Mariology and the papacy to identity

---

15. Prodi, *Paradigma tridentino*.
16. De Chirico, "Robert Bellarmine."

markers of modern Roman Catholicism. With Pius IX's *Syllabus of Errors* (1864), Rome condemned the modern world, just as the Council of Trent had anathematized Protestants. With the encyclical *Aeterni Patris* (1879), Leo XIII elevated Thomism to a system of Catholic thought against all the drifts of modern culture.

The Tridentine paradigm exalted the church of Rome and condemned its enemies. It established who was in and who was out. It defined Roman Catholic doctrine and rejected "Protestant" and "Modernist" heresies. It solidified Roman Catholic teaching and consolidated practices. It authorized controlled forms of pluralism but within the compact structure of the central organization. According to the Tridentine paradigm, it was clear who Catholics were, what they believed, how they were expected to behave, and how the church functioned.

Then, the world changed, and Roman Catholicism changed with it. The Tridentine paradigm gradually eroded with the Second Vatican Council (1962–65), not in a frontal and direct way but following the path of "development" and "aggiornamento" that Vatican II promoted. Of course, Rome does not make any U-turns or swerves sharply. Trent is still there, and the dogmatic and institutional structures of the Tridentine paradigm are standing. The Roman Catholic Church has begun to see its limits, wishing to overcome them by embracing a new posture in the world. Even if Paul VI immediately saw the risks of abandoning it, John Paul II tried to make the Tridentine paradigm elastic by extending it to the universal church. Benedict XVI coined the expression "reform-in-continuity" to try to explain the Catholic dynamic of change without breaking with the past.

The Pope who seems to perceive the Tridentine paradigm in negative terms is Pope Francis. His invectives against "clericalism" are directed at Roman Catholic people and practices nourished by the Tridentine spirit. The typical distinctions of the Tridentine paradigm are rendered fluid and are progressively dissolved: clergy/laity, man/woman, Catholic/non-Catholic, heterosexual/homosexual, married/divorced, etc. If the Tridentine paradigm distinguished and selected things and people, Francis wants to unite everything and everyone. The first paradigm separated Roman Catholicism from the rest; this Pope wants to mix everything. The first worked with the pair white/black, inside/outside, faithful/infidel. Francis sees the world in different shades of gray and welcomes everyone into the "field hospital" that is the church.

The "synodal" church dear to Francis seems to overturn the traditional pyramidal structure. The direction of the church is determined by the "holy people of God" made up of migrants, the marginalized, the poor, the laity, and people in irregular life situations.[17] Before there were heretics, pagans, and excommunicated, now we are "all brothers."[18] It is no longer the center that drives but the peripheries. It is not sin, judgment, and salvation that occupy the discourse of the church, but its message today touches on themes such as peace, human rights, and the environment. The church no longer wants to present itself as a "magistra" (teacher) but only as a "mater" (mother).

With its calls for the extension of the priesthood to women and the blessing of same-sex couples, the German "synodal path"[19] is effectively striking the Tridentine paradigm. The first results of the "synodal process" in European dioceses are attacks on the Tridentine paradigm. It is true that there are conservative circles (in the USA in particular) who claim the Tridentine paradigm and would like to revive it. However, the point is that Roman Catholicism globally is at a crossroads. Has the Tridentine paradigm reached the end of its journey? If so, what will be the face of Roman Catholicism tomorrow? Neither the Tridentine paradigm nor the various synodal paths dear to Pope Francis indicate an evangelical turning point in the Church of Rome. The Church of Rome was and remains distant from the claims of the biblical gospel.

In a Double Move, Francis Closes the Ratzinger Era. For Now. (August 1, 2023, Number 218)

Pope Ratzinger (1927–2022) died only seven months ago, but it is safe to say that on July 1st his era definitely ended, at least in the intentions of the reigning Pope.[20] In a double move that would make a skilled checkers player envious, Pope Francis put an end to an unwieldy presence in his pontificate. As a "Pope Emeritus" living in the Vatican (a situation that had never happened before in the millennial history of the Catholic Church), Ratzinger constituted a thorn in Francis's side, albeit a silent one at least on the outside. Light years removed in terms of theological

---

17. Karr, "No One Excluded."
18. De Chirico, "Vatican File 181."
19. De Chirico, "Vatican File 205."
20. De Chirico, "Pope Benedict XVI."

training and ideas about the church, Francis had assigned him the "wise grandfather" role—a vexatious way of saying that he was an old man rich in memory but lacking in future prospects.

Benedict XVI died at the end of 2022, but on July 1, his shadow receded further from the Vatican. Francis's first move was to dispatch Ratzinger's secretary, Msgr. George Gänswein, to Freiburg, Germany, without assignments: away from Rome, deprived of ecclesiastical responsibilities. The last rift between him and Francis had been the day after Ratzinger's funeral, with the publication of his book *Nothing but the Truth: My Life at the Side of Benedict XVI*, in which Gänswein had clearly spoken of the disagreements between the two popes.[21] Francis had not liked either the timing or the content. Now Gänswein, who is only 66 years old (a "young" age for the church in Rome), has received the reciprocation that tastes like revenge served cold: a one-way ticket and a future without appointments. The message is clear: cohabitation with Ratzinger and his "inner circle" is over.

But there was another move in contrast to the Ratzingerian age. Before becoming Pope, Ratzinger had been the powerful prefect of the Dicastery for the Doctrine of the Faith (formerly the Holy Office). Upon becoming Pope, in defense of Catholic doctrine, Cardinals Müller (German) and Ladaria (Spanish) had been appointed in his place. They are different in temperaments but both "conservative" or "moderate" like Ratzinger. The former had been his student, the latter had been secretary of the Dicastery in Ratzinger's time. Two "loyalists." There was no shortage of friction; Müller had said that Pope Francis needed "theological framing" and, in the face of this "offense," was promptly and abruptly dismissed by the Pope. Ladaria, a Jesuit like Bergoglio, has held a more defiladed and guarded position but certainly not in line with the evolution of Francis's papacy.

Now, coincidentally, on the very same day of Ratzinger's former secretary's departure, Ladaria, Ratzinger's appointee to the Dicastery, was also dismissed on grounds of seniority. In his place, Francis appointed Argentine Víctor Manuel Fernández. Not well known in international theological circles, Fernández is, however, a loyal follower of Pope Francis. He is said to have been the ghostwriter of *Evangelii Gaudium*,[22] the pontificate's programmatic manifesto calling for a "missionary conversion"

---

21. Coppen, "'Nothing but the Truth.'" See also, Italian edition: Gänswein, *Nient'altro che la Verità*.

22. De Chirico, "Vatican File 69."

of his church; *Amoris Lætitia*,[23] the exhortation that contains openings toward the Eucharistic inclusion of people in "irregular" states of life; and *Laudato Si'*,[24] the encyclical on environmental issues that is so popular in progressive circles. Virtually all the cornerstones of Francis's magisterium were written in consultation with Fernández. In the aftermath of *Evangelii Gaudium*, he had written a book presenting the new Papal course to the world—*The Project of Francis: Where He Wants to Take the Church*.[25] Now, this interpreter of Francis's thinking, far removed from Ratzinger's, became prefect of the Dicastery for the Doctrine of the Faith, the highest body for the promotion of Catholic doctrine. Francis has a very faithful and "young" theologian (sixty-two years old) in a position that can carry on his "project" even when he is gone. In Francis's view, this really is a big deal. The next two years will see two Synods of Bishops (gathering all Roman Catholic bishops from around the world) on the controversial topic of "synodality,"[26] i.e., a new way of proceeding in the church, with Rome becoming more inclusive and absorbing (catholic) and less marked by its traditional identity (Roman). Francis has now a trusted supporter and enthusiastic promoter of his view of "synodality."

In two moves, Francis has shrewdly weakened the "Roman-ness" of the church as interpreted by Pope Benedict XVI and scored a point in favor of the "catholicity" of the current fluid church, the one where we are "all brothers."[27] While physically frail, Francis has never been stronger than he is now.

---

23. Here is a recent summary of *Evangelii Gaudium* from the Pope himself: "Here we find the 'heart' of the evangelical mission of the Church: to reach all through the gift of God's infinite love, to seek all, to welcome all, excluding no one, to offer our lives for all. All! That is the key word." Holy See, "Audience to Pontifical Mission Societies."

24. De Chirico, "Vatican File 110."

25. Fernández, *Progetto di Francesco*.

26. Karr, "Synodality."

27. De Chirico, "Vatican File 181."

6

Mariology

Hurrah to Madonna. Pope Francis and the Re-Marianization of the Papacy (May 10, 2013, Number 58)

THAT POPE FRANCIS HAS a strong Marian devotion became immediately clear after his election. In his first speech as Pope he committed himself and the world to Mary. The following day his first visit outside of the Vatican walls was to the basilica of Saint Mary Major, where he prayed to Mary. In his homilies he has at times disseminated his Marian piety. Now that the liturgical Marian month (May) has begun, the Pope has further expressed his devotion. On May 3 he led the rosary in the same Marian basilica he visited after being elected and gave a public speech to the people that had gathered there.[1]

Mary, Salus Populi Romani

This particular basilica is known for hosting and displaying the icon of Mary who is called Salus Populi Romani (i.e., salvation of the Roman people). This is a Marian title that underlines her being the protector of the Roman people. In front of the icon, Pope Francis commented, "We

---

1. See Francis, "Recital of the Holy Rosary."

are all here in front of Mary; we prayed for her motherly guidance; we took her our joys and sorrows, our hopes and difficulties; we invoked her with the title *Salus Populi Romani* to ask for ourselves, for Rome and for the world the gift of health. Yes, she gives health, she is our health."[2] In expounding his teaching, Francis went on to talk about three ways in which Mary is our health: she helps us grow as men and women, just as a mother cares for her children; she helps us face our difficulties, just as a mother walks with her children; lastly, she helps us make right decisions in life, just as a mother wants her children to live responsibly. Outside of Roman Catholic piety, it is difficult to understand such a profound "motherly" language of devotion to Mary and to square it with a Christ-centered and a Bible-based faith which unequivocally points to Jesus Christ as the only Mediator between God and man. Biblically, these roles relate to the christological offices of Jesus as Priest and King. Yet Roman Catholicism attributes them to Mary as an extension of Christ's role as mediator. Out of its synergism the Roman Catholic faith allows, indeed demands, such a veneration of Mary which has theological, spiritual, and emotional dimensions. Mary is seen as the protector of life.

Papal Marianisms

In closing his speech, Pope Francis addressed the crowd by saying, "Thank you for your presence here in the house of the mother of Rome, our Mother. Hurrah to the Salus Populi Romani. Hurrah to Madonna. She is our Mother. Let us entrust ourselves to her because she cares for us like a good mother."[3] This time the devotional language matched that of sports enthusiasts: hurrah, hurrah! The magnitude of Mary's motherly role stirred the heart and soul of many people gathered there. Pope Francis has stressed the fact that he wants to emphasize his role as bishop of Rome and has begun to give this emphasis a distinct Marian flavor. We can now begin to see the trajectory of this present pontificate as far as his Marianism is concerned. The last Pope to share such a high view of Mary was John Paul II. His motto was "totus tuus" (i.e., totally yours), and his veneration of Marian icons and his practice of Marian devotions were very evident. Benedict XVI has been portrayed as a less Marian Pope, although he has always prayed to Mary on a daily basis and has included

2. Francis, *Holy Rosary Address*, 1.
3. Francis, *Holy Rosary Address*, 12.

many Marian elements in all his work. After a short recess, Mary is once again a prominent figure with Pope Francis. His pontificate seems to be significantly shaped by Marian theology and veneration.

The World Entrusted to Mary. Why? (October 16, 2013, Number 67)

"Where ever Mary is venerated, and devotion to her takes place, there the Church of Christ does not exist."[4] If Karl Barth is correct, the Church of Christ was not present yesterday (October 13) in St. Peter's Square, when Pope Francis entrusted the world to Mary. The occasion was offered by the veneration of the statue of Our Lady of Fatima, which had been brought to Rome for a special Marian day. Marianism is one of the keys to interpreting the present pontificate and this celebration further highlights its pervasiveness.

Entrusting the World to Mary?

If Francis appears to break with many conventions on the way he lives out his being Pope, he is very traditional as far as his Marianism is concerned. Entrusting the world to the Immaculate Heart of Mary was done by Pius XII during World War II (1942) and twice by John Paul II (1982 and 1984). Francis then follows an established 20th-century tradition that unites pre- and post-Vatican II Roman Catholicism. These acts are responses to the message that Mary supposedly gave to the three young shepherds in Fatima (Portugal) in 1917.

The entrustment of the world to Mary is therefore something that stems from a recent Marian vision, with no biblical support whatsoever. Entrusting the world is a very important act, but one wonders whether or not Christians are instead summoned by God's Word to entrust their lives to the Creator (e.g., 1 Pet 4:19) or to make their requests to God himself (e.g., Phil 4:6). The world was entrusted by God the Father to God the Son (1 Cor 15:27), and there is no Mariological development that can overturn this truth.

---

4. Barth, *Church Dogmatics*, I/2, 219.

The Act Itself

What did it mean for Pope Francis to entrust the world to Mary? Basically, the Pope prayed a Marian prayer that contained a number of far-reaching statements and commitments that, biblically speaking, are proper if addressed to the Triune God, but that were instead directed to Mary.

Here is a sample: "We are confident that each of us is precious in your sight and that nothing that dwells in our hearts is unknown to you." At this point an ordinary Christian would ask: does not the Bible say that we are precious in God's eyes (e.g., Isa 43:4) but never speaks of Mary in these terms? Moreover, does this statement imply that Mary knows the depths of our hearts? Is she omniscient, thus being referred to with attributes that belong to God alone? According to the Bible, God the Father knows the secrets of the heart (Ps 44:21), God the Son knows men's thoughts (e.g., Matt 9:4), God the Spirit intercedes for us with groanings too deep for words (Rom 8:26).

Here is another statement: "Guard our lives in your arms." Mary is depicted as defending and caring for us, yet another attribute that the Bible relates to God alone. God the Father preserves the lives of the saints (e.g., Ps 97:10) and the Lord Jesus guards those who were given him by the Father (John 17:12). It is God's power that guards his children through faith (1 Pet 1:5). Mary has no role in this. Moreover, it is God who gathers "the lambs in his arms" (Isa 40:11). Mary's arms stretched to baby Jesus, but nowhere in Scripture are we told that we can look for her embrace.

A final statement of the prayer contains the following invocation: "Revitalize and nourish faith; sustain and brighten hope; inspire and animate charity" as if Mary was assigned this role. The Bible teaches that believers ask Jesus to help them grow in their faith (e.g., Mark 9:24), have their hope in God (e.g., Acts 24:15), and know that love is the fruit of the Holy Spirit (Gal 5:22).

The problem with this Papal Mariology is that it is totally unwarranted if the Christian faith is to be based on the Word of God alone. In spite of all that is said in ecumenical circles about the re-approachment between Roman Catholics and evangelical Protestants on the Bible, this Act of Entrustment to Mary shows that their differences are not a matter of nuances but of fundamental issues that lie at the heart of the faith itself. Thankfully, "the earth is the Lord's and the fullness thereof" (Ps 24:1), and there is no need to entrust it to someone else.

"Without Mary the Heart Is an Orphan." Another Instance of Francis's Marianism (May 16, 2014, Number 80)

Francis's Marian devotion is one of the defining marks of his spirituality. From his very first acts as Pope to his daily speeches and practices, traditional Marian theology is basic to his Catholic worldview. To evangelical ears his language may at times seem Christ-centered and mission-oriented, but these apparent gospel emphases are always organically related to a strong Marianism that envelops the Pope's religious narrative and experience. The latest example of his profound Marianism occurred in a meeting with the seminarians in Rome on May 13. In answering their questions on various topics, the Pope made some interesting comments on the Marian framework that undergirds his theology of the Christian life.

Under the Mantle of the Holy Mother of God

Commenting on the need for vigilance in times of personal turmoil, Francis evokes the counsel of the Russian Fathers to run "under the mantle of the Holy Mother of God." This Marian protection—the Pope recalls—is also part of the liturgy whereby the faithful declare to find refuge under the "presidium" (haven) of Mary: "sub tuum presidium confugimus, Sancta Dei Genitrix." So, for a priest not to pray to Mary in times of difficulty is for him to be like an "orphan." When in trouble the first thing a child does is look for his mother, so too should it happen in the spiritual realm. The mediatorial work of Jesus Christ and his total understanding of our needs (the whole point of Heb 1–2 and 4:14–16) is here totally overlooked and is instead subsumed under the protection of Mary, who is the caring mother of those seeking help. Whereas the psalmist can cry "for God alone, o my soul, wait in silence, for my hope is from Him" (Ps 62:8), Francis's advice is to seek the "mantle" of Mary.

The Pope then goes on to underline the link between the motherhood of Mary and the motherhood of the church. According to him, those who have a "good relationship" with Mary will be helped to have a "good relationship" with the church and even with their own souls. All three have a "feminine element" which connects them in a transitive and motherly way. Again, there is strong emphasis on motherhood that runs through the Mariological worldview. Those who do not have a good relationship with Mary (assuming that this means praying to her, trusting her, and seeking her help) are like "orphans." The Bible, however, teaches that a good relationship with the church is made possible only through the head of the church, that is Jesus Christ, and this comes through the Holy Spirit (1 Cor 12). Francis, on the other hand, has a "motherly" way of getting that relationship right.

Either Mother or Mother-in-Law!

At this point the Pope recalls an episode that happened to him while visiting a family in Northern Europe thirty years ago. The members of the family were practicing Catholics and full of enthusiasm for Christ (perhaps influenced by the Protestant culture of their region?). In a conversation they said, "We have discovered Christ and—thank God—we have passed the stage of Madonna. We don't need her any longer." "No," replied the saddened Bergoglio. "This is not a mature faith. Forgetting the mother is always a bad thing, not a sign of maturity." Again, the question arises: is finding Christ and him alone a step towards or away from Christian maturity?

The last comment concerning this question seems more like a humorous joke. In wrapping up his Marian reflection, Francis concludes by saying, "If you don't want Mary as a mother, she will become your mother-in-law!" An intriguing way of further expanding the motherhood metaphor in non-biblical directions.

The point is that Pope Francis believes that a mariologically free or even mariologically light faith is an orphan-like and immature faith. The real question is whether or not a Christ-centered and mission-oriented faith should focus on Christ instead of intermingling the gospel with various motherhood ideas that obscure it.

The Marian Message of Pope Francis to Korea (August 22, 2014 Number 87)

The Papal visit to Korea (August 13-18, 2014) was his first trip to Asia, and many commentators have already highlighted different geopolitical aspects of it. Asia is one of the most promising regions in the world for the Roman Catholic in terms of potential growth. This is the reason why Pope Francis will visit Sri Lanka and the Philippines in January of 2015. Asia is inevitably related to China, where there is an ongoing diplomatic challenge for the Vatican and its prudent attempt to deal with the Chinese government and the unsettled situation of Christian churches there. This is why Francis extensively spoke on the theme of "dialogue" and the fact that Christians in no way intend to "invade" anyone or any place. He was in Korea but certainly had China in the back of his mind and wanted to send a message there as well. Korea itself is a divided nation and the Pope addressed the painful memories and the reality of the separation between North and South Korea. On a more symbolic level, Asia is also very evocative for Jesuits in general. Five centuries ago Matteo Ricci (1552–1610) was the first Jesuit to go to China, and so the Jesuit Pope also feels the Asian attraction that is typical of many Jesuits.

Geopolitical considerations aside, there were two main spiritual emphases of the visit: the usual Marian framework of Pope Francis and the elaboration of his missional view as far as the discipline of dialogue is concerned. This file concentrates on the first item, while another one will deal with the second.

Mary, Mother of Korea

The Papal visit coincided with the Asian Youth Day but most importantly with the solemn celebration of the assumption of Mary, body and soul, into the glory of heaven (August 15). This Marian dogma was promulgated in 1950 and fits very well the overall spirituality of Pope Francis. In his homily during the celebration, he invited the Korean audience "to contemplate Mary enthroned in glory beside her divine Son."[5] He called Mary "Mother of the Church in Korea," asking her help "to be faithful to the royal freedom we received on the day of our Baptism."[6] The queenly glory of Mary was coupled with the motherhood of Mary for the whole nation of Korea. Although the Bible teaches that "God is our refuge and strength, a very present help in trouble" (Ps 46:1), it was Mary that was presented to the faithful as an ever-ready helper on the spiritual journey.

In praising Mary, the Pope went on to say that "In her, all God's promises have been proved trustworthy."[7] Actually, the Bible says that "all the promises of God find their Yes in Him," i.e., in Christ (2 Cor 1:20). This is an example of how the logic of Catholic Mariology works its way

5. "Homily (Daejeon)," para. 2.
6. "Homily (Daejeon)," para. 4.
7. "Homily (Daejeon)," para 6.

through: it takes what belongs to Christ and extends it to his mother, although the Bible does not prescribe nor does it allow such an extension to take place.

The final invocation was also telling: "And now, together, let us entrust your Churches, and the continent of Asia, to Our Lady, so that as our Mother she may teach us what only a mother can teach: who you are, what your name is, and how you get along with others in life. Let us all pray to Our Lady."[8] Again, the motherhood of Mary was strongly emphasized to the point of attributing the discovery of our identity to her instead of Christ in whom we are saved and through whom we have received a new name. In so doing Mary joins Christ with the risk of taking his place.

Obtaining the Grace of Perseverance?

A final comment on the Mariology of the Papal visit is in order. During the Mass for the beatification of 124 Korean martyrs (August 16th), Francis ended his homily with these words: "May the prayers of all the Korean martyrs, in union with those of Our Lady, Mother of the Church, obtain for us the grace of perseverance in faith and in every good work, holiness and purity of heart, and apostolic zeal in bearing witness to Jesus in this beloved country, throughout Asia, and to the ends of the earth."[9] The idea is that the prayers of those whom the church proclaims to be blessed "obtain for us the grace of perseverance." Perseverance seems to be a human "work" that is obtainable through the efforts of the living and the dead.

In returning to Rome, after the long flight from Korea, Pope Francis stopped on his way to the Vatican at the basilica of Saint Mary Major, the largest Marian church in Rome, to thank Mary for the successful results of his trip to Asia. Saint Mary Major was the first church the Pope ever visited after becoming Pope and the dedication of his pontificate to Mary was the first official act of his reign. This church and what it represents is very dear to him. The point is that Francis's seemingly biblical language and "evangelical" attitude is always thought of and lived out in a thoroughly Marian framework, in both Rome and Korea alike.

---

8. Francis, "Homily (Vatican Basilica)," para 4.
9. *Catholic News Agency*, "Pope Beatifies 124 Korean Martyrs," para. 21.

Holy Mother of God! Three Times!
(February 12, 2015, Number 101)

In the Roman Catholic liturgical calendar the first day of the year marks the solemnity of Mary, the Mother of God. On this occasion the Pope delivers a Marian homily that highlights the unique status of Mary and her unparalleled role in Catholic doctrine and spirituality. Given the strong Marian devotion of Pope Francis, it is no surprise that he celebrated this solemnity with great enthusiasm that also included an unexpected finale. A recent book highlights the love of Pope Francis for the Madonna by collecting a number of Marian prayers and devotions which are extremely dear to him.[10]

Inseparable Mother

In his first speech of the year Francis offered a meditation on the inseparability of Christ and his mother.[11] He then elaborated on that inseparability by underscoring the relationship between Mary and the church and ultimately between Mary and the whole of mankind. "Jesus cannot be understood without his Mother," said the Pope.[12] This is true of course, but with certain limits and biblical distinctions. With the incarnation, the Son of God became a man by being born of Mary. He is the sinless God-man that brings forth the Father's grace through the Spirit, while his mother is a sinful creature that receives God's grace. That inseparability needs biblical qualifications; otherwise it can lead to the exaltation of Mary beyond what Scripture allows.

Having established the inseparability between Mother and Son, the Pope went on to apply it to another relationship: that of Mary and the church. Here is what he said: "Likewise inseparable are Christ and the Church—because the Church and Mary are always together and this is precisely the mystery of womanhood in the ecclesial community—and the salvation accomplished by Jesus cannot be understood without appreciating the motherhood of the Church."[13] The train of thought is that Mary is inseparable from Christ and from the church; therefore, Christ is

---

10. Sansonetti, *Francesco e Maria*.
11. Francis, "Homily (Vatican Basilica)."
12. Francis, "Homily (Vatican Basilica)," para. 4.
13. Francis, "Homily (Vatican Basilica)," para. 5.

inseparable from the church through Mary. Mary is the connecting point between Christ and the church. As she is inseparable from the former, she is also inseparable from the latter and mediates the relationship between the two. Thus, Mary is theologically central in the overall Roman Catholic scheme.

There is yet another step. As Mary is the mother of Jesus and the mother of the church, she is also deemed to be the mother of all mankind. The Roman Catholic transitive property of the inseparable link is at work here. In lyrical style, Francis concludes, "Mary, the first and most perfect disciple of Jesus, the first and most perfect believer, the model of the pilgrim Church, is the one who opens the way to the church's motherhood and constantly sustains her maternal mission to all mankind. She, the Mother of God, is also the Mother of the Church, and through the Church, the mother of all men and women, and of every people."[14] The human inseparability between Mary and Jesus is worked out in the inseparability between Mary and the church and then between Mary and the whole of humankind.

A Crescendo with a Marian Grand Finale

Francis's speech is a clear example of how Roman Catholic Mariology has been at work throughout the ages. An initial step with some biblical support (i.e., the Son-Mother link in the context of the incarnation) was developed in subsequent syllogisms that lacked biblical criteria (e.g., Mary Mother of the Church, Mary Mother of Mankind). The outcome is a brand-new theological framework that has little resemblance to how it began.

As an experienced bishop with pastoral warmth, Francis ended his homily with an unusual request that is hardly common in Vatican celebrations. "Let us look to Mary, let us contemplate the Holy Mother of God. I suggest that you all greet her together, just like those courageous people of Ephesus, who cried out before their pastors when they entered church: 'Holy Mother of God!' What a beautiful greeting for our Mother. There is a story—I do not know if it is true—that some among those people had clubs in their hands, perhaps to make the Bishops understand what would happen if they did not have the courage to proclaim Mary 'Mother of God'!

---

14. Francis, "Homily (Vatican Basilica)," para. 7.

I invite all of you, without clubs, to stand up and to greet her three times with this greeting of the early church: 'Holy Mother of God!'"[15]

Reports say that the puzzled crowd that was sitting and standing in the Vatican basilica shouted "Holy Mother of God!" three times as the Pope had instructed. Thus, the first day of the year was an occasion to introduce a highly sophisticated Mariological doctrine and a strongly felt Mariological devotion which were blended together by a committed Marian Pope. For those who desire to live according to the Word of God, it was not a very promising start to the year.

"The Only Creature Without Sin"—Pope Francis on the Immaculate Conception of Mary (January 1, 2017, Number 132)

On December 8 each year, the solemnity of the Immaculate Conception of Mary is celebrated. On this occasion the Roman Catholic Church contemplates the belief that Mary was preserved from original sin. This view had been part of Roman Catholic teaching and devotional practices for centuries, but it was not until 1854 that the Immaculate Conception was officially promulgated by Pope Pius as a dogma, i.e., a binding and unreformable belief of the church. Here is the precise wording of this dogma:

> We declare, pronounce and define that the doctrine which asserts that the Blessed Virgin Mary, from the first moment of her conception, by a singular grace and privilege of almighty God, and in view of the merits of Jesus Christ, Saviour of the human race, was preserved free from every stain of original sin is a doctrine revealed by God and, for this reason, must be firmly and constantly believed by all the faithful.[16]

In spite of the bold and conclusive language (declaring, defining, asserting), Protestants find it difficult to come to terms with this Marian dogma. This is due to not finding even a hint of evidence for this belief in the Bible. "How can such a view be elevated to dogmatic status if the Word of God is at best silent on it?" they ask. So, it is always interesting to listen to the way in which Roman Catholic theology argues for the Immaculate Conception of Mary by trying to relate it to Scriptural teaching.

---

15. Francis, "Homily (Vatican Basilica)," para. 9.
16. Pius IX, "Ineffabilis Deus," 34.

Marian Solemnity

The last occasion for this was given by Pope Francis on December 8. He spoke twice on the topic. The first was to a public audience in St. Peter's Square. He later spoke at a Marian prayer gathering in Piazza di Spagna, where a lofty statue of Mary towers above the space and where at the climax of the ceremony it is crowned with flowers. The Papal invocations[17] to Mary appealed to her "immaculate heart" to learn how to love, to her "immaculate hands" to learn how to caress, to her "immaculate feet" to learn how to take the first step.

The special Marian day of the Pope also included a visit to the Roman Basilica of St. Mary Major to venerate the ancient "Salus Popoli Romani"[18] (health or salvation of the Roman people) icon of Mary. The Pope travels to the basilica before and after every international trip he takes in order to entrust the voyage to the care and intercession of Mary, typically with flowers in hand. This is to say that we are not confronted with a marginal belief nor with a peripheral practice. Both the dogma and the devotions attached to it are encapsulated at the very core of the Pope's spirituality.

No Space For Sin?

In his speech, the Pope argued that "Jesus didn't come as an adult, already strong and full grown, but decided to follow the exact same path of the human being, doing everything in exactly the same way "except for one thing: sin." Because of this, "he chose Mary, the only creature without sin, immaculate," he said, noting that when the angel refers to Mary with the title "Full of Grace," it means that from the beginning there was "no space for sin" inside of her. "Also we, when we turn to her, we recognize this beauty: we invoke her as 'full of grace,' without the shadow of evil."[19]

It appears that the biblical reference the Pope recalls is Luke 1:28, where Mary is addressed by the angel Gabriel as a "favored" one. The Vulgate, the late fourth-century Latin version of the Bible, translates this expression as "gratia plena" (full of grace), thus opening up all sorts of misconceptions, as if Mary possessed the fullness of grace in herself. This

---

17. Francis, "Act of Veneration."
18. Wikipedia, "*Salus Populi Romani.*"
19. Harris, "Be Like Mary."

translation has been taken as implying that she was so full of grace that she must have been conceived without original sin. However, there is no hint in the text about the fact that Mary is "full" of grace and therefore "void" of sin. Being "favored" indicates that she is an unworthy recipient of God's grace, just as the rest of us. This is further reinforced by the fact that Mary calls God her "Savior" (Luke 1:47), indicating that she thinks of herself as needing God's salvation, just as the rest of us. There is nothing intrinsic in her apart from the divine favor and his presence with her. It seems, therefore, that a strong argument for the Immaculate Conception of Mary is based on a faulty translation of the passage, leading to an implausible doctrine impinging on anthropology and soteriology, i.e., something belonging to the core of the biblical gospel.

The fact that the Roman Catholic Church is fully committed to the Immaculate Conception of Mary still represents a serious question mark for all those who want to ground their faith in what the Bible teaches. Evidently Rome is not based on Scripture alone but is on a trajectory in which devotions and traditions can have the final say above (and contrary to) the Bible.

She is My Mamá—Pope Francis and Mary (December 1, 2018, Number 156)

Ella Es Mi Mamá[20] (*She Is My Mum*) is the title of a 2014 book written in Spanish that contains a long interview with Pope Francis by the Brazilian priest Alexander Awi Mello. During the interview, Francis highlights the filial affection and devotion that he has for Mary. Readers of the Vatican Files know that the Marianism of the Pope has often been covered and assessed on this blog. Here are some examples:

- "Hurrah to Madonna." Pope Francis and the Re-Marianization of the Papacy[21]
- The Word Entrusted to Mary. Why?[22]
- "Without Mary the Heart is an Orphan." Another Instance of Francis's Marianism[23]

20. Mello, *Ella es me mamá*.
21. De Chirico, "Vatican File 58."
22. De Chirico, "Vatican File 67."
23. De Chirico, "Vatican File 80."

- The Marian Message of Pope Francis to Korea[24]
- "Holy Mother of God!" Three Times![25]
- "The Only Creature without Sin." Pope Francis on the Immaculate Conception of Mary[26]

This book, which was recently translated into Italian[27] and includes a new preface, does not break any new ground in terms of the pervasive presence of the cult of Mary in Francis's spirituality. What is interesting, though, are the biographical details that help to explain the personal context of his "applied" Marianism.

First Personal Encounters

Born into a devout Roman Catholic family, the young Jorge Mario Bergoglio was exposed to the Marian dimension of the faith from his earliest days. He began praying using Marian prayers, and the first image he possessed was a little medal of Mary of Mercy. Marianism reached him intuitively as part of family life and was conveyed with deep affections and tender gestures. As Clodovis Boff argues, "The incubator of Mariology is the heart, not the mind."[28] In the cult of Mary, experiences and feelings precede and dominate everything else.

Bergoglio's first experiences of the Catholic Church were in a parish run by the Salesian order and dedicated to Mary the Auxiliatrix, so his first impressions of what "church" meant were thoroughly Marian. The most influential priest in his childhood was one who would impart Marian blessings and recite Marian prayers when visiting the Bergoglio family. As a child, Jorge Mario would regularly bring flowers to the statue of Mary. At nineteen years of age, he decided to become a priest while praying in the Marian chapel of his parish church. His sweetest memories and most decisive moments were punctuated by the "presence" of Mary surrounding him. In a telling passage of the book, we are told that "Mary entered progressively and profoundly in his life, never to leave it again."[29]

24. De Chirico, "Vatican File 87."
25. De Chirico, "Vatican File 101."
26. De Chirico, "Vatican File 132."
27. Mello, È mia Madre.
28. Mello, È mia Madre, 126.
29. Mello, È mia Madre, 49.

The Importance of Marian Sanctuaries

After becoming a priest, Bergoglio marked his pastoral activities around Marian devotions. The most popular ones were the diocesan pilgrimages to the Marian sanctuary of Our Lady of Luján (whose image oversees the room where he meets with Catholic bishops from around the world at the Vatican). It is here that he leads thousands of people to the sanctuary of the Blessed Virgin of the Rosary of Pompei. He has become so close to Our Lady of Luján that he carries close to his heart a little piece of cloth that was used to polish her statue back in Argentina. He wants a physical, ongoing touch with something Marian.

Apart from the influence of the Mexican cult Mary of Guadalupe and the devotions related to Mary Undoer of Knots, whose veneration he has introduced in Argentina, Bergoglio's life has also been shaped by the cult associated with Our Lady of Aparecida in Brazil. In visiting Aparecida for World Youth Day in 2013, the Pope said in his speech there:

> What joy I feel as I come to the house of the Mother of every Brazilian, the Shrine of our Lady of Aparecida! The day after my election as Bishop of Rome, I visited the Basilica of Saint Mary Major in Rome, in order to entrust my ministry as the Successor of Peter to Our Lady. Today I have come here to ask Mary our Mother for the success of World Youth Day and to place at her feet the life of the people of Latin America.[30]

Yet another link to a centrally important Marian sanctuary in the life of the Pope is Saint Mary Major in Rome. He pays a visit there before and after his journeys around the world in order to commit them to Mary and ask for her protection.

Blurred Theology

From childhood to adulthood, from Argentina to the Vatican, from piety to theology, in his daily spiritual practices and devotions, Marianism is perhaps the most significant factor shaping the Pope's life. The apartment he lives in is replete with Marian images. The rooms where he officially meets with people are furnished with portraits of Mary. His own daily clothes carry objects associated with Mary. His prayers are directed to her. His affections and tender thoughts are oriented to Mary. The interview

---

30. De Chirico, "Vatican File 64."

is a wide-open window into Francis's Mariological vision. All aspects of his life, thought, and ministry—none excluded—are strongly impacted by his Mariology.

Of course, the pervasiveness of Mary is argued for in theological terms as well. For instance, Jesus is presented as someone who does not want to do all on his own but instead wants Mary to collaborate in the work of salvation.[31] According to the Pope, Jesus always acts according to "the logic of inclusion," and Mary's mediation is therefore an example of such necessary mediation. Since there are "organic links" between the Son and the Mother, she is always involved in what the Son does. It is the "principle of incarnation" that sustains and supports Marian devotions and veneration.[32]

While Marianism has a primarily intuitive force and sentimental power, Mariology tries to connect it to Christology and therefore to Trinitarian theology, as Vatican II tries to do.[33] Quoting the 1979 Puebla document,[34] the Pope goes on to say that "she is the point of contact between heaven and earth. Without Mary, the gospel becomes disembodied, defaced and transforms itself in ideology, in spiritualistic rationalism."[35] So, in this high Mariology, Christology is also at stake. If Mary is the point of contact between heaven and earth, isn't Jesus Christ's uniqueness as the God-man imperiled? If the gospel becomes disembodied without Mary, isn't the incarnation of the Son blurred?

A Marian Gospel

A major assumption in most present-day ecumenical dialogues is that there is a solid agreement among all Christian traditions on basic orthodox Christology and thus that Protestants and Roman Catholics share the same Christology. However, a reading of this book challenges this poor argument, which is nurtured by theological myopia and invites us to take Roman Catholic Mariology seriously in all of its implications for Christology, salvation, grace, and prayer—in other words, the whole of theology and practice. If the Pope sees Mary everywhere, even when he

---

31. Mello, *È mia Madre*, 45.
32. Mello, *È mia Madre*, 86.
33. Second Vatican Council, "Lumen Gentium," 52–69.
34. CELAM, "Documento de Puebla,"
35. CELAM, "Documento de Puebla," n. 301.

thinks of Christ and the Trinity, salvation, and the Christian life; if Francis continually prays to Mary; if he strongly feels and seeks the maternal presence of Mary all the time, is his gospel a Bible-based, Christ-centered, and God-honoring gospel at all?

Soon after Bergoglio became Pope Francis in 2013, one of the Argentinian theologians who had influenced him the most, Juan Carlos Scannone, said about him, "He will emphasize popular piety and spirituality, especially the Marian devotion which is so typical of Latin America."[36] These words have proven true. Francis is promoting a "Marian" gospel that contradicts at fundamental points the biblical gospel of Jesus Christ.

---

36. Mello, *È mia Madre*, 138.

7

Universalism

A Mini-Assisi for the Holy Land?
(June 17, 2014, Number 82)

Assisi is the small town where Francis of Assisi (1181–1226) lived most of his life and is now a destination for thousands of pilgrims every year. Assisi is also the place where, in 1986, Pope John Paul II convened a prayer meeting for peace where different religious leaders came together to pray, each one in his own way and to his own G/god(s). This interreligious prayer initiative raised some concerns within the Catholic Church as well as outside of it. Was it an endorsement of religious universalism? Was it a way to downplay the exclusive claims of the gospel? Did it give the impression that all religions are equal? What kind of theology supported that interfaith and multi-religious prayer? Although Pope Benedict tried to address some of these issues, this debate continues.

Now Pope Francis has entered the debate in a most unpredictable way. During his recent visit to the Holy Land he invited the Israeli President Shimon Peres and the Palestinian leader Mahmoud Abbas to pray for peace in the region (June 8). In a way this was a mini-Assisi type of event.

The Power of Symbols and the Inherent Confusion

The prayer took place in the Vatican, but the scene was very similar to what happened in Assisi. The Pope (dressed in his usual white robes) sat at the center of a semi-circle, with the Israeli and Palestinian delegations (all dressed in dark black suits) at his right- and left-hand sides. St. Peter's cupola overshadowed them all. It was the same setting of Assisi with the Pope being recognized as the "center" of interfaith dialogue and presiding over interreligious prayers. In their short speeches both Peres and Abbas readily praised the strategic leadership of the Pope in bringing reconciliation. All the symbols present strongly supported the view that the Papacy is a key institution in bringing the whole of humanity together.

The main difference is that in Assisi John Paul II had invited religious leaders whereas Francis brought *political* leaders together to pray. No matter what one thinks of interfaith prayer, the 1986 event was at least coherent in that it called religious leaders to take part. Now, Francis wanted presidents to pray with him instead. The significance of this can be hardly overestimated. The Pope is also head of a state (i.e., the Vatican City) and therefore wears two hats, so to speak. He is a peer of both religious and political leaders. In asking the Israeli President to pray a Jewish prayer and the Palestinian President to pray a Muslim prayer, however, he wrongly attributed to them the role of being representatives of the majority religions of their countries. He exchanged their responsibilities of representing *all* citizens (e.g., Israeli Christians and Palestinian Christians included) by giving them the hat of Jewish and Muslim religious leaders.

The confusion lies at the heart of the Roman Catholic Church. Because the Pope is both a religious leader and a head of state, the distinction between what belongs in the realms of both religion and state is significantly blurred. Francis invited his fellow heads of state and asked them to perform a religious duty as if they were religious leaders. He projected his own dual-identity (religious and political) onto his guests. This in no way represents a healthy relationship between the two spheres.

Standing Perplexities

The 2014 mini-Assisi gathering also used similar language that was used in 1986. In his prayer Francis invoked God as "God of Abraham, God of the Prophets, God of Love" who calls us to live "as brothers and sisters." He strongly advocated the idea that we have to "acknowledge one another as children of one Father." "Brother" was the most frequently used word in his speech, and the universal Fatherhood of God was the theological framework of the event.

Now this whole language is ambiguous at best. It can be used to indicate the need for peoples of different backgrounds and religions to live together in peace as if they were brothers and sisters. Or it can mean that they are already brothers and sisters, children of the same Father, no matter what their religious convictions are. The stress on the "same God" idea strongly suggests that the latter interpretation is what Francis really meant. The fact that a Christian prayer (with a final invocation to Mary, "the daughter of the Holy Land and our Mother"), a Jewish prayer, and a Muslim prayer were offered one after the other, all containing references to the "same God, same humanity," points to the idea that all religions are in the end good in themselves, provided that they restore and maintain peace. This is actually what most people took from the mini-Assisi of Pope Francis. After the cautious reservations of Pope Benedict, the "spirit of Assisi" still breathes in the Vatican.

Redefining Fraternity. At What Cost? (August 11, 2014, Number 86)

"Where is your brother?" asked God to Cain (Gen 4:9). This standing question challenges all people not to harm one's brother. The assumption though is that the identity of the brother is clear enough. Therefore, the issue is, Who is my brother? The Bible has two answers to this question: brothers and sisters are those who belong to the same family group. Jesus had brothers and sisters (Matt 13:55–56), i.e., people who were part of his inner family circle. According to Scripture brothers and sisters are also those who do the will of the Father who is in heaven (Matt 12:50), i.e., people who belong to the same spiritual family that has God as Father, Jesus as Lord and Savior, and the Spirit as guarantee. On the one hand there is the natural family (or people group), and on the other there is the "household of faith" (Gal 6:10).

What about the rest? The Bible says that all other people are "neighbors," people who are around us, near or far, but who live where we live and share part of our journey. "Who is my neighbor?" (Luke 10:29) is the other standing question for all people. Neighbors are all those who are next to us, and we are called to love them as ourselves (Matt 22:39).

Towards a Genuine Fraternity Between Christians and Muslims?

The Bible draws a distinction between natural or spiritual brotherhood and general neighborhood, though the Vatican no longer recognizes such a distinction. In a message sent to Muslims at the end of Ramadan and significantly entitled "Towards a Genuine Fraternity Between Christians and Muslims" (June 24, 2014), the Pontifical Council for Inter-Religious Dialogue reaffirmed the idea that Christians and Muslims are "brothers and sisters." The message itself traces the origin and the official endorsement of this language from John Paul II to Francis:

> Pope Francis . . . called you "our brothers and sisters" (*Angelus*, 11 August 2013). We all can recognize the full significance of these words. In fact, Christians and Muslims are brothers and sisters in the one human family, created by the One God. Let us recall what Pope John Paul II said to Muslim religious leaders in 1982: "All of us, Christians and Muslims, live under the sun of the one merciful God. We both believe in one God who is the creator of man. We acclaim God's sovereignty and we defend man's dignity as God's servant. We adore God and profess total submission to him. Thus, in a true sense, we can call one another brothers and sisters in faith in the one God." (Kaduna, Nigeria, 14 February 1982).[1]

What is happening here is the blunt redefinition of what it means to be brothers and sisters. First, while being "in Christ" becomes only one way of being brothers and sisters, fraternity is extended to all those who live "under the sun," i.e., "the one human family." Secondly, as far as Muslims are concerned, fraternity is further consolidated by the shared belief in "one God" whom is adored by both Christians and Muslims. The result is that they are truly "brothers and sisters in faith in the one God."

An Unwarranted Stretch

The redefinition of what it means to be brothers and sisters is an attempt to blur what the Bible expects us to distinguish. Neighbors become brothers and sisters. Our common humanity takes over the spiritual connotation of being "in Christ" as the basis for the shared fraternity. What are the implications of such a stretch? Here are two main ones.

---

1. Pontifical Council, *Towards Genuine Fraternity*, para. 2–3.

First, Popes John Paul II and Francis are taking the responsibility to reconstruct biblical language forsaking its own meaning and reshaping it at the service of the Roman Catholic view of the church representing the whole of humanity, Muslims and all others included. The assumption is that the finality of Scripture is undermined, the clear meaning of Scripture is questioned, and the living tradition of the church is thought of being entitled to "actualize" Scripture by way of changing its plain message.

Second, there is a whole set of crucial issues related to this redefinition. What does "genuine fraternity" mean in theological and soteriological terms? It seems to mean that the biblical God and the Muslim Allah are the same God who accepts worship indifferently, both in the Christian way and in the Muslim way. After all, we are all "brothers and sisters" under him. Moreover, it seems to imply that, as brothers and sisters "in faith in the one God," Christians and Muslims will ultimately be saved as Christians and Muslims. The universality of salvation is clearly envisaged if not openly stated. This message is a further extension of the very "catholic" theology stemmed from Vatican II, which shifted the locus of salvation from the profession of the faith in Jesus Christ to the shared humanity of all created beings. However, it remains to be seen whether or not this is biblical at all.

Beside these serious biblical flaws, you don't need this redefined fraternity to love Muslims and to seek to live in peace with them, as the Vatican message wants everybody to do. There is no reason to distort the plain words of Scripture: a biblically defined neighborhood is more than sufficient to promote civic engagement and peaceful coexistence with all men and women.

Is Unity Like a Sphere or a Polyhedron? (September 18, 2014, Number 89)

Pope Francis does not like spheres: he likes polyhedrons. In various recent speeches and in different contexts he used the image of the polyhedron to illustrate what he has in mind when he thinks of unity, i.e., Christian unity and the unity of mankind. In elementary geometry, a polyhedron is a solid of three dimensions with flat faces, straight edges and sharp corners or vertices. Without going into too many technical details, the basic idea is that a polyhedron lacks the harmony and proportions of a sphere but retains the unity of a solid. Not only that—it has variable distances from its center and not a single way of being related to it. It may be an awkward type of unity, but it still holds the solid together.

Unity in the Global World

Francis first began talking about the polyhedron in the context of globalization. In a message to a festival on the Social Doctrine of the Church which addressed the issue, he said, "I would like to translate the theme into an image: the sphere and the polyhedron. Take the sphere to represent homologation, as a kind of globalization: it is smooth, without facets, and equal to itself in all its parts. The polyhedron has a form similar to the sphere, but it is multifaceted. I like to imagine humanity as a polyhedron, in which the multiple forms, in expressing themselves, constitute the elements that compose the one human family in a plurality. And this is true globalization. The other globalization—that of the sphere—is an homologation."[2]

According to this vision, globalization as a sphere can lead to cultural uniformity and social homologation whereby one model of development and one way of life become the center of what it means to be human and the whole world must conform to it. Globalization as a polyhedron, on the other hand, allows for multiple solutions that are all different from one another while still maintaining vital relationships between its components. In the latter, homogeneity is not imposed and multiplicity is encouraged. In his 2013 apostolic exhortation *Evangelii Gaudium*, Francis elaborated on the dangers of reducing the world to a single economic pattern and a monolithic cultural paradigm. This globalization brings "an economy of exclusion," "the new idolatry of money," "a financial system which rules rather than serves," and "inequality which spawns violence." Globalization, by desiring to mould the world into a single pattern, kills it. Conversely, if it celebrates the world's diversity, it causes it to flourish. The center of this polyhedron is the common humanity that all human beings share while the different faces represent the cultural particulars that cannot be squeezed nor overlooked by globalization.

---

2. Francis, "Video Message of Pope Francis," para. 2.

Christian Unity

What is interesting in Francis's use of these geometric images is how he applies them to the realm of ecumenism. Christian unity has its own biblical metaphors, such as that of a single body with a head and many organs and parts (1 Cor 12). In his visit to the Italian Pentecostal Church (August 28, 2014), Francis developed his idea of ecumenism as a polyhedron: "We are in the age of globalization, and we wonder what globalization is and what the unity of the Church would be: perhaps a sphere, where all points are equidistant from the center, all are equal? No! This is uniformity. And the Holy Spirit does not create uniformity! What figure can we find? We think of the polyhedron: the polyhedron is a unity, but with all different parts; each one has its peculiarity, its charism. This is unity in diversity."[3]

Reading between the lines, it seems clear that unity as a sphere is pre-Vatican II Roman Catholic ecumenism whereby other Christians were drastically invited to "come back" into the Catholic fold and to conform to its doctrines and practices under the rule of the Pope. With Vatican II, Roman Catholicism updated its ecumenical project and embraced a concentric circle type of unity in which the one and only church "subsists in" the Roman Catholic Church and other churches and communities gravitate around this center according to their degree of nearness or distance from it. According to Vatican II and subsequent magisterial teachings, Christian unity is threefold: 1. Professing the same faith; 2. Celebrating the same Eucharist (i.e., the Roman Catholic way); and 3. Being united under the same sacramental ministry in apostolic succession (i.e., under the Pope).

How does a polyhedron kind of unity as advocated by Pope Francis fit this view of unity? For example: as far as the second mark of unity is concerned, is the Pope saying that the sacrificial understanding of the Eucharist and the theology of transubstantiation belong at the center of Christian unity or are they particulars that can accommodate differences? Or is the Pope saying that apostolic succession, which is the basis of the hierarchical structure of the Roman Catholic Church, is still part of the center or is it a variable that is secondary to Christian unity?

Polyhedrons are fascinating solids, and Francis's use of the image of a polyhedron is thought-provoking. However, the problem for Christian unity does not primarily lie in the metaphors used but in the theological

3. Fournier, "He Went to Find Brothers," para. 18.

vision that nurtures it. If the Catholic Eucharist and the Catholic sacramental system are part of the center of Christian unity, one can make reference to spheres or polyhedrons all he likes, but the substance of the problem is that unity still gravitates around the Roman Catholic Church and its distinct outlook and not around the biblical gospel that calls all Christians to conform to the mind of Christ.

An Atonement-Free Mercy? (March 1, 2016, Number 120)

"Mercy" is by far the most-used word by Pope Francis. Actually, it is the interpretative key of his whole pontificate. A book on mercy by Cardinal Kasper was on Bergoglio's bedside table when he was elected Pope, thus shaping his own personal reflections as he prepared to become pontiff. Mercy was the main rubric of the Synod of the Family when the Pope urged his church to apply less rigorously the "letter" of the teachings on sexuality and to listen more to the "spirit" of inclusion for those who live in various forms of irregular relationships. Mercy is the overarching theme of the Jubilee Year which Francis indicted in order to offer a year-long display of mercy through the system of indulgences. It is not surprising, therefore, that mercy is also the main theme of his recent speeches where he expounds it and unfolds it. The last instance was the general audience given on February 3 in Saint Peter's Square.[4]

Mercy and Justice

The vexed question of the relationship between mercy and justice is central to the Pope's meditation. Here is how he sets the tone of it: "Sacred Scripture presents God to us as infinite mercy and as perfect justice. How do we reconcile the two?" There seems to be a contradiction between God's mercy and God's justice. One way of connecting mercy and justice is through "retributive justice," which "inflicts a penalty on the guilty party, according to the principle that each person must be given his or her due." Justice is done when one receives what is owed to him. Francis makes reference to a couple of Bible verses that show retributive justice at work, but he wants to challenge it. "This path does not lead to true justice because in reality it does not conquer evil, it merely checks it. Only by

---

4. Francis, "General Audience, Saint Peter's Square."

responding to it with good can evil be truly overcome." The unnecessary implication here is that retributive justice never produces any good. Does it not?

There is a far better way of doing justice, according to Francis. "It is a process that avoids recourse to the tribunal and allows the victim to face the culprit directly and invite him or her to conversion, helping the person to understand that they are doing evil, thus appealing to their conscience. And this is beautiful: after being persuaded that what was done was wrong, the heart opens to the forgiveness being offered to it. This is the way to resolve conflicts in the family, in the relationship between spouses or between parents and children, where the offended party loves the guilty one and wishes to save the bond that unites them." According to the Pope, mercy achieves justice by avoiding tribunals, sentences, and prices to be paid. A whole chunk of what the Bible teaches on justice is chopped out and replaced by a merciful and atonement-less justice. Is it God's justice, though?

This is God's paradigm of mercy, says Francis. "This is how God acts towards us sinners. The Lord continually offers us his pardon and helps us to accept it and to be aware of our wrong-doing so as to free us of it."[5] What is happening here? No reference is made to the cross, the penalty of sin that was paid there, the wonder of Jesus Christ being punished on our behalf, the need for repentance and conversion for those who believe. Mercy seems to relinquish the cross. The point is that biblical atonement is totally missing here, and the resulting view of mercy and justice is severely flawed.

What About Atonement?

Unfortunately, this is a seriously faulty teaching. Atonement-free justice is one of the popular ways to re-imagine God's dealings with sin which is practiced by significant trends in contemporary theology. All that sounds connected to punishment, in execution of a lawful sentence, objectively imparted, etc., is seen as belonging to an old-fashioned, patriarchal, legalistic understanding of justice that needs to be overcome by a merciful, restorative, loving extension of pardon. In other words, what contemporary theology seems to reject are the basics of covenant justice instituted by the covenant God of Scripture. This justice presents a righteous Father

5. Francis, "General Audience, Saint Peter's Square," para. 5.

who is also love, who sent his Son, the God-man Jesus, to pay for sin in order to bring salvation. Fulfilling the Old Testament, Jesus is the Lamb of God who takes away the sin of the world (John 1:29). Through his sacrifice, he is God's provision for the forgiveness of sin.

Biblical justice has the cross of Christ at the center (1 Cor 1:23): Jesus Christ bore our sin on the cross (1 Pet 2:24). Mercy is possible not because tribunals and sentences are left out and made redundant by an all-embracing love. Mercy is accomplished and displayed exactly because justice was satisfied: "Without the shedding of blood there is no forgiveness of sin" (Heb 9:22). Not by us but by our Substitute, Jesus Christ, who died on the cross for us (Rom 5:8). When Pope Francis speaks of mercy, is he missing this fundamental biblical truth?

Would You Ever Ask Muslims to Pray for You? Pope Francis Did (July 1, 2017, Number 139)

In our fragmented and violent world, peaceful and respectful relationships between people of different religions can be crucially important. Such relationships can help us avoid tragedies of religious extremism, such as terrorists attacking their neighbors or political authorities mistreating religious minorities. Pope Francis is working hard to establish and maintain friendly relationships with peoples of all religions, Muslims in particular. In his 2013 programmatic document, he wrote that "interreligious dialogue is a necessary condition for peace in the world, and so it is a duty for Christians as well as other religious communities."[6] His relentless encouragement for mutual listening and even cooperation is a clear indication that this is one of the top priorities of the pontificate.

More Than Friendships

But there is another side of the coin. Based on Pope Francis's words and his interfaith activities and dealings, it is evident that something more is at stake than an attempt at fostering peace and freedom in our world. In a video[7] released in 2016, the Pope appeared with several religious leaders. One after another, each leader affirmed his or her beliefs in a celebration of religious pluralism and fraternity. At the end of the video the Pope

---

6. Francis, "Evangelii Gaudium," 250.
7. Vatican Archives. "Pope Francis' Prayer Intentions."

concluded by arguing that "there is only one certainty we have for all: we are all children of God." The message could have hardly been clearer. "We are all children of God" sounded like an endorsement for a pluralistic religion whereby all different theologies and worldviews are legitimate and truthful ways to live out one's own faith, with the Pope of the Roman Church ultimately endorsing their validity.

For those Christians who are committed to the words of Jesus as the Way, the truth, and the life (John 14:6) and the words of the apostles according to whom there is no other name (i.e., Jesus Christ) by which men can be saved (Acts 4:12), Pope Francis's statement that "we are all children of God" was puzzling and perplexing to say the least.

"Pray for Me"

A new and surprising instance of the Pope's interfaith theology came more recently. While meeting a delegation of Muslim leaders from Great Britain (April 5, 2017),[8] and after praising the value of listening to one another as "brothers and sisters," Francis ended his brief speech by saying, "When we listen and talk to each other, we are already on the path. I thank you for taking this path and ask almighty and merciful God to bless you. And I ask you to pray for me." The official text of the Pope's greeting is in Italian and was published in the daily Vatican bulletin.[9]

"Pray for me." The audience of this prayer request was a group of Muslim leaders, worshippers of Allah, bound to the authority of the Koran, denying the Triune nature of God and the divinity of Jesus Christ, following a work-based religion. The Pope went beyond diplomatic politeness or even the cordial, interreligious tone of the conversation. He addressed these Muslims by asking for their prayers, using language that is ordinarily used among fellow Christians.

Massive Implications

The theological implications of this prayer request are massive. Let's briefly point to some of the most obvious ones. "Pray for me" is an expression of deep fellowship among fellow believers. Pope Francis often asks people to pray for him, but the general context in which this request normally

---

8. *Local*, "Pope Francis Praises British Muslim Leaders."
9. Holy See, "Udienza ad una delegazione."

takes place is when he gathers with those who share his faith. This time it happened in the context of an interreligious meeting. This request shows that when the Pope talked about all religious people being "children of God," he did not simply mean members of the human family. He meant those belonging to the same spiritual family, all part of the same people of God. Buddhists, Christians, Muslims, etc., are all "children of God" to him. Biblically speaking, however, does the "children of God" include all religious people, in spite of their beliefs and allegiances?

"Pray for me" also implies that when Muslims pray, they pray to the same God of the Bible. This is the conviction held by the Pope from the Second Vatican Council (1962–65), according to which Muslims "profess to hold the faith of Abraham, and together with us they adore the one, merciful God, who will judge humanity on the last day."[10] With his request, however, the Pope goes even further, inferring that the God of the Bible is not only worshiped by Muslims, but he even responds to their petitions as if they were his children. Does not the Scripture teach that our confidence in prayer lies in Jesus being the High Priest and in whose name we can boldly approach the throne of grace (Heb 4:14–16)?

Asking Muslims to pray for you goes way beyond the good intention of cultivating friendly and peaceful relationships. It is a theological statement that impinges on basic biblical doctrines such as the Trinity, the divinity of Jesus, the authority of Scripture, and salvation in Jesus Christ alone. In other words, the very biblical gospel is at stake. The Pope's dismaying request has significantly distorted it.

Do Atheists Go to Heaven? Pope Francis Says Yes (May 1, 2018, Number 149)

Recent weeks have seen Pope Francis attracting media attention for statements that sound controversial even among Roman Catholic circles. Recently he was quoted using ambiguous language—to say the least—regarding the existence of hell[11] for those who don't believe. The Vatican Press office quickly responded to the controversy, saying that the Pope's words on hell should not "be considered as a faithful transcription of the

---

10. Second Vatican Council, "Lumen Gentium," 16.
11. Giuffrida, "Vatican Scrambles."

Holy Father's words."[12] In doing so, the Vatican made a journalistic point but failed to clarify the Pope's actual teaching on hell.

More recently (April 15, 2018), Pope Francis claimed that atheists get to heaven,[13] thus reinforcing the impression that his opinions on the afterlife are somewhat clumsy when compared to standard biblical views. Both statements, in fact, have to do with the eternal destiny of people, the former suggesting the prospect of annihilation (i.e., the waning away of the soul) and the latter implying a form of universalism (i.e., all will ultimately be saved regardless of their faith in Christ).

"Be Sure, He is in Heaven with Him"

This public comment by the Pope was given in the context of a visit paid to a parish in the suburbs of Rome. While meeting kids and responding to their questions, a boy went to him in tears, telling the Pope the story of his recently deceased father and asking whether or not he is now in heaven. The boy made sure to inform the Pope that his father, though wanting his children to be baptized, was himself an atheist.

So, what to say to this boy mourning his father and asking for information on his eternal destiny? Here is the answer given by Pope Francis:

> "God has the heart of a father, your father was a good man, he is in heaven with Him, be sure. God has a father's heart and, would God ever abandon a non-believing father who baptizes his children? God was certainly proud of your father, because it is easier to be a believer and have your children baptized than to be a non-believer and have your children baptized. Pray for your father, talk to your father. That is the answer."[14]

One needs to appreciate the emotional challenge of having to answer a boy in pain and tears. Talking about a dear one who has recently died is always difficult. Having said that, the first commitment of a Christian should always be to be true to the biblical gospel and then to convey what the Bible says in pastorally appropriate and sensitive ways. This is exactly what the Pope failed to do, in more ways than one. He certainly showed sympathy, but was he faithful to the Word of God?

---

12. Giuffrida, "Vatican Scrambles," para. 5.
13. Agasso, "Child Cries."
14. Agasso, "Child Cries," para. 7.

The Pope made several incorrect claims that need to be briefly mentioned. First, the connection he made between the father being a "good person" and him being with God. Is being a good person sufficient to be accepted by God? Does not the Bible say that no one is righteous before God (e.g., Rom 3:10–12) and that our only hope is because Jesus Christ was the only "good person" through whom we can be accepted by God the Father (e.g., 2 Cor 5:21)?

Second, does having one's own children baptized equate with trusting the Lord Jesus for our salvation? Is this not a version of salvation by works that is always opposed in the Bible (e.g., Eph 2:8–9)?

Third, the assurance given to the boy was issued on the basis of whose authority? How can a person—even a Pope—be confident enough to say that an atheist is in heaven? Don't Christians have to rely on the authority of the Word of God, which clearly teaches that those who don't believe will be condemned (e.g., John 3:18)? Has the Pope the authority to change that, or is his authority superior to plain biblical teaching?

And fourthly, how can the encouragement to pray for the father and to talk to him be squared with the clear biblical teaching that warns us not to talk to the dead (e.g., Deut 18:9) and to pray only to Jesus Christ, the only Mediator between God and men? Instead of leading the boy to Jesus Christ, why did the Pope point him to his dead father?

"We Are All Children of God"

In this answer the Pope gave voice to a whole theological vision that may sound compassionate and warm but which is ultimately misleading and deviant because is not truthful to Scripture. Even more troubling, the answer did not occur in a vacuum. It was instead the climax of a previous comment in which the Pope said that we are all children of God. Here is how the Pope articulated this thought:

> "We are all children of God, all, even the unbaptized ones, yes, even those who believe in other religions, or those who have idols. Those of the mafia are also children of God but prefer to behave like children of the devil. We are all children of God, God created and loves us all and placed in each of our hearts the consciousness of distinguishing good from evil. With baptism the Holy Spirit entered and strengthened your belonging

to God. The 'mafiosi' are also children of God, we must pray for they go back on their ways and recognize God."[15]

Here Pope Francis reiterates his attempts at redefining what it means to be a child of God.[16] For him, children of God are all people: Christian believers, baptized people, unbelievers, atheists, people of other religions, idolaters, etc. He grounds this claim in creation and relates it to the human conscience.[17] No mention is made of sin and separation from God. He refers to baptism as "strengthening" our belonging to God, intensifying it, making more relevant something that is already there before baptism takes place. The idea that all people are children of God means that all people will ultimately be saved, thus blurring the distinction between nature and grace, between being a created person and being a saved person. Evidently for the Pope this was the background for him assuring the boy that his atheist father is now in heaven.

There are serious distortions in this Papal teaching. All Bible believers, even among Roman Catholic circles, should begin to biblically question the wayward theological system of Pope Francis.

Inter-Faith Prayers for the Pandemic to Cease? What Is at Stake is Bigger Than What You Think (July 1, 2020, Number 177)

Can you imagine an apostle Paul who, at the Areopagus in Athens (Acts 17), invites his listeners (followers of various philosophical schools and ancient cults) to unite in prayer, each to his own god/ideal as a sign of fraternity? Can you imagine an apostle Peter who, in writing to Christians at the four corners of the Roman Empire (1 Pet 1:1), recommends that they raise petitions together with the faithful of the Eastern, Greek, and Roman religions to invoke the end of a pandemic? For those who have a basic grasp of the biblical faith, this is pretty absurd. Not for Rome, though. Indeed, the Roman Catholic Church organized a "Day of Prayer and Fasting Addressed to Believers of All Religions" (May 14)[18] under the auspices of the Higher Committee for Human Fraternity[19] to pray

15. Agasso, "Child Cries," para 4.
16. De Chirico, "Vatican File 86."
17. De Chirico, "Vatican File 65."
18. *Vatican News*, "COVID-19."
19. https://www.forhumanfraternity.org.

together. Catholics, Muslims, and people of other religions or of no religion were all encouraged to pray to her/his own god or personal ideal for the pandemic to cease.

Biblical Proximity Is Not Universal Fraternity

Before examining the theological problems behind the interfaith prayer promoted by the Roman Catholic Church, it is important to be aware of the context of this initiative. The aforementioned Higher Committee for Human Fraternity was established in 2019, a few months after the meeting in Abu Dhabi between Pope Francis and Ahmed al-Tayyeb, Grand Imam of al-Azhar, the Muslim University in Cairo (Egypt). That meeting was centered on the signing of the controversial *Document on Human Fraternity for World Peace and Living Together*.[20] In spite of the praise gathered in interfaith circles, it is a controversial document for a simple reason: it joins the commendable attempt to build a peaceful society (especially in areas where the relationship between the Muslim majority and the Christian minority is tense) with the idea that Muslims and Christians are "brothers and sisters" praying to the same God. In so doing, it wrongly exchanges proximity with fraternity, i.e., our being neighbors with all men and women, with our being brothers and sisters with those who belong to the family of God in Jesus Christ. While proximity connects people of different faiths and backgrounds and calls them to live in peace, fraternity is a spiritual bond that unites believers in Jesus Christ as brothers and sisters in him.

The *Document on Human Fraternity* blurs the distinction and changes the meaning of fraternity, extending it to the relationships between peoples of different religions, as if Muslims and Christians are "brothers and sisters" praying to the same God.

An Ever-Expanding "Catholic" Trajectory

This day of prayer witnessed the participation of believers of all religions, but also of those who do not believe, united "spiritually" to pray to their divinity or ideal, all pleading for the end of the pandemic. Each participant was called to address his god/ideal in a spirit of fraternity that embraced everyone. What is at stake theologically is enormous. Moving beyond the

---

20. Francis and Ahmad Al-Tayyeb, *Document on Human Fraternity*.

perimeter of the biblical faith, Roman Catholicism legitimizes prayers to other deities or religious ideals, silencing the prophetic message of Scripture that we either serve the biblical God or idols. It fails to bear witness to the claims of Jesus Christ as the God-man who came to save those who believe in him and instead changes the meaning of fraternity by stretching it indiscriminately to all humanity[21] rather than believers in Jesus only. In so doing, the tenets of the biblical faith are trampled on.

This is a further move away from biblical Christianity. Not being anchored in Scripture alone, not being committed to Christ alone, Roman Catholicism is anxious to extend its ever-expanding catholicity (i.e., all-encompassing embracement) in all directions, even those clearly contrary to the basics of the Christian faith. This is not even something new that was introduced by the current Jesuit Pope, with his "uncertain" magisterium. It is rather a confirmation of the slippery slope of the "development" of what is already contained in Vatican II,[22] with its universalistic bent, which was visually represented at the interreligious prayer of Assisi (1986, convened by John Paul II) and then confirmed by Francis's apostolic exhortation of 2013,[23] eventually culminating in the *Document on Human Fraternity* in 2019.

Present-day Roman Catholicism, while open to ecumenism with liberal Protestants, Eastern Orthodox, and evangelicals, does the same with Muslims, Buddhists, men of goodwill, etc. For Rome, unity is not only among Christians but among all women and men as human beings. This "unity" is based on the "gospel" of our common humanity, to which everyone belongs regardless of faith in Jesus Christ as Savior and Lord. The question remains, though: is this the biblical gospel?

Back to Paul and Peter

Biblical proximity does not require common prayer and does not entail fraternity. At the Areopagus, while respectfully engaging various people in various contexts, Paul preached the gospel by calling all to repent and believe in the Man appointed by the Father who was raised from the dead, i.e., Jesus Christ (Acts 17:31). He was a good neighbor, but he did not call the Athenians "brothers and sisters," nor did he ask them to pray

---

21. De Chirico, "Vatican File 86."
22. Second Vatican Council, "Lumen Gentium," 16.
23. Francis, "Evangelii Gaudium," 244–54.

with him. To the Christians scattered all over the world, Peter did not give the advice of uniting in prayer with the peoples around them, but he did teach them to always be prepared to make a defense of the gospel (1 Pet 4:15). Peter wanted them to be good neighbors (e.g., 1 Pet 2:12) but always ready to proclaim the excellencies of him who had called them out of darkness into his marvelous light. If Paul and Peter were informed of the "Day of Prayer and Fasting Addressed to Believers of All Religions,"[24] they would ask themselves, "Is this biblical Christianity?"

Pope Francis, the Chaplain of the United Nations? (February 1, 2021, Number 184)

The pandemic hit hard in 2020. Disruption broke in at all levels. The Vatican, as the headquarters of the Roman Catholic Church, was no exception. Programs in Rome were canceled or held in a low-key form. Was it then a standby or—even worse—a wasted year? Not at all.

The year of 2020 was one filled with intense activity behind the scenes, especially in the area of expanding the borders of Rome's "catholicity." The catholicity of Roman Catholicism is one of the two pillars of the whole system: while it is "Roman"—i.e., centered on Rome's hierarchical institution, focused on Rome's catechism and canon law, based on its sacramental machinery—it is also "Catholic"—i.e., ever-expanding its synthesis, assimilating trends and movements, aiming at becoming more fully universal through absorbing the world. Outside of the spotlight of media attention, it was the catholicity of Rome that gained a great deal from the COVID year.

While its ordinary events were negatively impacted, the long-term, "catholic" vision of the Roman Church was fueled with impressive consequences. Pope Francis was the architect and proactive director of all these moves. In observing the recent global activities of the Pope, the Argentinian philosopher Rubén Peretó Rivas compared them with those of an international organization and asked whether Pope Francis aims at becoming the "Chaplain of the United Nations."[25] His 2020 "universal" initiatives indeed look like those of the United Nations in language, scope, and content. Three projects deserve to be mentioned in this respect.

---

24. "COVID-19: Faithful Respond."
25. Valli, "Dilemma."

"All Brothers"

It has been rightly called the "political manifesto" of Pope Francis's pontificate. In fact, there is a lot of politics and a lot of sociology in the latest encyclical *All Brothers*[26] (October 3, 2020). In it, Francis wants to plead the cause of universal fraternity and social friendship. To do this, he speaks of borders to be broken down, of waste to be avoided, of human rights that are not sufficiently universal, of unjust globalization, of burdensome pandemics, of migrants to be welcomed, of open societies, of solidarity, of peoples' rights, of local and global exchanges, of the limits of the liberal political vision, of world governance, of political love, of the recognition of the other, of the injustice of any war, of the abolition of the death penalty. These are all interesting "political" themes which, were it not for some comments on the parable of the good Samaritan that intersperse the chapters, could have been written by a group of sociologists and humanitarian workers from some international organization. The vision proposed by *All Brothers* is the way in which Rome sees globalization with the eye of a Jesuit and South American Pope.

Its basic message is sufficiently clear: we are all brothers as children of the same God. This is Pope Francis's theological truth. When *All Brothers* talks about God, it does so in general terms that can fit Muslim, Hindu, and other religions' accounts of god, as well as the Masonic reference to the Watchmaker. To further confirm this, *All Brothers* ends with a "Prayer to the Creator" that could be used both in a mosque and in a Masonic temple. Having removed the "stumbling block" of Jesus Christ, everyone can turn to an unspecified divinity to experiment with what it means to be "brothers"—brothers in a divinity made in the image and likeness of humanity, not brothers and sisters on the basis of the work of Jesus Christ who has died and risen for sinners. *All Brothers* has genetically modified the biblically understood meaning of fraternity by transferring it to common humanity. In doing so, it has lost the biblical boundaries of the word and replaced them with pan-religious traits and contents. The Papal document is deist, at best theistic, but not in line with biblical and Trinitarian Christianity.

All Brothers shows that the mission that Pope Francis has in mind is not the preaching of the gospel in words and deeds but the extension to

---

26. Francis, "Fratelli Tutti."

all of a message of universal fraternity.[27] This is the theological framework of the Pope as he stretches the boundaries of the catholicity of his church.

The Global Compact on Education

Soon after releasing *All Brothers*, there was another indication of Pope Francis's universalist agenda. In a video message[28] aired on October 15, 2020, he commended the "Global Compact on Education" (GCE),[29] i.e., an ambitious plan in the field of education worldwide to bring about a "change of mentality." The GCE is worked out with Mission 4.7,[30] a UN-backed advisory group of civil and political leaders aiming to meet the educational target (numbered 4.7) of the UN's Sustainable Development Goals (SDGs).[31]

SDG number 4 strives for "quality education," and within that goal, target 4.7 aims to "ensure all learners acquire knowledge and skills needed to promote sustainable development, including among others through education for sustainable development and sustainable lifestyles, human rights, gender equality, promotion of a culture of peace and non-violence, global citizenship, and appreciation of cultural diversity and of culture's contribution to sustainable development."

This is the UN's globalist language, but the Roman Catholic language significantly overlaps with it. GCE speaks of "human fraternity" regardless of and beyond religious beliefs. In the plan, the watchwords are wholly secular. The dominant formula is "new humanism," explained in terms of "common home," "universal solidarity," "fraternity" (as it is defined in *All Brothers*), "convergence," "welcome," overcoming "division and antagonism" . . . The "new humanism" is coupled with the "universal brotherhood" so as to embrace the whole of humanity in a human, common project. In the "new humanism" Rome reads its increased catholicity, the UN its globalist agenda.

In the video Francis also praised the UN's role and contribution in offering a "unique opportunity" to create "a new kind of new education" and quoted St. Paul VI's 1965 message of appreciation of the UN in which

27. De Chirico, "Vatican File 181."
28. Francis, "Videomessaggio."
29. https://www.educationglobalcompact.org/en/
30. https://www.mission4point7.org/
31. https://sdgs.un.org/goals

he lauded the institution for "teaching men peace." Francis is certain that this plan will bring about "the civilization of love, beauty and unity." No explicit Christian reference is made, and there is no indication that the root problem is human sin. It seems that as we will have better education opportunities for all, the "new humanism" will come. This is in line with the UN vision, but is it realistic from a Christian viewpoint?

The Economy of Francesco

If *All Brothers* is the theological framework and GCE is the project in education, a third area that Pope Francis has strongly pushed forward is an initiative in the field of economics. Making reference to Francis of Assisi's reconciled view between humanity and the earth and drawing inspiration from it, the initiative was called the "Economy of Francesco" (EF).[32]

In a video broadcast on November 21st,[33] the Pope called young economists, entrepreneurs, and business leaders "to take up the challenge of promoting and encouraging models of development, progress and sustainability in which people, especially the excluded (including our sister earth), will no longer be—at most—a merely nominal, technical or functional presence. Instead, they will become protagonists in their own lives and in the entire fabric of society." The goal is to strive towards "a pact to change the current economy" and to "give a new soul to the global economy"—and indeed to radically overthrow it in the wake of the "popular movements."

Again, this project is another extension of the catholicity of the Roman Catholic Church, with no explicit reference to a Christian framework but falling in line with an apparently globalist view of an economic reality marked by the "new humanism."

As Francis promoted EF, he also included as partner in the initiative the "Council for Inclusive Capitalism,"[34] meaning the magnates of the Ford Foundation, Johnson & Johnson, Mastercard, Bank of America, the Rockefeller Foundation, and the like. The council is formed by around five hundred companies, which together represent 10.5 trillion dollars in assets under management and two hundred million workers in over 163 countries. This is to say that simply painting Rome's catholicity as

---

32. https://francescoeconomy.org/
33. Francis, "Video Message."
34. Kelly, "Pope Francis Partners."

anti-capitalist is wrong. Pope Francis aims at including all parties in his "new humanism." In these relationships with the global companies there are also strategic opportunities for funding the initiatives of the Roman Catholic Church. It's a win-win relationship.

As already mentioned, Francis's activism on the global scene in 2020 prompted someone to label him as "Chaplain of the United Nations" because of the striking convergence between the "new humanism" that he has been advocating in the areas of fraternity, education, and the economy and the goals of the UN. In doing what the Pope does, the impression is not to be given that Francis is awkwardly operating outside of Roman Catholic principles and convictions. While there are apparent similarities with the ethos of an international organization such as the UN, what the Pope did in 2020 is an attempt to implement the vision cast at the Second Vatican Council (1962–65).

In one of its foundational documents on the church, Vatican II argues that the church is a "sacrament." Here is how it explains what this means: the church is a "sacrament" because she is "a sign and instrument both of a very closely knit union with God and of the unity of the whole human race."[35] The idea of the global "human fraternity" and the Roman Church being a sign and instrument of it is embedded in the self-understanding of Rome. With these recent projects, Pope Francis is making it plain what it means for the Roman Catholic Church to be a "sacrament" in the world in the realms of global politics, education, and economy, i.e., uniting the whole of humanity around itself.

In his 2013 document *Evangelii Gaudium*, Francis wrote that "initiating processes rather than possessing spaces"[36] is what he wanted to achieve. "All brothers," GCE, and EF are all processes initiated by the expansion of Rome's catholicity. Those who are used to think of Roman Catholicism as a "Roman" system (e.g., dogmatic, rigid, locked-in) and not as a "Catholic" project (e.g., open-ended, absorbing and expanding) may be surprised and even puzzled. But Roman Catholicism demands that its Roman-centered institution be unceasingly fertilized by its evermore Catholic horizon, and vice versa.

---

35. Second Vatican Council, "Lumen Gentium," 1.
36. Francis, "Evangelii Gaudium," 223.

Children of Abraham? Pope Francis's Equivocation (April 1, 2021, Number 186)

Whenever we talk about lands tormented by decades of wars and violence, sometimes perpetrated in the name of religions, divinities, and faiths, we must do so with sobriety and circumspection. It is easy to pontificate from a distance, comfortably seated and safe, forgetting the tragic context and the widespread suffering in the situation you want to talk about. This is to say that commenting on Pope Francis's recent trip to Iraq can become a pretext for easy criticism if one does not try to enter the complexity of the situation and the tragedy of the hour. Therefore, it must be acknowledged that the Roman Pope's call to religious freedom and freedom of conscience was very good. His appeal to respect for minorities was extremely helpful. His invitation to national conciliation and solidarity between the various components of society was also commendable.

Having said that, the theological framework of his visit to Iraq cannot be overlooked. The climax of his journey was the address given at the interreligious meeting at the Plain of Ur (March 6).[37] In a very evocative and emotional way, his speech was centered on the figure of Abraham as the father of Jews, Christians, and Muslims. According to Francis, "Abraham our father" is common to all: Jews, Christians, and Muslims are the "descendants" promised by God to Abraham and therefore "brothers and sisters" among them. These three groups are called by God "to bear witness to his goodness, to show his paternity through our fraternity." In the name of Abraham, they experience the same human (in Abraham) and divine (in God) fatherhood, thus being brothers and sisters. Applying it to today's situation, according to the Pope, "there will be no peace as long as we see others as *them* and not *us*."

All Brothers and Sisters

After laboring the point of the shared brotherhood in God and in Abraham, Francis ended his address in a way that boils down his vision:

> Brothers and sisters of different religions, here we find ourselves at home, and from here, together, we wish to commit ourselves to fulfilling God's dream that the human family may become

---

37. Francis, "Interreligious Meeting."

hospitable and welcoming to all his children; that looking up to the same heaven, it will journey in peace on the same earth.[38]

This heartfelt appeal was followed by the "Prayer of the Children of Abraham" (recited with the Christian and Muslim representatives present at the meeting) in which, among others, these expressions are striking:

> As children of Abraham, Jews, Christians and Muslims, together with other believers and all persons of good will, we thank you for having given us Abraham, a distinguished son of this noble and beloved country, to be our common father in faith.[39]

And again:

> We ask you, the God of our father Abraham and our God, to grant us a strong faith, a faith that abounds in good works, a faith that opens our hearts to you and to all our brothers and sisters; and a boundless hope capable of discerning in every situation your fidelity to your promises.[40]

Abraham is presented as "our common father in faith" and the prayer is addressed to "our God" without mentioning the name of Jesus Christ, taking for granted God's fatherhood not as Creator of all things but as "our God," God of us "brothers and sisters."

In addition, by concluding his address with an interreligious prayer, the Pope shifted the focus from a religious speech to a form of "spiritual ecumenism," i.e., joint prayer. For him, speaking about universal fraternity and praying as brothers and sisters to the same God are one and the same. Interreligious dialogue becomes a spiritual form of unity based on the conviction that all humanity shares faith in the same God. In the Roman Catholic understanding and practice of ecumenism and interreligious dialogue, joint prayer is always in view when talking about "unity."

The Papal address and his interreligious prayer require a "grammar" to be fully understood. It is easy to stop at the level of a convinced call for religious freedom and peaceful coexistence. It would be reductive and not in line with the intentions of the pontiff. What Francis said and did is embedded in a truly Roman Catholic theology of the unity of the human race as it is made up of sisters and brothers, all children of the same God who, as such, can and must pray together.

---

38. Francis, "Interreligious Meeting," 11.
39. Francis, "Interreligious Meeting," 13.
40. Francis, "Interreligious Meeting," 18.

The Pope's Slippery Slope

There is an evident slippery slope in this train of argument related to the themes of otherness and coexistence between different people. Apart from the heavy implications of universalism (i.e., the idea that all religions lead to God), the Pope says that in order to not be in conflict with one another, people must be friends; to be friends, they must be brothers and sisters; and to be brothers and sisters, it is necessary to refer to the same divinity which, although differently constructed on the theological level, is the same God. The train of thought ends in this way: being all children of the same God, we must pray together.

If we consider all the steps involved in this argument, we are faced with an impressive concentration of what the Roman Catholic vision looks like.

There are strong *theological* implications as far as the doctrine of God is concerned: is the Muslim Allah the same as the Triune God of the Bible? If we are praying as brothers and sisters together, the Pope's answer is *yes*.

There are evident *soteriological* consequences: are we all saved, regardless of faith in Jesus Christ the incarnate Son of God? If we pray to the same God as brothers and sisters, implying that we are all accepted in his eyes, the Pope's answer is "YES," even though the language of "universal salvation" is not explicitly used.

There are also *missiological* overtones: what about the great commission to go into the whole world and proclaim the gospel in view of the conversion of the lost? If we are already brothers and sisters, praying together to the same God, the Pope's answer is that the church's mission is to make visible and concrete what is already true: no one is really lost, and as human beings, we are already part of God's family.

The Roman Catholic "Logic" and its Dangers

If one accepts this Roman Catholic "logic" of Pope Francis, in order to live in peace among those who are different, one must recognize the pan-religion that unites everyone. Having a common religion is foundational for striving towards peace. According to the Pope, peace is possible among brothers and sisters who are children of Abraham and who are ultimately children of God.

Those who do not accept this "logic," i.e., those who believe that one should not have to have the same faith to live together in peace, that one should not have to pray together to love the neighbor as Christ commands us, that one should not have to resort to the rhetoric of "we are all brothers and sisters" to work together for the common good, they sow enmity, foment violence, and create conflicts. The slippery slope of the Pope's speech is extremely dangerous. It undermines the Christian "scandal" according to which Jesus Christ is the only way to the Father (John 14:6) and, at the same time, Christ's disciples are called to live in peace with everyone (Rom 12:18), regardless of their religious beliefs and practices. This is the Christian claim: in the process of loving the neighbor and living in peace, one should never fudge the gospel that says that apart from Jesus Christ there is no salvation (Acts 4:12). On the contrary, the Pope thinks that in order to have peace one *must* profess the universal religion of "we-are-all-brothers-and-sisters-praying-to-the-same-God." His is not the Christian way.

A final word on Abraham. What the Pope said about the patriarch, the apostle Paul would not have said. For Paul, Abraham is the father of the believers in Jesus Christ (Rom 4:11–12). For Paul, the descendants of Abraham are the disciples of Jesus Christ from every nation (Rom 4:16–17): his inheritance, in fact, does not follow the biological line of flesh and blood but is received and transmitted "by faith" in Jesus Christ (4:16). Jesus himself questioned ethnic and cultural appropriations of the common fatherhood of Abraham (John 8:39), saying that Abraham rejoiced in waiting to see the day of the Lord Jesus (John 8:56). Without Jesus, and outside of faith in Jesus Christ, being children of Abraham can be a cultural identity marker but not the basis for unity in faith and prayer.

"God Has Many Ways to Save." Cardinal Cantalamessa and Roman Catholic Universalism (January 1, 2023, Number 209)

Like every Christmas season, the tradition of the "advent sermons," whereby the preacher of the Papal household addresses the Pope and the community working in the Vatican, was repeated this past December when Cardinal Raniero Cantalamessa, a capuchin, preached three sermons. This preaching role is important because it is officially appointed by the reigning Pope and assigned to a priest, whose task is to preach to the community working and living in the Vatican (Pope included) on special liturgical festivities. More generally, the Vatican preacher contributes to setting the standard of Roman Catholic homiletics, even beyond the little community of the recipients, and is looked upon as a "model" for good Roman Catholic preaching. For these reasons, it is always useful to have an eye on what he says and how he says it.

In 2022, the first Advent sermon (December 5)[41] had the theological virtue of faith at its center and was followed by one sermon on hope and charity, i.e., the three theological virtues. With faith being the general heading, one of the focuses of the cardinal's sermon was the breadth and scope of salvation. The Italian edition of the Vatican News website effectively summed it up with the headline "God Has Many Ways to Save."[42] In a nutshell, according to the cardinal, all human beings will be saved by Christ, with or without faith in Christ.

This is how Cantalamessa presents the issue:

> If faith that saves is faith in Christ, what to think of all those who have no chance of believing in him? We live in a pluralistic society, even religiously. Our theologies—Eastern and Western, Catholic and Protestant alike—developed in a world where practically only Christianity existed. It was, however, aware of the existence of other religions, but they were considered false from the start, or were not taken into consideration at all.[43]

After acknowledging the traditional position of the church(es), whereby salvation is given to those who "believe" in Christ and therefore do manifest a personal commitment to him, the cardinal goes on by saying:

> Today this is no longer the case. For some time there has been a dialogue between religions, based on mutual respect and recognition of the values present in each of them . . . With this recognition, the conviction has taken ground that even people outside the Church can be saved.[44]

Notice that he brings with him an argument stemming from the "development" of doctrine and practice due to the adaptation to time and culture. "Today this is no longer the case": not because Scripture has changed but because "dialogue" has introduced a new perception of religions that has

---

41. Cantalamessa, "Gate of Faith."
42. Vatican News, "Cardinale Cantalamessa."
43. Cantalamessa, "Gate of Faith," para. 11.
44. Cantalamessa, "Gate of Faith," para. 12.

led to a revision of the traditional view. A new conviction has emerged and become mainstream in post-Vatican II and ecumenical theology, i.e., "even people outside the Church can be saved."

The problem with this Roman Catholic view of development is always the same: what are the biblical boundaries of such a "development"? For example, can the church develop its Mariology to the point of elevating two Marian *dogmas* (like the 1854 dogma on Mary's immaculate conception and the 1950 dogma of Mary's bodily assumption) without any biblical support? In other words, "development" without the biblical principle of *sola Scriptura* (i.e., the Bible as the supreme authority for the church) safeguarding and guiding it can become a self-referential principle at the service of the institutional church. If the church can "develop" her own traditions even outside of the perimeter of the written Word of God, is it not a questionable development?

How does this updated theology work in salvation? Here is how Cantalamessa explains it:

> God has far more ways to save than we can think of. He has established "channels" of his grace, but he has not bound himself to them . . . It is one thing to affirm the universal need of Christ for salvation and another thing to affirm the universal necessity of faith in Christ for salvation.[45]

Translated in simpler language, this means that it is always Christ who saves, but believing in Christ is not necessary for salvation. All people (believers and non-believers) are saved, even those who do not believe in Christ. Faith in Christ is important but not necessary for salvation. Christ saves us all, with or without faith in him.

> Is it superfluous, then, to continue proclaiming the Gospel to every creature?—then asks the Cardinal. Far from it! It is the reason that must change, not the fact. We must continue to proclaim Christ; not so much for a negative reason—otherwise, the world will be condemned—as for a positive reason: for the infinite gift that Jesus represents for every human being.[46]

According to the cardinal, the gospel is only a positive message and contains no judgment against anyone. There is no condemnation for sinners, no reprobation. God's judgment is no more. God's mercy has swallowed it. The gospel only has "positive" reasons. We (the whole of humanity)

45. Cantalamessa, "Gate of Faith," para. 17.
46. Cantalamessa, "Gate of Faith," para. 19.

are all already saved by Christ with or without faith in Christ. If how we are saved changes, the Christian mission changes too. Evangelizing today means "dialogue" with other religions always assuming the universal salvation of all in the presence or absence of faith in Jesus Christ.

The cardinal is neither the first nor the only to support this Roman Catholic account of the universalist reinterpretation of the gospel. Sadly, he is in good company; his position is the mainstream, present-day Roman Catholic view. It has its background in Vatican II texts (for example, *Lumen Gentium*[47]) and Pope Francis (for example, the apostolic exhortation *The Joy of the Gospel*[48] and his latest encyclical, *All Brothers*[49]). It is the position of present-day Rome which believes that the church, as the sacrament of salvation, includes (willy-nilly) the whole of humanity and that Christ saves us all, whether someone believes in him or not. The Roman Catholic gospel used to be compromised by its rejection of the biblical truth that we are saved by Christ alone through faith alone. Now, it is further compromised by its universalism, whereby all will be saved by Christ, with or without faith in him.

Cardinal Cantalamessa's sermon has provided further clarification on what "salvation" and "faith" mean for the present-day Roman Catholic Church. They are biblical terms that are reinterpreted in such a way that their biblical meaning is reshaped to fit the Roman Catholic version of universalism. This is another instance of Roman Catholics and evangelicals using the same words but meaning very different things.

The whole of Roman Catholicism is "developing" towards becoming less "Roman" (hierarchical, top-down, doctrinaire) and more "Catholic" (embracing, inclusive, universalist). The Roman Catholic gospel was flawed when it had a more "Roman" focus, and it continues to be so with the new "Catholic" emphasis, though the accents are put differently.

---

47. Second Vatican Council, "Lumen Gentium," 16.
48. De Chirico, "Vatican File 69."
49. De Chirico, "Vatican File 181."

8

Ecumenism

Ecumenism of Blood (December 20, 2013, Number 72)

THE FACT THAT POPE Francis gives interviews to both the religious and secular press is no longer a surprise. *Time* magazine chose him as "Man of the Year" because of his more relaxed and open approach to the media. This attitude was expressed in an interview that was published in the Italian daily newspaper *La Stampa* on December 15. The conversation began with a reflection on Christmas but then proceeded to other topics including interesting comments on the Pope's views on Christian unity.

Is Christian Unity a Priority for You?

It was this question that was abruptly posed to Pope Francis during his interview with *La Stampa*. He responded with the following:

> "Yes, for me ecumenism is a priority. Today there is an ecumenism of blood. In some countries they kill Christians for wearing a cross or having a Bible and before killing them they do not ask them whether they are Anglican, Lutheran, Catholic or Orthodox. Their blood is mixed. To those who kill we are Christians. We are united in blood, even though we have not yet managed to take necessary steps towards unity between us and perhaps

the time has not yet come... Those who kill Christians don't ask for your identity card to see which Church you were baptized in. We need to take these facts into consideration."[1]

These are important words that take into account what happens around the world. Christians who are persecuted in different minority situations belong to different churches and traditions, but they are persecuted mainly because their public faith stirs opposition. Their ecclesiastical identity is definitely secondary. More than their attachment to a church (whatever it might be), what comes first is their allegiance to Christ and his gospel. It is their personal faith as followers of Jesus that incites persecution against them. In the global world, the neat denominational distinctions and ecumenical complexities make very little sense. The heart of the matter is the heart of the gospel.

What Is Unity Based On?

There is still something to be said about what the Pope states concerning the "ecumenism of blood." It seems that while recognizing the astonishing reality of Christians being persecuted, notwithstanding their secondary labels, the Pope still thinks about unity in terms of the old Roman Catholic and ecumenical categories. When he refers to "baptism" as marking the Christian identity, he echoes the mainstream idea in ecumenical circles, i.e., that Christian unity is based on baptism. According to this view, to be baptized means to be Christian and thus to be united with God and with other Christians. This is the standard Roman Catholic doctrine[2] and ecumenical teaching.[3]

The ecumenism of blood is instead based on a personal faith in Jesus Christ. It is not opposed to baptism, of course, but it is not based on it. It is likely that some of these martyrs are not even baptized or do not formally belong to any historic Christian church. Yet they are believers in Jesus Christ, and this is what really counts for their salvation and our unity as a whole as a body of believers. On the other hand, many who are baptized and are canonically members of a religious institution are not Christian at all. The phenomenon of nominalism in the West demonstrates that one can be baptized and yet be totally opposed or indifferent

1. Tornielli, "Never Be Afraid," para 14.
2. Holy See, "Unitatis Redintegratio," ch. 3, 22.
3. World Council of Churches, "Baptism, Eucharist and Ministry."

to the gospel and its message. Christian unity is not based on baptism but on a personal faith in Jesus Christ. Those who are united are those who are Christian believers in the biblical sense.

Rethinking Ecumenism

The ecumenism of blood should serve as an encouragement in the rethinking of our theology concerning Christian unity, beyond sentimental accounts of the persecuted Christians and towards a better biblical grasp of what it means for the church to be "one, holy, catholic and apostolic." According to Vatican II and subsequent magisterial teaching, Christian unity is threefold: professing the same faith, celebrating the same Eucharist, and being united under the same sacramental ministry in apostolic succession in submission to the Papal office. Paradoxically, this understanding of unity is one of the greatest obstacles to Christian unity because it derives unity from a sacrament administered by a church and confuses unity with being under a specific religious institution. The martyrs that the Pope refers to do not fit this definition of unity, and yet they are nonetheless considered to be truly unified Christians.

The ecumenism of blood shows that these dimensions are not necessary for real unity to take place. Instead, they only serve as additional burdens and add-ons. Pope Francis has, however, rightly emphasized the reality of the ecumenism of blood. But time will tell whether or not his "ecumenical priority" will stop paying lip service to it or will instead encourage him to think of ecumenism beyond mere ecumenical stereotypes and towards more biblically warranted patterns. The unity of these martyrs with the Roman Catholic Church may be "imperfect," but their unity with Christ is perfect, and this is what really matters.

Restoring Full and Visible Unity?
(January 29, 2014, Number 73)

"Has Christ been divided?" This is the question that Paul rhetorically asks the Corinthians (1 Cor 1:13), and this is also the question that Pope Francis commented upon in his homily at the end of the Week of Prayer for Christian Unity at the Basilica of St. Paul Outside the Walls in Rome. His brief meditation shows the passion that is a defining mark of the present pontificate, but it also restates important aspects of the traditional Roman Catholic view of unity that has been expounded since Vatican II.

A Given and a Goal

The first remark has to do with the understanding of unity as a "goal." In commenting on the developments of the ecumenical movement, he speaks of "journeying together on the road towards unity," implying the idea that unity stands ahead of us as if it were a goal to be eventually reached. Unity is therefore in the future tense. What exactly does unity mean here, and why is it in the future tense? Later on, the Pope makes a comment that sheds light on these issues. He refers to the prospect of "restoration of full visible unity among all Christians" as the future climax of the ecumenical path. There is need, however, to unpack such a statement.

Firstly, there is the idea of "restoration." According to this view, there was a time in the life of the church when full and visible unity existed. It is not explicitly stated here, but what is perhaps referred to is the "undivided" first millennium of the church before the East-West Schism (1054 AD) and the Protestant Reformation of the 16th century. This view is common in ecumenical circles but highly problematic from both historical and theological points of view. From its very early years and on, the church has constantly been dealing with inner divisions and conflicts, as the Pauline text testifies. Before there was a Pope and even after the papacy came into existence, a "golden age" of Christian unity never existed, even within the Roman Catholic Church itself! Unity always stands in tension and under attack. Rather than restoring unity, the Bible urges us to "maintain" the already-given unity (Eph 4:3) and to equip the body of Christ in order to "attain" the unity of faith (4:13). In other words, from the beginning of the church, unity is both a given and a goal. It is a gift and a task. The restoration model wrongly implies that unity was full in the first stages of the church and was then lost along the way and now needs to be recovered. Christian unity is instead a given reality amongst those whom the Father has given to the Son (John 17:9) that must be protected and lived out.

Secondly, the Pope makes reference to a "full" and "visible" unity as the goal of ecumenism. According to the Roman Catholic view, "full" means sacramentally full, i.e., same baptism, same eucharist, same ministry. Given the self-understanding of the Roman Church, it means adhering and submitting to the sacramental theology of Rome and the hierarchical nature of its priesthood. "Visible" means that unity needs to accept the visible Papal structure of the Roman Catholic Church as the divinely appointed way for the One Church of Christ. The ecumenical price for full and visible unity is the acceptance of the Roman Catholic view of the church. All other views are defective and, in the end, partial and invisible.

Prayer to Paul?

In closing his homily, Pope Francis reports that he had previously visited Paul's tomb in the Basilica with other Christian leaders, and they exhorted one another with these words: "Let us pray that he (Paul) will help us on this path as we advance towards unity." Is Paul really the one to pray to for the advance of unity? Is he really in the position to help? Here again, another fundamental obstacle towards unity arises. According to the Pope, Paul can be prayed to, but the same Paul that taught us about unity was the one that wrote: "I bow my knees before the Father" (Eph 3:15). The restoration of gospel purity and the keeping of Christian unity (as a gift and a task) belong together. Paul was the great apostle of the gentiles and pointed out the Triune God as the model for our unity (Eph 4). We should not seek Paul's help beyond what God inspired him to write in his letters.

What Francis Really Thinks of the Reformation (and of Calvin in Particular) (June 23, 2014, Number 83)

Friendly. Appreciative. Always wanting to stress commonalities and to lay aside differences. This has been the popular image of Pope Francis in his dealings with non-Catholics thus far. Many are impressed by his easygoing style that often seeks to affirm others. This may have been the rule, but now there is an exception—and a very significant one. The recent republication of a lecture on the history of the Jesuits that Archbishop Bergoglio gave in Argentina in 1985 indicates the kind of harsh assessment that he gave of the Protestant Reformation in general and of John Calvin in particular. The lecture was republished in Spain in 2013 and then translated into Italian in book form.[4] Since there is no indication that he has changed his mind, we have to consider the contents of the book an accurate reflection of what Francis still thinks of the Protestant Reformation.

Protestantism as the Root of All Evils

In examining the history of the Jesuits, Bergoglio gives special attention to their interactions with the Reformation and their role in the Latin American missions. According to him the inevitable consequences of the Reformation are the annihilation of man in his anxiety (resulting in existential atheism) and a leap in the dark by a type of superman (as envisaged by Nietzsche). Both outcomes lead to "the death of God" and a kind of "paganism" that manifests itself as Nazism and Marxism. All this originating from the "Lutheran position"! Bergoglio argues that the Reformation is the root of all the tragedies of the modern West, from secularization to the death of God, from totalitarian regimes to ideological suicides.

There is nothing new under the sun. This disparaging and appalling view of the Reformation has been the common reading of modern European history by scores of Counter-Reformation Catholic polemists until recent decades. Bergoglio did not invent it. He rather reaffirms it as if more thorough historical research and theological and cultural analyses never took place after the Council of Trent. What can we make of his friendly tones towards Protestants if he really thinks that the "Lutheran position" is to be blamed for all the evils of Western civilization?

John Calvin the Spiritual Executioner

There is more. Bergoglio makes a distinction between Martin Luther the "heretic" and John Calvin the "heretic" and "schismatic." The Lutheran heresy is "a good idea gone foolish," but Calvin is even worse because he also tore apart man, society, and the church. As for man, Bergoglio's Calvin split reason from the heart, thus producing the "Calvinist squalor." In society, Calvin pitted the bourgeoisie against the other working classes, thus becoming "the father of liberalism." The worst schism happened in the church, however. There, Calvin "beheaded the people of God from being united with the Father." He beheaded the people of God from its patron saints. He also beheaded it from the mass, i.e., the mediation of

---

4. Bergoglio, *Chi sono i gesuiti*.

the "really present" Christ. In summary, Calvin was an executioner that destroyed man, poisoned society, and ruined the church!

To say that Bergoglio does not like Calvin is an understatement. He has strong feelings against him. But are we sure that he understands Calvin beyond totally biased and outdated clichés? The year 2017 will mark the five hundredth anniversary of the Protestant Reformation and will be an opportunity for Francis to go back to more recent history books and get a fairer and more accurate picture of what happened from the 16th century onwards. If he does not revise his assessment of the Reformation all "ecumenical" language will be a superficial mask hiding a real hatred for Luther and (especially) Calvin.

Francis's Apology To Pentecostals In Search of Significance (August 3, 2014, Number 85)

Offering apologies is a highly regarded habit even in secular circles. We are surrounded by words of apology everywhere, as customers on the metro, on trains, and on TV. But in the midst of all the rhetoric of apology are there ways to discern the truthfulness of it all? Parents quickly learn to assess their children's apologies. To say "I am sorry" is not in and of itself a true apology. One needs to show a sense of guilt—of being aware of what he is asking apology for—and to do something about what went wrong. Pope Francis's words of apology to Italian Pentecostals were considered the high point of his visit to his pastor friend Giovanni Traettino (July 28). They referred to the nasty discriminations that Pentecostals had to suffer under the Fascist regime in the thirties when they were deemed a threat to the stability of the social order and severely ostracized.

A Confusing Apology

The Pope's "apology" was curious. The persecutions of 1935 against Pentecostals were implemented by the Fascist government and police, not by the Catholic Church. However, Francis offered his apology for these persecutions. The Catholic Church had no direct role but was the main social agent that supported the culture of discrimination. What he could have apologized for, however, was the centuries-long sin of the Catholic Church that has constantly been against religious freedom. Interestingly, Francis never mentioned religious freedom but only made reference to one single episode of intolerance. Then in his apology, he did not speak of the Catholic Church as being responsible for opposing religious freedom, but he only spoke of the sin of "catholic brothers and sisters" who persecuted Pentecostals. While the Catholic Church of the time was totally in agreement with the Fascist regime in opposing minorities and providing its cultural legitimacy in exchange of favors and privileges, Francis downplayed the role of the church and focused on individuals. He apologized as "pastor" of those individuals who persecuted Pentecostals, but he did not take responsibility for the church they represented and that he represents. According to Catholic teaching, the church never errs per se; it is only the children of the church that sin. On the one hand, then, he apologized for the sins he did not commit. On the other he didn't apologize for the sins his church committed. A confusing way of offering an apology.

An Inconsequential Apology

Furthermore, spiritually speaking, any apology is real if it implies restoration and compensation for those who were wronged, at least to some extent. The Pope's apology was rhetorical but not practical. He did not speak of a commitment to finally accept and implement full religious freedom in Italy. The Catholic Church is the main obstacle in recognizing equal rights and opportunities to all religious groups, but Francis was silent on the whole issue. He only spoke words of "apology" without having institutional title to do that, without being serious about the sins of the church and without suggesting practical ways towards a better solution for religious freedom for all. Fascism is over, persecutions against Pentecostals are over, but religious freedom is still an issue for the country that the Catholic Church considers "home." What's the significance of offering an apology if there is no change of mind with practical steps towards a better settlement for religious freedom?

One positive aspect of his apology was his rejection of the word "sect." "You are not a sect," he said to his Pentecostal audience. The label "sect," applied to evangelicals and Pentecostals, was regularly used by John Paul II and Benedict XVI, Francis's immediate predecessors. No word of apology was offered for such derogatory language that has been standard in many Papal speeches concerning evangelicals. Here he could have offered an apology on behalf of his church and its leaders, but he remained silent. Apologies are less significant for things that belong to a distant past than for things that are happening now. In spite of all the emotional fuss that his apology originated, Francis chose a confusing and inconsequential way of saying "sorry" while maintaining the idea that his church never makes mistakes.

Ecumenism in All Directions. Pope Francis and the Unity of the Church (October 8, 2014, Number 91)

Nothing is substantially new, but everything is affirmed and lived out in a really new way. This is how Cardinal Walter Kasper, former head of the Pontifical Council for Christian Unity, summarizes Pope Francis's approach to ecumenism. In a foreword to a book that analyzes the major Papal speeches and acts as far as the unity of the church is concerned,[5] Kasper argues that from his first address after being elected to his daily words and gestures, ecumenism has been central to what Francis has been doing thus far.

As is often the case in the Roman Catholic Church, there is no substantial change in the overall doctrinal framework. The Catholic approach to ecumenism is still the same without additions or subtractions. The final goal of ecumenism is to bring the whole church *cum Petro* (with Peter, i.e., in fellowship with the Pope) and *sub Petro* (under Peter, i.e., in submission to the Pope). Having said that, emphases and attitudes do change, and this Pope certainly has a distinct way of interpreting his mission as a chief promoter of the ecumenical cause.

Ecumenism of Friendship

The book reflects the ongoing commitment of Pope Francis to foster his view of Christian unity. After reading it, here are some observations that can be made. His ecumenical initiatives are based more on personal contacts with leaders of different churches and organizations than on institutional channels. In performing his role, the Pope does not totally depend on Vatican bureaucracy but instead retains his own sphere of initiative. This relational aspect is often underlined as the primary way to foster mutual trust and deeper relationships. In Francis's view, theological dialogues are less important than personal acquaintances. Nothing changes as far as the long-term goal of the Pope presiding over the whole church

---

5. Burigana, *Cuore Solo*.

is concerned, but this is not the issue that the Pope likes to focus on. The important thing for him is to say that we are friends, brothers, sisters, already "one" in some sense.

He wants different ecumenical partners and friends to be valued, listened to, cared for, and even admired. He wants to affirm them and wants them to feel appreciated. Theological and ecclesiastical alignments are secondary. Anyone interested in what is happening with this Pope should note that the paradigm he is operating under is that of an ecumenism of friendship rather than one of convictions. The two are not opposed, but the emphasis for him lies on the former, not the latter.

In his 2013 exhortation *Evangelii Gaudium*, Francis made clear that time is more important than space. What he meant is that those who set their lives in long-term trajectories are better suited to achieve something than those who concentrate on the here and now. The overwhelming appreciation of the ecumenical partners and the ongoing investment in personal relationships are two tracks of the ecumenical path that is consistent with this view.

Closer to All?

Another impressive mark of Pope Francis's ecumenism is that he manages to get closer to all his ecumenical partners without making distinctions between them. He has similar words, attitudes, and approaches to Eastern Orthodox of various stripes, Liberal Protestants, Anglicans, evangelicals, Pentecostals, and other kinds of Christians. Theologically speaking this is rather awkward because the closer you get to the sacramentalism and the devotions of the East, the farther away you go from the liberal agenda of most Western Protestant churches, and vice versa. Furthermore, as you draw nearer to the "free" church tradition of Pentecostalism, you at the same time distance yourselves from the highly hierarchical and sacramental ecclesiology of both the Roman and the Eastern traditions. Not so for Pope Francis. As already pointed out, this is not his approach. He invests in relationships with all people while leaving aside theological traditions and ecclesiastical settlements. He wants to get closer to all.

A further illustration of this point is that as he draws nearer to all Christians, Pope Francis is also determined to draw nearer to all people, be they religious or secular. The same brotherly and appreciative afflatus is what marks the Pope's attitude towards Jews, Muslims, and agnostic intellectuals. Divisive issues are left aside, whereas the "brotherly" dimension is always in the foreground. The Pope is clearly pushing with the same intensity the relational side of ecumenism and interreligious dialogue as if they were two intertwined paths to achieve the overall catholic goal: *cum Petro* and *sub Petro*.

The point is that one's objective is to draw nearer to everyone: this means that the driving concern is not biblical truth and love that is a principled and discerning criterion but the catholicity of friendship that is much more flexible and fluid. While appreciating the friendly tone, the keeping of Christian unity cannot be a matter of friendship alone. Unity in truth is what Jesus prayed for in John 17, and unity in truth and love is what Paul wrote about in Eph 4.

Turkey, Gateway To Interreligious Dialogue and Ecumenism (December 12, 2014, Number 87)

Pope Francis's visit to Turkey (November 28–30, 2014) was significant for a number of reasons. The two most outstanding reasons concern the ability of the Roman Catholic Church to engage in "dialogue"—that is, dialogue with Islam and dialogue with the Patriarchate of Constantinople. The former takes the form of interreligious dialogue, the latter is primarily an expression of ecumenism. Turkey is a threshold into the Muslim world. The country borders Syria and Iraq, places where Islamic fundamentalism threatens the sheer survival of the local Christian communities. Turkey is also the historical see of the "second Rome," i.e., Constantinople, an influential center of Eastern Orthodoxy. The focus of the visit was therefore twofold: to foster mutual understanding with the "moderate" Islam and to advance the ecumenical agenda with Constantinople.

Your Prayers for Me

Pope Francis had several meetings with various Muslim leaders. In each of them he stressed the commonalities between Christians and Muslims in terms of them worshipping the All-Merciful God, having Abraham as father, practicing prayer, almsgiving and fasting, and sharing a religious sense of life that is foundational for human dignity and fraternity. In addressing Muslims, the Pope used the language of brotherhood and focused on what they have in common. This same approach was used in Turkey.

One interesting albeit striking element emerged as he spoke on November 28 to the Department for Religious Affairs in Ankara.[6] After referring to the common themes that we already mentioned, he said, "I am grateful also to each one of you, for your presence and for your prayers which, in your kindness, you offer for me and my ministry."[7] Pope Francis is used to asking for prayers for himself and to thanking people who pray for him. But in this case he was speaking to Muslims, and he nonetheless thanked them for their prayers for him. It seems that in this case he went further than simply underlining commonalities in basic theology and spirituality. He went as far as recognizing Islamic prayers as legitimate, and even useful, acts of intercession. Should a Christian be thankful to Muslims for their prayers? Are these prayers accepted by God? Didn't the Pope unwarrantedly stretch the interfaith theology that assumes that all prayers are pleasing to God and answered by him? Didn't he further blur the distinction between the Christian faith and the Muslim religion by implying that Christians and Muslims can pray for each other, as if God accepts their respective prayers as they are?

Back to the First Millennium

The other focus of the visit was to strengthen the ecumenical relationships with the Patriarchate of Constantinople. According to the Roman Catholic principles of ecumenism, the Eastern Orthodox churches are close to "full communion" with Rome because they profess the same apostolic faith, they celebrate the same Eucharist and they have maintained the apostolic succession in their priesthood. From a theological point of view, the role of the papacy is the only imperfection that inhibits them from full communion. The Papal office as it developed after the schism of 1054 AD makes Eastern Orthodox churches unwilling to accept the primacy of the Roman Pope as it stands. In their view, certain monarchial aspects of the Petrine ministry that were introduced in the second millennium (e.g., the infallibility of the Pope as he speaks *ex cathedra*) go against the collegiality principle of Orthodox ecclesiology.

Being aware of these complexities and yet wanting to promote an ecumenical breakthrough, Pope Francis said that he is willing to envisage a way forward: the Roman Church is open to concede that in order

---

6. Francis, "Address (Ankara)."
7. Francis, "Address (Ankara)," para. 9.

to enter into full communion with Rome, Eastern Orthodox churches need to accept the Papal office as it was understood and practiced in the first millennium, when the church was still "undivided." This is not a new idea—even Joseph Ratzinger was in favor of it—but it is important that Francis made it his own.[8] It seems that the way forward is to first go backwards. The Roman Church is willing to exercise its catholicity, i.e., being flexible enough to accommodate a different point of view, all while maintaining its distinctive outlook without renouncing any of it. This suggestion needs to be worked out historically and theologically. What exactly were the forms of the papacy in the first millennium? How can they be implemented after so many centuries? How can an institution such as the Papacy that the Roman Church couched with dogma (i.e., the infallibility) be diluted for non-Catholic Christians? How can one be *cum Petro* (with Peter) without being *sub Petro* (under Peter)?

While ecumenical theologians have some homework yet to do in this field, a final comment is warranted. In the end, even the Protestant Reformation was a cry to go back to the written Word of God, i.e., *sola Scriptura*! In calling for a new season under the rule of the Jesus Christ of the Bible, the Reformation beckoned the church to rediscover the Scriptures and re-submit to them. Back to the Word was a way of saying, "Back to Jesus Christ, back to the gospel!" The Catholic Church of the 16th century was, however, unwilling to receive this challenge and wanted a way forward without giving thought to the need of going backward. The Council of Trent (1545–63) imagined a renewal without a reformation, a way forward without having to go backward. Now, Rome is ready to go back to the first millennium and fully embrace the Eastern Orthodox churches. Why not go a bit further than the first millennium? A return to *sola Scriptura* should be the real starting point for a much-needed breakthrough.

Still "Our Holy Mother the Hierarchical Church" (February 28, 2015, Number 102)

A church more interested in promoting mission than keeping traditions. A church less concentrated on theological boundaries and more focused on expanding its loving appeal to all men. A church whose unity is like a polyhedron and allows multiple relationships with her. This is the picture

---

8. Francis, "Address (Ankara)."

of the church that Pope Francis has been presenting since his election in 2013. Overall, the secular public opinion resonated well with this seemingly "lighter" form of Roman Catholicism, i.e., a more relaxed church in terms of faith and morals living out its message in more organic and relational ways. In Francis's preferred metaphor, the church is a "field hospital" welcoming the irregular ones more than an impressive cathedral assembling the liturgically righteous. This is only one side of the coin, however. While it is true that Francis's emphasis has been consistently put on the missional side of the church, it is also true that he has occasionally but consistently restated the full, heavy, and thick traditional understanding of the church.

Holy Mother

The last instance was during a recent catechesis on the topic of the church.[9] In introducing the role of the Bishop, Francis said, "In the presence and ministry of the Bishops, of Presbyters and of Deacons we can recognize the true face of the Church: it is the Hierarchical Holy Mother Church."[10] Notice the reference to the "true face" of the church, which is shown in the hierarchical structure of the church thought of as the mother. This is a very propositional statement about the church. Two dimensions are particularly stressed: the hierarchical and the motherly aspects of the church, which form the backbone of its self-understanding.

According to Francis, as mother the church "generates us in Baptism as Christians, making us reborn in Christ; she watches over our growth in the faith; she supports us between the Father's arms, to receive his forgiveness, she prepares for us the Eucharistic table, where she nourishes us with the Word of God and the Body and Blood of Jesus; she invokes upon us God's blessing and the strength of his Spirit, sustaining us throughout the course of our life and enveloping us with His tenderness and warmth, especially in the most difficult moments of trial, of suffering and of death." This is a breathtaking list of verbs: generating, making reborn, watching over, supporting, nourishing, sustaining, enveloping . . . these are the maternal roles of the church that always accompany the Christian life. Their cumulative force is overwhelming and makes them resemble the role of the Head of the Church, Jesus Christ. Actually, this is what

---

9. Francis, "General Audience Catechesis."
10. Francis, "General Audience Catechesis," para. 3.

they are meant to be. Christ continues his mission through the mother church.

If one wants to come to terms with Roman Catholicism at all levels, she needs to grapple with this deeply felt sense of motherhood, which is also the theological and devotional architecture of the Roman Catholic Mariology. It is Mary, the mother *par excellence*, who embodies the motherly care of the church and who is by no chance always invoked to ask for motherly protection and care.

The Hierarchical Church

The maternal principle of the church lies at the heart of Francis's vision of the church. There is also an intertwined element to this. The motherly dimension is organically connected to the hierarchical structure of the church. The Pope goes on to say that in the Bishop, the hierarchical top of the motherly church, "is Christ Himself who renders Himself present and who continues to take care of His Church."[11] The presence of Jesus Christ is made present in the motherly role of the church through its hierarchical structure. It is curious to notice that in his earthly ministry Jesus showed the Father, whereas now He carries on his mission in and through the motherly face of the church. It is through the hierarchy that "the Church exercises her maternity."

According to the Pope then, the "true face" of the church is where the maternal and the hierarchical dimensions are intimately connected to one another and form the core of the church's identity. In churches where the motherhood of the church is less explicit because it is defined by the sobriety of biblical boundaries and where the hierarchical structure is lived out against the background of the headship of Christ and the universal priesthood of all believers, the church loses her "true face." So, on the one hand, Francis is sending the message that Christian unity and human brotherhood are at hand in a loosely articulated vision of unity; on the other, he maintains the traditional understanding of the Roman Catholic Church, which stemmed out of the Council of Trent.

At a superficial level Christian unity under Pope Francis may seem "easier" for non-Catholic Christians, but a closer look shows that the theological issues of the historic differences, at least with evangelical Christianity, are still standing.

11. Francis, "General Audience Catechesis," para. 2.

Should Evangelicals Love Pope Francis? (April 13, 2015, Number 106)[12]

On the day before Easter, Peter Wehner, a columnist for the New York Times (NYT), wrote an interesting and thought-provoking article titled "Why Evangelicals Should Love the Pope."[13] Three main concerns about it can be raised and briefly presented.

The Straw Man

Pitting Franklin Graham against Pope Francis on how to address the moral crisis of our time is very easy but totally arbitrary. With his seemingly harsh language and judgmental arguments against homosexuality, Franklin Graham represents a still significant portion of US evangelicals yet a minority of evangelicals globally considered. In speaking to the US context, Graham may have right-wing political overtones that do not fit the whole evangelical family. North American sociopolitical categories are not useful to account for its complexity. Lots of evangelicals, both inside and outside of the US, deal with the same issues with a different attitude and language. On the other hand, Pope Francis speaks on the same issues in more pastoral terms, and in doing so he is able to overlook specific situations. When he does address concrete cases, he does so using strong language. For instance, in his recent visit to the Philippines (January 16, 2015), he spoke about the prospect of introducing same-sex marriage as an "ideological colonization" of family life to resist and fight against. Not exactly the tender tone that Wehner wants us to believe. Francis may seem softer and milder only because he speaks about these issues "in general" and in a more pastoral tone. Before contrasting Graham and Pope Francis, Wehner should wait until the Pope visits the US this coming September, when he will speak at the World Meeting of Families. Is he so sure that Francis will speak merciful words only? Until then, he should have instead compared Franklin Graham and Cardinal Timothy Dolan, the staunch Archbishop of New York. Perhaps the difference between the two is not so sharp as it appears to be between Graham and the Pope. In the article Graham is depicted as the Shakespearean fool and Francis as the wise man of the story: a much too simplistic picture of reality to be true.

---

12. This Vatican file was written together with Reid Karr, a dear friend and a colleague in gospel ministry in Rome.

13. Wehner, "Why Evangelicals."

The Tip of the Iceberg

In calling evangelicals to love the Pope, the NYT article has a sentimentalized view of the Pope. It focuses on some aspects of the Papal language but fails to give readers the fuller picture. In the same period in which Francis met with prisoners and social outcasts, he also presided over pompous Easter celebrations in St. Peter's Basilica, with all the richness and power of the Roman Catholic Church on full display. Where was Francis's humility in all these splendorous liturgies and costly events? Moreover, about the same time in which Francis spoke about the church being a "field hospital," he confirmed and reinforced the existence and necessity of the Vatican bank, which is a worldwide power structure that deals with all sorts of financial activity. Wehner highlighted the "loving" words of the Pope and overlooked the rest. This is a common practice in the religious analysis of the papacy: a carefully selected picture of the Pope becomes his full representation, thus failing to provide an accurate account of the whole. The humble and frugal aspects of the Pope as a person have little to do with the political and imperial aspects of his role. Below the surface and the tip of the iceberg is the iceberg itself, which in this case is the last absolutist monarchy that can be found on earth. Serious reflection should be devoted to the reality of the iceberg rather than focusing on the tip only.

What About the Gospel?

"Welcoming all," "showing compassion," and "all-inclusive" seem to be the mainstream and politically correct expressions of the "gospel of the day." Pope Francis is a champion of this kind of gospel presentation. Many secular people, as well as many evangelicals, are fascinated by the seemingly generous scope of his message. In his article Wehner quotes Pope Francis as saying, "Without mercy, we have little chance nowadays of becoming part of a world of 'wounded' persons in need of understanding, forgiveness and love." Truer words could not be spoken. But this statement represents the tip of the iceberg. We should be responsible and look below the surface and identify what is giving form to and supporting the Pope's words and actions.

Where does sin fit into the Pope's view? What about repentance and faith in Christ alone? What about turning back from idolatry and following Christ wholeheartedly? What about putting the Word of God first?

After visiting the prisoners in Naples and speaking words of mercy and forgiveness, the Pope went to the city cathedral to kiss the liquefied blood of St. Gennaro, a medieval practice related to the beseeching of a blessing of the patron saint upon the city. Where is the biblical gospel in this?

What should concern every Christian above all else is the salvation of those who don't know Christ as Savior. We can talk about mercy and forgiveness and love and taking Christ to the farthest and darkest places of the earth all we want, but what really matters is the message we proclaim and embody to the lost and hurting we encounter. What then is the message of salvation? If asked how one is forgiven and saved from his or her sins, how would Pope Francis respond? The article does not delve into these controversial waters. He and other evangelicals who share his sentiments would do well to examine what's below the tip of the iceberg.

We Are Not Puritans, Are We?
(August 1, 2015, Number 111)

The Puritans do not generally enjoy good press. For most people the term Puritanism is synonymous with religious bigotry and judgmental moralism. This is especially true in neo-Latin cultures, where the word "Puritan" is normally associated with a derogatory caricature of Puritanism. In these contexts, Puritan is referred to as a kind of cerebral Christianity, overwhelmingly interested in outward and formal purity at the expense of human warmth and personal proximity. Pope Francis is no exception. On a recent occasion he made an *impromptu* reference to the Puritans. The term slipped out of his mouth as he was telling a story of a priest with a negative attitude.

What Are We, Puritans?

In delivering a meditation on priesthood to thousands of priests from around the world at the Basilica of St. John Lateran in Rome on June 12, the Pope recalled a priest who found it difficult to baptize the child of a single mother who had asked him to do so. The priest had opposed the idea because the woman was not married and the child had been born outside of marriage. The then Archbishop Bergoglio reacted with outrage and vehemently replied, "What are we, Puritans?" In his mind there was no better description of this hypocritical and arrogant approach than naming it "Puritan"! Are we Puritans? Absolutely not! "Please"—the Pope went on in his meditation—"let's not have a Church without Jesus and without mercy. Don't scare the faithful people. When this happens, when the priest's heart is bureaucratic and attached to the letter of the law, the Church, which is Mother, is transformed, for so many faithful into a stepmother. Please, make them feel that the Church is always Mother."[14]

What does Puritan mean, according to Francis? Apparently, it means to have a church without Jesus, a church that scares people rather than welcoming them, a bureaucratic church obsessed with the letter of the law, a church that is a rigid stepmother rather than a loving mother. In Francis's vocabulary there was no better term to discredit this merciless form of Christianity than referring to it as "Puritanism." But is this a fair theological and historical description of Puritanism? Surely not.

There are tons of evidence that support a very different portrait. Here is how C. S. Lewis sketches it: "We must picture these Puritans as the very opposite of those who bear that name today: as young, fierce, progressive intellectuals, very fashionable and up-to-date. They were not teetotalers; bishops, not beer, were their special aversion."[15] Instead of being cold and detached Christians, they were "worldly saints" (L. Ryken), combining a radical biblical faith with a down-to-earth interest in the whole of life.[16] Again C. S. Lewis is helpful here: "To be sure, there are standards by which the early Protestants could be called 'puritanical'; they held adultery, fornication, and perversion for deadly sins. But then so did the Pope. If that is puritanism, all Christendom was then puritanical together. So far as there was any difference about sexual morality, the Old Religion was the more austere. The exaltation of virginity is a Roman, that of marriage, a Protestant, trait."[17]

An Unsettled Relationship with Historic Protestantism

Against the term "Puritan," Francis encouraged the priests to "be merciful, be merciful"—"mercy" being the key word with which to understand

14. For the full speech, see Zenit, "Pope Francis' Meditation at 3rd Word Retreat."
15. Lewis, *Studies*, 121–22.
16. De Chirico, "Vatican File 111."
17. Lewis, *English Literature*, 35. Other interesting quotes by C. S. Lewis on the Puritans can be found at https://tidesandturning.wordpress.com/2012/12/26/c-s-lewis-defining-and-defending-the-english-puritans/. I wish to thank Greg Pritchard for pointing this website to me.

the Pope and the program of the fast approaching Jubilee of Mercy—as if Puritanism was opposed to a biblically defined mercy.

Pope Francis is not new in showing profound uneasiness—even repulsion—towards what historic Protestantism stood for. In his 1985 lecture on the history of the Jesuit order he wrote severe evaluations of Luther (a "heretic"), and especially of Calvin (a "heretic" and "schismatic"), bringing about the "Calvinist squalor" in society, in the church, and in man's heart.[18] According to that lecture, Protestantism lies at the root of all evils in the modern West. The fact that this lecture was republished unchanged in 2013 in Spanish and translated in 2014 in Italian with his permission, but without a mitigating word of explanation, indicates that this assessment still lingers in the Pope's heart and mind.

In spite of the much applauded yet inconsequential "words of apology" recently extended to Pentecostals and Waldensians, Pope Francis still demonstrates he has mixed feelings about the whole of the Protestant Reformation, its main architects (e.g., Luther and Calvin), and some of its historical representatives (e.g., the Puritans). In his *impromptu* reaction, Francis echoed widespread prejudices. Surely the Puritans deserve a much fairer treatment than what the Pope gave his audience. They were not merciless Christians. In J. I. Packer's words, the Puritans were "God's giants" who embraced wholeheartedly a version of Christianity that paraded a particular blend of biblicist, pietist, churchly, and worldly concerns.[19] The Pope is among those who, instead of caricaturing Puritanism, should take the opportunity to better grasp it historically, theologically, and pastorally.

Evangelicals and Catholics: A New Era? (May 1, 2016, Number 124)

A talk given to the Annual General Assembly of the Italian Evangelical Alliance (Rome, April 8, 2016).

Is This a New Era for Evangelicals and Catholics?

To give an answer we need to place this question in a wider historical and theological context, because otherwise we risk reducing everything

---

18. See De Chirico, "Vatican File 183."
19. Packer, *Among God's Giants*, 433.

to the here and now. This preliminary observation about method is always valid, but even more so when analyzing Catholicism, which is an institution that boasts two thousand years of history with its doctrinal, institutional and cultural heritage. Roman Catholicism has to be assessed using macro-categories able to hold together the largest possible number of elements. Failing to do this will lead to a collection of fragments, just pieces of Catholicism, which will not allow a real understanding of its dimensions, depth, connections, and projects. A "spiritual" assessment cannot ignore the fact that while we are dealing with a system made up of people, they are in fact people within a framework that has a history, a doctrine, a bond to the sacraments, a political commitment, a financial system, popular piety, a plurality of spiritual expressions, etc., all of which are nonetheless connected to an institutional center and a theological heart. To speak of a "new era" it is important to remember that along the course of its history, Catholicism has known some particularly significant eras. Here is a brief summary:

The Era of Imperial Catholicism

After the Constantinian turning point, Catholicism quickly transformed into a religious empire, forged in the institutional mold of the empire and animated by an imperial ideology. From the ashes of the Roman Empire rose the imperial church that assumed a pyramidal institutional structure, clothing it with Christian language and symbols. The imperial hubris of Roman Catholicism (that is, its desire to be both church and state) is its original sin, which has never been seriously questioned, let alone refuted. The orthodoxy of primitive Christianity has been gradually broadened in the attempt to assimilate new beliefs and new practices, causing the Christian faith to become contradictory. The desire to represent all of humanity has moved the point of entry into the church from conversion to Christ to the baptism administered by the church, leading to the establishing of a church composed of baptized people and not of believers. Biblical revelation has in fact been relativized due to the growing role of the church's tradition. The church has become a nominal church made up of baptized people who are not necessarily believers. The grace of God has become the property of a religious institution that claims it can administer and dispense it through its sacramental system. The imperial era has given rise to an imperial DNA that Catholicism has never laid aside. In this era all biblical renewal movements were either fought against or assimilated through a policy of domestication to the imperial ideology. Niches of different forms of spirituality were carved out so as to be inoffensive and lifeless and thus maintain the status quo.

The Era of Oppositional Catholicism

The second great age was that of the Counter-Reformation, structured around two central moments: the Council of Trent (1545–63) and the Vatican I (1869–70). The Roman Catholic Church's long trajectory is characterized by a doctrinal trend which is at the same time abrasive, dulling, and interested in affirming the centrality and superiority of the church. It is the age in which the modern Catholic doctrine based on the prerogative of the church as alter Christus is formed; it is the age in which the doctrine of the two sources of revelation is expressed—Scripture and tradition; it is the age in which the church elevates itself to the point of thinking that its imperial structure is the divine will of God. Confronted with the Protestant Reformation, which invited the church to rid itself of its self-referentiality and rediscover the gospel of God's grace, Rome strengthened a sacramental system that made the church mediator of divine grace. Confronted with modernity that pushed for a review of the prerogatives of the church over people's consciences and society, Rome elevated its main institution (the papacy) to an even more accentuated role, as well as dogmatizing some Marian beliefs without any biblical support whatsoever. This recovery of a robust identity also led to a missionary expansion of Catholicism and the development of mystical and Marian forms of spirituality.

The Era of a Compliant and Captivating Catholicism

The oppositional method led to isolation and a marginalized role for Catholicism. The change took place with Vatican II (1962–65). The new era began there, when instead of siding against the modern world, Rome changed strategy, choosing to assimilate it, to penetrate it from within without changing in its own essence. Now it adopted the method of "updating": adjustment without structural reform, incorporation without loss or cost, expansion of the system without purification, development without renunciation of tradition, a continuous adding without subtracting anything. Vittorio Subilia has rightly spoken of the "new catholicity of Catholicism": a different posture, a new style, a new language. In every direction, however: in the direction of theological liberalism, making room for a critical reading of the Bible and universalism of salvation; in the evangelical direction, learning the linguistic code of evangelical spirituality (personal relationship with Christ, etc.); in the direction of Marian theology, traditionalism, ecumenism, etc. A 360-degree expansionary catholicity that still maintains the sacramental, hierarchical, devotional, and imperial structures (certainly made more discreet but definitely still present), all of which revolve around an abnormal and dilated ecclesiology and around the fundamental pillars of traditional doctrine.

The Question for Us

Without quoting it often, Pope Francis incarnates the catholicity of Vatican II: open to dialogue, merciful, pleasing but without paying any dogmatic, theological, or spiritual price. The imperial and Counter-Reformation framework of the former ages remains, only "updated" to the new requirements of the contemporary global world. He speaks all languages: evangelical, ecumenical, interreligious, secular, traditional. He seems to draw close to everyone without actually moving. He seems to reach out to everyone without going very far. And then, the fact that everyone (from secularists to Muslims, and including liberal Protestants and evangelicals) considers him close to them must make us ask, Is he really near to anyone? In other words, the strategy of the "polyhedron" seems to be the instrument of catholicity that has its roots in Vatican II and that fulfills it: all have to relate to a Roman church that has axes of various lengths in order to reach everyone but without shifting its center of gravity. Rome has already reached such a well-oiled homeostatic balance that it can play on more than one table at the same time without altering the overall framework.

In this climate, some people claim that the Reformation has practically finished because there no longer exists the oppositional Catholicism that rejected it. Catholicism has widened its synthesis and has also made room for the concerns of the Reformation, though trimmed of their groundbreaking character and bent to enable them to coexist, to cohabit, to live side-by-side with other demands opposed to the gospel within a Catholic system which is even more eclectic and plural but still Roman and Papal. Catholicism continues to add places to the table and extend the menu; it variegates more and more the codes, to fulfill its vocation to unite the world inside the net of catholicity and under the effective or honorary jurisdiction of a head.

In the new era of captivating catholicity there will be a niche for the evangelicals who have made peace with the imperial structures of the church of Rome and its abnormal theology and who are no longer concerned about a comprehensive reform in accordance with the gospel. These evangelicals instead are content to be able to integrate their own spirituality into a system that is more fluid but still vertebrate, that is programmatically open to everything and yet opposed to everything. The criterion of the system is not the gospel of Christ but a version of the gospel that guarantees the universalist and Rome-centered strategy of Catholicism.

The new era between evangelicals and Catholics requires us to ask the question which is both old but also relevant for every generation of believers: can the church of Rome be renewed in accordance with the gospel from within, or do we have to envisage moving past it and leaving it behind in the name of the gospel? With its encumbrance of unreformable dogmas, imperial institutions, projects of omnivorous catholicity, can the church of Rome be impacted by the gospel in its propulsive heart? In other words, is the gospel just one option amongst many possibilities, or is it the radical "yes" to the Word of God that says "no" to all forms of idolatry? Can a church, whichever one it is, be programmatically open to a multitude of offers, or, if it wants to be a church, must it be founded exclusively on the biblical gospel?

Thus, evangelical theology has the necessary instruments to focus consistently on the gospel without degenerating into sectarian and spiritually autistic attitudes. As is stated in the document *An Evangelical Approach Towards Understanding Roman Catholicism*:

> 12. What refers to the Catholic Church in its doctrinal and institutional configuration cannot necessarily be extended to all Catholics as individuals. The grace of God is at work in men and women who, though considering themselves Catholics, entrust themselves exclusively to the Lord, cultivate a personal relationship with Him, read the Bible and live as Christians. These people, however, must be encouraged to reflect on whether their faith is compatible or not with belonging to the Catholic Church. Moreover, they must be helped to critically think over

what remains of their Catholic background in the light of Biblical teaching.

Criticism of the Catholic system must not indiscriminately group together all people on their spiritual journeys. Furthermore, it is possible, and even necessary, to create opportunities for cobelligerence in areas of common commitment:

> 13. In fulfilling the cultural mandate there can be agreement, collaboration and communal action between Evangelicals and people of other religious and ideological leanings. Wherever shared values in the ethical, social, cultural and ideological fields are at stake initiatives of cobelligerence are desirable. These forms of necessary and inevitable cooperation must not be mistaken for ecumenical initiatives, neither must they be considered expressions of a new-found doctrinal consensus.[20]

A new era between evangelicals and Catholics? A long look at history, the spiritual discernment of the gospel, the overall view the Spirit leads us to answer "yes" and "no." Certainly, with Vatican II a different period began that needs to be understood. It is wrong to have a flattened or static view of Catholicism. On the other hand, Vatican II and Pope Francis, who is its most successful incarnation, are only the latest evolutionary step in a system that was born and developed with an "original sin" from which it has not yet been redeemed but which instead has been consolidated. No ecumenical diplomacy will be able to change it, not even the addition of a new evangelical offer to the traditional menu. The invitation of the Lord Jesus applies to everyone: "The time is fulfilled, and the kingdom of God is at hand; repent, and believe in the gospel" (Mark 1:14). The real new time, God willing, will be when Roman Catholicism breaks the imperial ecclesiological pattern and reforms its own catholicity, basing it no longer on its assimilation project but on the basis of faithfulness to the gospel.

After Lund, What Remains of the Protestant Reformation? (November 9, 2016, Number 131)

While Pope Francis was taking part in the ecumenical events in Lund and Malmoe commemorating the Protestant Reformation, the giant screens in St. Peter's Square—the heart of the Roman Catholic Church—invited

---

20. Istituto di Formazione Evangelica, "Orientamenti evangelici per pensare il cattolicesimo."

all to assemble around the statue of St. Peter to recite the Holy Rosary. Mere coincidence? Perhaps. It is striking, though, to notice that in Lund the intention was to bridge over the distance between Rome and the Protestant Reformation, while in Rome the clear indication was of a strong commitment to the Marian and Petrine marks of the Roman Church, which in modern times have been defined in light of all that the Reformation stood for. In assessing the ecumenical scene, the risk of looking at Lund without being aware of what happens in Rome is real. Yet both belong to the ecumenical landscape of our time.

So, after Lund, what remains of the Reformation? The document "Is the Reformation Over?,"[21] signed by dozens of evangelical theologians and leaders around the world, clearly suggests that the Reformation is in fact not yet over. The question is open, though. In a pointed article in *First Things*, for instance, Dale M. Coulter criticized the statement of being theologically outdated and typifying an unhelpful bunker mentality. According to him, the document "seeks to define Protestantism over against the Catholic Church out of a concern that evangelicals do not have a clear view of Catholic teaching." In doing so, "It simultaneously sets forth a misguided view of *sola Scriptura* as implying that tradition has no role to play in Protestant understandings of authority and interpretation, and a reductive view of Catholicism that extracts Papal infallibility and Marian dogma out of the hierarchy of truths and the structure of Catholic teaching within which they fall."[22]

The reality is that the document affirms that the main thrust of the Reformation was mainly theological and in essence centered on the recovery of the authority of Scripture and the biblical gospel of salvation by faith alone. These two pillars of the Christian faith are its standing legacy after five hundred years. This is the theologically positive thrust of the Reformation, both then and now. As a matter of fact, to be "protestant" does not primarily mean reacting against something but standing *for* something. In the 16th century *pro-testare* meant testifying to the truth of the gospel. The Reformation was a positive affirmation of what the church needs always to be reminded of: God's written Word is the supreme norm for the whole of life, and salvation is a God-given gift from beginning to end. The word "protestant," therefore, has a theologically positive tone. In

---

21. Reformanda Initiative, "Is the Reformation Over?"
22. Coulter, "Pope, Protestantism, and Reformation."

this sense, all Christians need to be protestant, i.e., affirming, witnessing, and publicly heralding the gospel.

With various degrees of theological consistency, the Reformation tried to define itself *according* to the teaching of Scripture. At least in principle, it was Scripture that determined what was acceptable and what was not acceptable in the Roman Catholic Church of the time. The Reformation did not pit the Bible against tradition in abstract terms, but being fully aware of the unavoidable role of tradition anchored it to the sure foundations of the Bible. For the Reformers, *sola Scriptura* was an issue of authority, not of hermeneutics. They accepted tradition and practiced it insofar as it was *under* God's written Word. This is its standing legacy. It is also the vantage point from which all churches and traditions ought to critically assess themselves in light of Scripture. That is, the "Is the Reformation Over?" document does not attempt to defend the Protestant Reformation per se. Instead, it simply seeks to reaffirm in our age the two main commitments which are integral to the Christian faith.

The Council of Trent provided alternative accounts of the authority of Scripture and salvation by faith alone and condemned Protestant positions. The reverse was true as well. Protestant confessions condemned Roman Catholic doctrines and practices. Since then, however, much water has flown through the Tiber River. It is a given, though, that the three Roman Catholic modern dogmas (Mary's immaculate conception [1854] and bodily assumption [1950] and Papal infallibility [1870]) rest on tradition as their supreme authority, thus running the opposite direction than that of the Reformation. Tradition has become magisterial rather than ministerial.

The post-Vatican II Roman Church, while being more open and nuanced (might we say more ambiguous?) towards biblical authority and salvation by faith alone, still retains a significantly different theological orientation from the classical understanding of Scripture and salvation of the Reformation. *Dei Verbum*[23] (the Vatican II dogmatic constitution on divine revelation) is a masterful exercise of theological *aggiornamento* according to the "both-and" pattern of Roman Catholicism at its best. Still, it's not what the Reformation understood concerning *sola Scriptura*. The 1999 Joint Declaration on the Doctrine of Justification[24] (JDDJ), signed by Roman Catholics and Lutherans, comes close to what the Reformation

---

23. Second Vatican Council, "Dei Verbum."
24. Lutheran World Federation, "Joint Declaration."

stood for in recovering the good news of salvation as a Christ-given gift, but it tends to blur lines on significant points. As evangelical theologian Mike Reeves[25] has shown, in JDDJ, "The matter of the Reformation was not accurately addressed there, and still stands: are believers justified through faith in Christ *alone*, or is eternal life 'at one and the same time, grace and the reward given by God for good works and merits'?" This is why the Reformation is not over.

"Is the Reformation Over?" is a statement characterized by a biblical "parrhesia," i.e., the bold conviction deriving from being persuaded by the gospel truth which, after all, was recovered at the Reformation. The document reaffirms that on these two issues the Reformers were simply recovering the biblical gospel, and therefore so should we. After suggesting what was at stake during the Reformation and why it is still relevant, the last section of the document "looks ahead" towards better clarification and cooperation on the basis of the gospel, while recognizing the value of respectful and friendly dialogue and even cooperation with the Roman Catholic Church. Contrary to Coulter's straw man, there is no bunker mentality in the statement but instead a willingness to engage Roman Catholicism.

Returning from Lund to Rome, Pope Francis remarked in his in-flight interview that "in Catholic ecclesiology there are two dimensions to think about. The first is the Petrine dimension, which is from the apostle Peter, and the Apostolic College, which is the pastoral activity of the bishops. The second is the Marian dimension, which represents the feminine dimension of the Church."[26] The Reformation, on the other hand, would recommend the biblical dimension, and that dimension alone, as sufficient. In a nutshell this is why the Reformation is not yet over.

What Kind of "Reformation" Does Pope Francis Have in Mind? (February 1, 2017, Number 133)

"Christ summons the Church as she goes her pilgrim way . . . to that continual reformation of which she always has need, insofar as she is a human institution here on earth."[27] These words by Pope Francis, which are actually a quotation from Vatican II, reflect a deep conviction

---

25. Reeves, "Joint Declaration."
26. Francis, "Full Text: Pope Francis' In-Flight Presser."
27. Francis, Evangelii Gaudium, 26

concerning the need for an ongoing reformation in the church. The question is, What kind of reformation does he have in mind?

The recent book *La riforma e le riforme nella chiesa*[28] helps answer the question. This is the publication of the proceedings of an international conference held in Rome in 2015, organized by the Jesuit magazine *La Civiltà Cattolica*[29] on the subject of church reform. The size of the book, containing thirty papers, and the proximity of the editors to the Pope (Spadaro is the Jesuit editor of the magazine, and Galli is an Argentinian theologian), contribute to making the book an important tool to dig into what the Pope thinks of reformation.

Not a New Word

In the Western church, talks about reform have been going on since the Councils of Vienne (1312), Constance (1414–18) and the Lateran V (1512–17). The word is therefore part of the language of the church, even before the Protestant Reformation. The Council of Trent (1545–63) used it abundantly to promote changes at the level of ecclesiastical organization. In subsequent centuries the word was treated with caution, if not suspicion, given its Protestant flavor. It was Vatican II (1962–65) that began to circulate it[30] also using "aggiornamento" (updating) and renewal. Typically, the Catholic sense of reformation is continuity in change and change in continuity. Again, it's Vatican II that sets the tone for interpretation when it says that "every renewal of the Church is essentially grounded in an increase of fidelity to her own calling."[31] In reforming itself, the Roman Catholic Church does not lose anything of the past but rather tries to become more faithful to what she is already. The criterion of reformation is not external and objective, as would be the case with recognizing it in the Word of God, but always internal and ecclesial, i.e., the church itself setting the parameters of its own renewal.

Against this background, Pope Francis has been talking about reformation in the context of calling the church to re-launch its missionary impetus. No reformation of doctrine and devotions is in view.

---

28. Spadaro and Galli, *Riforma*.
29. http://www.laciviltacattolica.it.
30. See Second Vatican Council, "Lumen Gentium," 4.
31. Holy See, "Unitatis Redintegratio," 6.

In the Papal narrative, reformation means accelerating the process spurred by Vatican II.

Two Axes

Francis's own understanding of the reformation of the church has two main pillars. This book contains ample evidence affirming both. The first has to do with the increase of "synodality," i.e., the involvement of many players in the decision-making process. The Pope wants to change the way the universal church is governed in such a way that the local church—dioceses, bishops' conferences—plays a much larger part in the decisions that affect it, without questioning the universal ministry of the Pope. In short, Francis wishes to shorten the distance between Rome and the local church, to ensure that they act better together. In a programmatic summary the editors write, "The reform of the church is the synodical reform of local churches and of the whole church."[32] Reformation is therefore a participatory dynamic that introduces some minor structural changes in the internal organization of the church.

The other axis has to do with the "revolution of tenderness" that Francis has been talking about since his election in 2013. According to this program, the primacy of mercy needs to be recognized and implemented at all levels. The recently-ended Year of Mercy[33] has indicated the inclusive and embracing nature of what it means for the Pope to insist on mercy, at times neglecting aspects of the biblical teaching concerning repentance from sin and turning to Christ alone to be saved from our separation from God.

Synodality and mercy are the two qualifiers of reformation the Pope has in mind. There is no hint of what the Reformation of the 16th century meant for the church, i.e., the recovery of the supreme authority of the Bible and the message of salvation by faith alone. There is no hint of it in the Papal dream for a reformation. According to Francis's view, the future of the Roman Catholic Church will make room for more discussion and involvement of different subjects at all levels and will be marked by the pervasiveness of mercy. This is perfectly legitimate on his part and even admirable. The following question remains though: is *this* a reformation according to the gospel? Does it really recognize the primacy of God to

---

32. Spadaro and Galli, *Riforma*, 12.
33. De Chirico, "Vatican File 109."

call the church back to the whole counsel of God, to repent from deviations from the gospel and renew its commitment to be faithful to it? In its concerns with structures and attitudes, does it properly deal with the need for a reformation of doctrine and practice according to the Word of God?

Some evangelicals seem to be fascinated by the phenomenology of Pope Francis, although they do not always understand his theological vision. Addressing the issue of the "reformation" is a significant entry point in his world and gives to opportunity to begin to understand it. As the Pope commemorates the five hundredth anniversary of the Protestant Reformation,[34] what he has in mind is an altogether different kind of reformation, i.e., a reformation that will make his church more catholic and more Roman, doubtfully more evangelical.

Where Does Pope Francis Stand on the Doctrine of Justification? (November 1, 2017, Number 143)

"Here I stand": these are the famous words spoken by Martin Luther in front of the Diet of Worms in 1521. Questioned about his convictions as they had been outlined a few years before in the Ninety-five Theses, Luther stood firm on the truth of the Bible and its good news: sinners can be justified by Christ alone through faith alone. It was clear to all what he believed.

The Council of Trent (1545–62) was the official response of the Roman Catholic Church to the issues raised by the Protestant Reformation. By rejecting the tenets of the Protestant understanding of the gospel and declaring its proponents anathema, Trent endorsed the view that sinners could not be justified by faith alone; instead, Catholicism insisted on an ongoing journey of good works punctuated by the sacraments administered by the church. Where Trent stood was and is crystal-clear.

In recent decades, though, the situation has become blurred. The 1999 Joint Declaration on the Doctrine of Justification (JDDJ)[35]—signed by mainstream Lutherans and the Church of Rome—introduced ambiguities in language, juxtaposition of terms, and theological nuances that make it difficult to understand where the signatories stand in comparison to Luther's and Trent's viewpoints. After the declaration, Rome's position

---

34. De Chirico, "Vatican File 131."
35. De Chirico, "Vatican File 140."

on justification is harder to ascertain. This ambiguous context is Pope Francis's framework when he speaks on the topic.

The Essence of Human Existence?

In the ecumenical ceremony that commemorated the Reformation in Lund (Sweden) in 2016, Pope Francis made a perfunctory reference to the doctrine of justification. In a generally positive comment on Luther, the Pope argued that "the doctrine of justification expresses the essence of human existence before God,"[36] thus seeming to be in accord with what evangelicals might say on the doctrine. Recognizing justification as something essential is surely a pointer toward its primary importance for the Christian life. But notice that the Pope speaks of the essential role of justification in "human existence" in general, not just in the Christian life. The context of this statement does not restrict it to Christians, nor to believers in Christ or disciples of Jesus. The Pope is not referring to the essence of the Christian life but to human existence as a whole.

Here is the ambiguity. Does this mean that justification is essential for all human beings, regardless of whether or not they are Christians? Does it mean that justification is a constitutive component of life in general, a defining mark of the existence of all men and women? Does it mean that all those living a "human existence" are essentially justified? Certainly, this is not the meaning that either Luther or the Council of Trent gave to justification. For Luther, there was a sense in which justification could be defined as "the essence of human existence before God," with the caveat that this would refer only to those who have received the grace of God by faith alone. In other words, justification is the essence of the *Christian life*, not of human life in general.

On the surface, then, the Pope's comment on justification seems to be very biblical and indeed very Protestant. At a closer look, though, things are not as clear as they appear. While affirming the importance of justification, Pope Francis seems to confuse it with a universal property that all human beings share. If this is what the Pope meant, we are very far from what both Luther and Trent stood for. Indeed, we are very close to a universalist, all-embracing, humanistic "gospel" that betrays the biblical gospel of salvation in Christ alone by faith alone for those who repent and believe.

36. Francis, "Homily of His Holiness," 7.

Faithful to One's Own Conscience?

Arguably, what Pope Francis said in Lund on justification is generic and can be interpreted in different ways. It is not possible to say for sure that this is what he had in mind. Therefore it is important to look for other references to justification in his thought elsewhere and give him another chance to explain what he means.

Here is another quotation that is worth pondering. In his widely acclaimed 2013 exhortation *The Joy of the Gospel*,[37] the programmatic document of his pontificate, Francis writes that "non-Christians, by God's gracious initiative, when they are faithful to their own consciences, can live justified by the grace of God."[38] This section of the exhortation deals with ecumenical and interreligious dialogue in the context of mission. According to Pope Francis, non-Catholic Christians are already united in baptism,[39] Jews don't need to convert,[40] and with believing Muslims the way is "dialogue" because "together with us they adore the one and merciful God."[41] Other non-Christians are also "justified by the grace of God" and are linked to "the paschal mystery of Jesus Christ."[42]

Justification, according to the Pope, seems to be receivable by following one's own conscience. It is still "by God's gracious initiative" (although not necessarily by his grace alone), but it is no longer by faith—even by faith alone. It is through the conscience that men and women are linked to the paschal mystery of Jesus Christ, i.e., the work of Christ as it is reenacted at the Eucharist, the chief sacrament of the church. Faith in Jesus Christ is gone. The gospel appears to be not a message of salvation from God's judgment but instead a vehicle to access a fuller measure of a salvation that is already given to all mankind through the conscience. What about faith in Jesus Christ? What about his justice being credited to the sinner? Are, therefore, all human beings justified ultimately by following their conscience? By grace but not by faith?

At this point, it becomes clear that the Lund reference to justification being "the essence of human existence" was purposefully and

---

37. Francis, "Evangelii Gaudium."
38. Francis, "Evangelii Gaudium," 254.
39. Francis, "Evangelii Gaudium," 244.
40. Francis, "Evangelii Gaudium," 247.
41. Francis, "Evangelii Gaudium," 252; quotation of Holy See, "Lumen Gentium," 16.
42. Francis, "Evangelii Gaudium," 254.

intentionally designed to mean that justification defines everyone's life, not only that of the believing Christian. This reference in *The Joy of the Gospel* makes it abundantly clear that the Pope, while using the language of justification, has radically altered its meaning and made it synonymous with a universal existence embracing the whole of humanity. He is using the word in an ambiguous way, but a closer inspection reveals its non-biblical content.

Is Pope Francis's justification what Luther stood for? And, more decidedly, is this what the Bible teaches about justification? As we celebrate the five hundredth anniversary of the Protestant Reformation, with its recovery of the doctrine of justification by faith alone, we know where Luther stood and, in contrast, we know where Trent stood. Where does Pope Francis stand? He is saying radically different things. Therefore, before listing Pope Francis as a friend of the evangelical faith, we must understand what he is saying on his own terms. Beyond commonalities in the use of words, he belongs to a different world.

Eucharistic Hospitality? Between a Catholic "Yes" and a Roman "No" (July 1, 2018, Number 151)

"Can a non-Catholic be given the Eucharist in the Catholic Church?" When asked this question by a Lutheran woman married to a Catholic man during his 2015 visit to a Lutheran Church in Rome, Pope Francis gave a convoluted answer,[43] the gist which was "perhaps yes," "perhaps no," "I don't know," and "look at your conscience." This was a personal question highlighting a thornier and more general issue. In times of increased ecumenical friendliness, when reconciliation among Christians is often portrayed as a given, people are asking why that purported unity is stopped by the Catholic Church when it comes to the Eucharist. This is especially true in countries like Germany, where many couples are made up of Lutheran and Catholic spouses (and are therefore called "inter-confessional" families) who live together during the week and yet are divided on Sunday.

---

43. Francis, "Address (Christuskirche Parish)."

A Predominantly German Concern

This issue made headlines recently. In a nutshell, this is the background story: on February 22 of this year, the German Bishops' Conference announced the publication of a pastoral guide on the sharing of the Eucharist by inter-confessional couples, providing some openings for the admission of the Eucharist to non-Catholic partners. The proposed opening was not yet generalized—it would have had to be decided on a case-by-case basis by individual bishops. Controversy arose immediately. In the weeks that followed, seven German bishops addressed the Vatican to seek clarification on an initiative that they believed violated the unity of the church and undermined standard Catholic doctrine concerning the sacraments.

Pope Francis exhorted the German bishops to continue in dialogue and possibly reach a unanimous decision. A unanimous decision was not reached, and therefore the Congregation for the Doctrine of the Faith (i.e., the Vatican office responsible for doctrinal issues) made it clear with a letter endorsed by the Pope himself that the text presented by the Bishops' Conference raises considerable problems. The resulting decision: "The Holy Father has reached the conclusion that the document has not matured enough to be published."[44]

A Specifically "Roman" Response

In the Vatican letter, the two main reasons for stopping the process are listed as follows:

a. The question of admission to communion for evangelical Christians in inter-confessional marriages is an issue that touches on the faith of the Church and has significance for the universal Church.

b. This question has effects on ecumenical relations with other Churches and other ecclesial communities that are not to be underestimated.[45]

Here are some brief remarks. First, the Vatican reaffirms that, in dealing with the Eucharist, one touches on "the faith of the church," one of the main tenets of what Roman Catholicism stands for. Given the fact

---

44. Wooden, "Pope Francis Asks German Bishops," para. 3.
45. Montagna, "Pope Francis Blocks Proposal."

that the Eucharist is the "source and summit" of the Christian life,[46] the pastoral issues raised by inter-confessional couples need to be addressed within the dogmatic framework of Eucharistic doctrine, not at the expense of it nor even at the relaxing of its parameters. Rome can be very flexible and nuanced (i.e., "catholic") when it comes to discussing justification, conversion, mission, etc., but the Eucharist is what constitutes the sacramental self-understanding (i.e., Roman) of the Catholic Church and is one of its pillars. Rome could, therefore, sign the 1999 Joint Declaration on the Doctrine of Justification[47] with the Lutherans without changing its eucharistic doctrine and practices, thus showing flexibility on the one hand and rigidity on the other. In 2016, the Pope could speak words of reconciliation and unity at the joint commemoration of the Protestant Reformation[48] with the Lutherans in Lund (Sweden), but those kind words have no effect on the "real" unity around the Eucharistic table. Francis was very ecumenical then, and now he is very "Papal" and "Roman."

Secondly, the Vatican letter also shows concern that the openings envisioned by the German bishops would have an impact on other realities, such as couples formed by, say, Catholic and Methodist, Catholic and Anglican, or Catholic and Baptist spouses, thus paving the way to widespread and unwarranted Eucharistic hospitality. This "domino effect" is something that Rome is not prepared to accept if the doctrinal essence of the Catholic Eucharist is imperiled. Again, Rome can be very soft and adaptable in many respects, but the Eucharist is the core of its "Roman" identity, and so it is strictly safeguarded.

In spite of the fact that Francis is perhaps the most ecumenical Pope that the Catholic Church has ever had, for the time being, no Eucharistic hospitality is on the horizon. And this is not by accident. This decision reflects the nature of Roman Catholicism, which is catholic in attitude only insofar as the Roman structures are maintained and reinforced. Rather than submission to biblical teaching, it is the dialectic between the "Roman" and the "Catholic" poles that governs the self-understanding and the policies of the Roman Catholic Church.

---

46. Holy See, "Lumen Gentium."
47. Lutheran World Federation, "Joint Declaration."
48. De Chirico, "Vatican File 131."

9

Morals

Peter Didn't Have a Bank, Did He?
(April 15, 2014, Number 79)

"Peter didn't have a bank, did he?" Shortly after his election Pope Francis asked this rhetorical question. Peter did not have a bank, of course, but the Vatican does have a bank, and it's called the Institute for the Works of Religion (Istituto di Opere Religiose, IOR). Its operations have been well known by the public for its record of financial scandals over the last thirty years, often exchanging the "works of religion" for reckless banking. The peak of mismanagement and distrust was reached during Pope Benedict XVI's reign and was certainly one factor that contributed to his resignation. Pope Francis called for an investigation and formed a commission to help him make decisions concerning the future of IOR.

The Vatican Keeps the Bank

Francis has been working hard to bring a breath of fresh air both inside and outside the Vatican walls. In many ways he is a Pope who is trying to renew the system from the inside out by giving a personal example of a sober lifestyle full of religious enthusiasm. His statement about Peter and the bank raised some expectations that he would also touch on significant structural changes as far as the institutions of the Vatican are concerned.

Some commentators went as far as saying that the Pope was ready to shut the IOR down, thus opening a season of disestablishment of the political adds-on at the center of the Catholic Church.

Last week the decision was finally announced: the Pope confirms "the importance of the IOR's mission for the good of the Catholic Church, the Holy See and the Vatican City State."[1] In other words, the bank will continue to exist as is but with more transparent policies, all while its banking profile remains untouched. For all that Francis is changing, the financial system of the Vatican will not change. Peter did not have a bank but popes do, and despite of all his "missional" emphases, Francis is no different than his predecessors.

The Thick "Hardware" of the Vatican

What is becoming more and more apparent is that Francis is focusing on the "attitude" of the church, but he is hardly interested in revising the basic "structure" of the Vatican. His remarks on the outgoing "mission" of the church revolve around the "operative system" of the church but leave its "hardware" as it stands. The bank is only one piece of a much larger picture. The Vatican is a state, and the Pope is a political leader. The Vatican has a territory, an army, a diplomatic body, civil and penal courts, a prison, and a bank. It issues passports and participates in the international political scene as a sovereign state. The Roman Catholic Church is a church which operates with a state as its center. Its two-sided face is both religious and political.

The political "hardware" exchanges the church with a political body trusting in man's protection, rather than encouraging God's people to serve God's mission in God's way. The usual justifications for the "hardware" of the Vatican are that it is the result of its long history and it helps to serve the mission of the church. These are of course pragmatic reasons rather than biblical ones. Moreover, these justifications have caused the church to become something that goes ways beyond the way Jesus wanted the church to be. "Peter did not have a bank, did he?" was a promising start. In fact, the church does not need to own a bank, nor did Jesus ever say or even suggest that the church is supposed to be a political state at heart. Francis's subsequent reinforcement of the IOR shows that in the

---

1. Holy See, "Communique," para. 1.

system as it stands the reason of state prevails over biblical principles, even for a "revolutionary" Pope.

Where Is the Catholic Marriage Going? (March 21, 2014, Number 77)

The family is at the center of Vatican concerns and activities. A Synod of Bishops is due to meet this coming October and then again in 2015. These important gatherings will address the challenges that the Catholic Church is facing concerning the difficult task of maintaining its traditional teaching in relationship with today's realities, e.g., many broken families, many divorces, many "new forms" of family even amongst practicing Catholics, not to mention what happens in secular society. Of course, the issue is huge and multifaceted.

One has to bear in mind that the present-day Catholic concern focuses primarily on the sacramental dimension of the problem. In other words, what does the church do with the many Catholics who are divorced and are therefore excluded from the Eucharist? Should the church soften the ban? Should it make provision for more "pastoral" approaches that could allow their admission under certain circumstances? Ultimately, should the church change its rigid sacramental categories and come to terms more with the "human," frail, and transient aspects of marriage?

Kasper's Way Forward

In preparation for the Synod, Cardinal Walter Kasper was asked to introduce the discussion. His lecture (February 20) has stirred the internal debate and is polarizing opinions between reformists and traditionalists. The latest book by Kasper has a programmatic title—*Mercy: The Essence of the Gospel and the Key to Christian Life*[2]—and was publicly praised by Pope Francis as the best book he had personally read for some time. It is no chance that Francis has been insisting on "mercy" as the attitude that needs to characterize the church in all its dealings with people.

Kasper's lecture is a theological feast that blends biblical exegesis, patristic writings, canon law, and magisterial teaching throughout history. After revisiting all this against the background of the present-day crisis, Kasper envisages some possible "open doors" for those who have

---

2. Kasper, *Mercy*.

had failed marriages and whose conditions of life prevent them from any possible reconciliation. He makes references to the practice of the early church that used to readmit people who divorced in some specific cases and that is still kept in the Eastern Orthodox churches.

How can a well-established Roman Catholic teaching change? Kasper is aware of the newness of his proposal and suggests that the current situation is analogous to that of the Second Vatican Council on issues of ecumenism and religious freedom. The church had been against both issues for centuries, but "the Council opened doors" by deciding that a "development" should take place and therefore recognized religious freedom and embraced ecumenism. What should prevent the same from happening with the admission of divorced couples to the Eucharist?

The "Sacramental" Bottom Line

Non-Catholics may fail to understand the depth and the intensity of the problem. It is not so much about the indissolubility of marriage per se and the realization that divorce is part of the fallen world. It has to do with the sacramental theology that lies at the heart of the Roman Catholic religion. According to Catholic doctrine, marriage is a sacrament, i.e., an "efficacious sign of grace, instituted by Christ and entrusted to the Church, by which divine life is dispensed to us."[3] The essence of marriage is not a human covenant before God but a divinely appointed channel of grace that is administered by the church. "Normalizing" the failure means downplaying the sacrament and therefore shaking the sacramental institution that dispenses it. The fact that the discussion is also about the admission to the Eucharist, i.e., another sacrament, nay the chief sacrament, further amplifies the issue.

Any talk about marriage, divorce, remarriage and the Eucharist is a talk about the sacramental nature of the church. Kasper quoted the "development" that took place during Vatican II concerning ecumenism and religious freedom. This is true, but neither of those issues impinged on the sacramental structure of the church. They were sacramentally free developments, so to speak. Readmitting divorced people to the Eucharist surely has a "pastoral" dimension to it, but it is essentially a dogmatic issue in that it revolves around the identity of the sacrament, i.e., a divinely appointed efficacious sign of grace entrusted to the church.

3. *Catechism of the Catholic Church*, § 1131.

The Roman Church is built around the notion of the sacrament. It is a thoroughgoing sacramental institution. Cardinal Kasper (along with Pope Francis?) wants to emphasize the need for "mercy," but is he counting the dogmatic weight of such a move? A more "human" and "merciful" sacrament will mean a more humble and modest church, certainly not the Catholic Church that stemmed out of the Councils of Trent, Vatican I, and Vatican II.

Paul VI, A Beatus to Reassure the Perplexed Conservatives (October 24, 2014, Number 92)

The Roman Catholic Church has another *beatus*, or blessed one, whom the church recognizes as having the capacity to intercede on behalf of individuals who pray in his or her name. On October 19 Pope Francis beatified Giovanni Battista Montini (1897–1978), who became Paul VI (1963–78). A reserved and sophisticated intellectual, well versed in modern French literature and theology, Montini became Pope during the Second Vatican Council and was given the difficult task of concluding the council and handling the turbulent years that followed. Paul VI had to wrestle with the "spirit" of the council that for many inside and outside the church meant an adaptation to the radical changes that Western society was going through during the sixties. Not a natural leader, Montini embodied the drama of a church that had just reached out to the world with its optimistic words of appreciation but had to also retreat to more cautious attitudes.

The Timing of the Beatification

Paul VI's beatification comes at the end of a Synod that discussed the possibility of a repositioning of the Catholic Church on matters concerning the family. This gathering of bishops openly debated the readmission of divorced people to the Eucharist, as well as a more positive approach towards new forms of family, e.g., civil unions and homosexual relationships. No final decision was made, but the fact that certain changes were envisaged and even advocated for by some progressive voices made traditional hardliners fear that a significant paradigm shift was about to occur. Pope Francis called the Synod and appeared to welcome these changes, always insisting that the church needs to be open-minded. At the same time, though, he did not want to give the impression of entirely siding with those who want to re-discuss the Catholic moral assessment of different human relationships.

At this point the beatification of Paul VI comes to the fore. In Catholic circles Paul VI is always portrayed as the Pope who with his 1968 encyclical, *Humanae Vitae*, opposed contraceptive methods and stuck to traditional Catholic morality in the midst of the "sexual revolution."[4] It is feasible that Francis knew that the Synod could have broken new ground in the Catholic understanding of the family and that conservatives would have been upset by these changes. Yet he wanted Paul VI to be beatified at the end of the Synod to send the message that, on the one hand, the Catholic Church can update its vision and, on the other, honor its traditions. It is both a living and a traditional reality. Therefore, the timing of the beatification demonstrates the cleverness of an institution that is traditional without becoming traditionalist or, to put it differently, that changes without losing its heritage. The beatification was a reassuring message to that section of the Catholic constituency that felt puzzled and perplexed with the outcome of the Synod.

The *Lausanne Covenant* and *Evangelii Nuntiandi*

Paul VI should also be remembered for an interesting parallel to what was happening in the Evangelical Movement during his pontificate. In 1974, as a result of the Congress on World Evangelization convened by Billy Graham and shaped by John Stott, the *Lausanne Covenant* called the church to be engaged in evangelizing the world with the biblical gospel.[5] Up to that point the word "evangelization" and the vocabulary associated with it had been treated with suspicion in Roman Catholic circles due to its "protestant" usage and overtones. Mission and catechesis were more traditional and were the preferred terms for a long time.

It is only after Vatican II that the language of evangelization began to be used. It was actually Paul VI, with his 1975 apostolic exhortation *Evangelii Nuntiandi*,[6] that helped the Catholic Church to accept and use the word "evangelization," giving it a Catholic connotation. It is interesting that it was after Lausanne that the Catholic Church understood

---

4. Paul VI, "Humanae Vitae."
5. See Lausanne Movement, "Lausanne Covenant."
6. See Paul VI, "Evangelii Nuntiandi."

the importance of the term for its mission. While resisting the relaxation of Catholic morality, Paul VI caught the need for the church to explore the significance of evangelization. Now Pope Francis speaks more about "mission" than "evangelization" and wants the church to be "an open house" for all human beings, leaving aside the concerns that completely wore out Paul VI.

After the Synod on the Family, What? (December 1, 2015, Number 116)

Two sessions in two consecutive years (2014 and 2015). Two full months of intensive discussions among Catholic bishops gathered in Rome from around the world. Several controversies between conservative and progressive voices discussing the state of the family in today's world and, more specifically, whether or not to admit divorced and remarried Catholics to communion. Now that the Synod is over and its *Relatio Finalis* (*Final Report*) was voted and released,[7] it is finally possible to ask the question, What was its outcome?

Letter vs. Spirit

The answer comes from the mouth of the Pope himself. At the end of the Synod he delivered a speech that provides his interpretation of the document. A closer look reveals that his approach to the text is actually an overall framework of his papacy. Referring to a language used by Paul (e.g., 2 Cor 3:6) and Origen (e.g., *On First Principles* 4,2,4), the Pope pitted the "letter" against the "spirit" of any given official teaching.[8] One the one hand, the "letter" of canon law is rigid and protective; on the other, the "spirit" of the same teaching needs to be elastic and embracing.

According to Pope Francis, there are those who want to defend the "letter" in the attempt to safeguard its purity and definitiveness. If this happens, the attitude towards those who are outside of its boundaries becomes harsh and judgmental to the point of excluding those who do not fit its criteria. This is why he urged his church to implement the "spirit" of its traditional teaching in view of the fact that the church is for the

---

7. Synod of Bishops, "Final Report to Pope Francis."
8. Francis, "Address (Synod Hall)."

whole of humanity. In theory, the "spirit" does not annul the "letter" but practically it overcomes and eventually will supersede it.

Pitting the "letter" over against the "spirit" in this way has far-reaching consequences. In fact, distancing from the clear-cut "letter" and searching for the merciful "spirit" of traditional Catholic teaching seems to provide a fitting hermeneutic of the Pope's attitude as a whole. This tension helps come to terms with what he has been saying and doing so far. The Pope seems to think that the "letter" is a straitjacket to the mission of the church and needs to be replaced by the "spirit" of it.

Where Is the "Spirit" Leading?

The "spirit" requires a big-tent approach that paves the way for developments. Applying this "letter vs. spirit" dialectic to the issues at stake at the Synod, it is not surprising to read Pope Francis encouraging his church to address the divorced and remarried Catholics not according to the sheer "letter" of their traditional exclusion from communion but following the all-embracing "spirit" that will look for ways to include them on a case-by-case basis. Each confessor will have to decide, opening the possibility for different criteria to be used. The "letter" of the report does not openly speak about readmitting them to communion, but the "spirit" of the Synod endorsed by the Pope does indicate that there must be a way to achieve this. The text is at least ambiguous, and the "spirit" will eventually help to clarify it.

The final report only contains recommendations, but the final decisions will be made by the Pope himself in the form of an "exhortation," i.e., a written Papal document that becomes official teaching. Commenting on the outcomes of the Synod, the Italian senior journalist Eugenio Scalfari wrote that in a recent phone interview with the Pope, Francis told him, "The diverse opinion of the bishops is part of this modernity of the Church and of the diverse societies in which she operates, but the goal is the same, and for that which regards the admission of the divorced to the Sacraments, [it] confirms that this principle has been accepted by the Synod. This is [the] bottom line result: the *de facto* appraisals are entrusted to the confessors, but at the end of faster or slower paths, all the divorced who ask will be admitted."[9] According to this view, the "spirit" of a text may take time to become "letter" but nonetheless indicates the way

9. Rorate Cæli, "Bombshell."

forward and the expectations of the process. It is true that the Vatican Press Office said that Scalfari's report was not reliable,[10] but these alleged Papal statements are completely in line with the "spirit" with which Francis understands the results of the Synod. Moreover, the same "spirit" exactly reflects the pastoral approach that Archbishop Bergoglio followed in Buenos Aires before becoming Pope, when he applied very inclusive patterns of admission to communion. The way he is leading towards is the same way he is coming from.

Pope Francis is working hard to change the overall narrative of the Roman Catholic faith, wanting it to be marked by mercy and inclusivity at the expense of tradition and rules. The "letter vs. spirit" dialectic helps him to pursue his goal. Roman Catholicism has always played with this dialectic in order to account for its "development": the development of doctrines, traditions, and practices. Vatican II has been a monumental exercise of the "spirit vs. letter" tool. With its numerous ambiguities disseminated in the texts, it has given rise to an ongoing debate between conservative letter-bound interpreters and progressive spirit-evoking voices. The Synod is the latest instance of this lively confrontation that is intrinsic to a complex system like Roman Catholicism. What is new is that, whereas the previous Pope was a defender of the "letter" of the magisterial heritage, Pope Francis advocates for the "spirit" of it. We will see which "developments" this "spirit" will lead to.

The Decentralization of Catholic Bioethics in the Time of Francis (April 1, 2017, Number 135)

Since the beginnings of modern bioethics in the 1970s, the Roman Catholic Church has taken the hard line of defending human life from conception to natural death, protecting the concept of marriage between a man and a woman, and guarding the limits of scientific research within the parameters of human dignity. Not only did the Catholic Church strongly argue for traditional moral convictions over secular redefinitions of life and reproductive "rights," but it also put such issues at the forefront of its action in the public arena. Those days are over. With Pope Francis we are witnessing a shift in the posture of the Catholic Church as far as public debates on bioethics are concerned.

---

10. Pentin, "Fr. Lombardi."

A recent study by Luca Lo Sapio[11] documents the transition we are witnessing in the attempt by Pope Francis to invest the public voice of his church away from bioethical controversies, which clash with secular culture, and toward a number of social issues (e.g., immigration, poverty, the environment), which seem to resonate with the secular world.

What Happened to the Non-Negotiable Principles?

The differences between John Paul II and Benedict XVI, on the one hand, and Pope Francis, on the other, are becoming apparent. When dealing with bioethics, the two former popes often spoke of "non-negotiable principles" in staunchly defending the Catholic positions on life issues. Moreover, they wanted these principles to be at the heart of the church's agenda in the modern world no matter how much controversy they generated in public opinion.

The official teaching of the church on bioethical issues supported the strong stance taken by these popes. Encyclicals like *Veritatis Splendor*[12] and *Evangelium Vitae*,[13] exhortations like *Familiaris Consortio*,[14] and documents like *Donum Vitae*[15] and *Dignitatis Personae*[16] all univocally pointed to the clear-cut teaching of the church in dealing with abortion, euthanasia, genetic engineering, and the like and showed the willingness of the church to relentlessly advocate for it.

Francis's Detente Strategy

The outcome of such a posture was an ongoing and intense "culture war" against secular bioethics. The Roman Catholic Church has been considered a "militant" army fighting for the sacredness of life on the battlefield of bioethics. With Pope Francis, Rome has significantly changed strategy. The overarching narrative of the relationship with the world has been modified. One of his preferred metaphors for the church is that of a "field hospital for the wounded." The time of "culture wars" against the West

---

11. Lo Sapio, *Bioetica Cattolica*.
12. John Paul II, "Veritatis Splendor."
13. John Paul II, "Evangelium Vitae."
14. John Paul II, "Familiaris Consortio."
15. Holy See, "Instruction on the Respect for Human Life."
16. Holy See, "Instruction Dignitas Personae."

is over, and the task of the church is to convey forgiveness and mercy. The secular world is not to be fought against but cared for. From being the bulwark of the defense of life, the church is now a place where the wounds can be healed.

How does this narrative work in his pontificate in relation to bioethics? Lo Sapio convincingly argues that Francis has little interest for "doctrinal bioethics" and is more concerned with concrete and individual life situations. His approach is existentialist rather than theological (or content/truth-driven). He wants to be close to people, even at the cost of appearing to be less faithful to principles. He focuses on the primacy of conscience rather than the prescriptive nature of law. He wants to be a warm and welcoming pastor and has reservations over the dangers of being a cerebral and judgmental theologian. The center of gravity of his pontificate is forgiveness and mercy rather than truth and deontological ethics. His preference goes with the messiness of life rather than the neatness of systems. Rather than talking about embryos and stem cells, Francis often speaks of poor children, displaced people, and abandoned old people. Rather than condemning wrong actions, he looks for ways to go alongside people, notwithstanding the morality or immorality of their lives.

Francis is not outspokenly changing the traditional Roman Catholic positions on bioethics. The official teaching is still there. What he is doing is decentralizing its role, de-emphasizing its importance, and displacing its centrality. His overall strategy looks for ways to engage the secular West on grounds that are more palatable to it, while leaving the controversial issues to the side. Where this strategy will lead the Roman Church is difficult to know. Certainly, all those who looked to Rome for clarity, vigor, and proactive actions on bioethical issues may find it necessary to look elsewhere. Pope Francis has little time for them.

The Icing on the Cake of Pope Francis: The Blessing of Same-Sex Unions (December 20, 2023, Number 223)

The Roman Catholic Church officially opens for the blessing of same-sex unions. After much winking and hinting that this would be the outcome of the current pontificate, the official statement came out, putting pen to paper. "One should neither provide for nor promote a ritual for the blessings of couples in an irregular situation. At the same time, one should not prevent or prohibit the Church's closeness to people in every situation in which they might seek God's help through a simple blessing."[17] So says the declaration *Fiducia Supplicans* by the Congregation for the Doctrine of the Faith, with explicit approval from Pope Francis.

The die is cast. What had been a decade-long debate between those who hoped for this opening, considering it an advancement of Catholic morality toward greater inclusiveness, and those who saw it as a sign of Roman Catholicism's irreversible ruin is now resolved. With a "declaration" of high hierarchical value in the authority of Vatican pronouncements (observers note that the Congregation's last statement was Joseph Ratzinger's *Dominus Iesus*[18] dating back to 2000), Roman Catholicism is now officially in favor of blessing gay unions, as are many liberal Protestant churches around the world.

It all began with "who am I to judge?"[19] to "all, all, all"[20] at the Lisbon Youth Day (2023). The trajectory was clear from the start: Pope Francis's inclusive, embracing, "Catholic" afflatus and his distance from positions that he calls "clerical" and "backwardism" but that are also part of the doctrinal baggage of Roman Catholicism. In between are many steps, not the least of which is the appointment of trusted Argentine theologian Víctor Manuel Fernández as Prefect of the Congregation for the Doctrine of the Faith,[21] who signed the declaration. Now Francis has his back covered, even within the Vatican's "official" theology. Indeed, *Fiducia Supplicans* openly contradicts another 2021 document of the same congregation, when Cardinal Ladaria was Prefect. Then, responding to "doubts" precisely about the possibility of blessing same-sex unions, the Vatican had still responded with a (somewhat) clear "no." Two years later, however, the answer is "yes." Evidently, the evolution toward Roman Catholic inclusion has accelerated further.

Of course: the Vatican says that there is no question of recognizing gay unions as marriage, that Catholic doctrine does not change, that the blessing is not a sacrament but a sacramental . . . all secondary doctrinal clarifications that do not modify the main point. The Roman Catholic Church today officially offers blessing to same-sex couples: something,

17. Francis, "Fiducia Supplicans," 38.
18. Congregation for the Doctrine of the Faith, *Dominus Iesus*.
19. De Chirico, "Vatican File 93."
20. Francis, "Address (Lisbon)."
21. De Chirico, "Vatican File 93."

moreover, already in place (and for years) in Roman Catholic churches in many European (e.g., Germany and Belgium) and Latin American (e.g., Argentina) countries.

Roman Catholics must ask themselves whether *Fiducia Supplicans* is consistent with the previous magisterium or is in open conflict with it. By its nature, Roman Catholicism is constantly on the move to possibly encompass the whole world within the institutional-sacramental structures of its Roman system. Not being hinged on and guided by the biblical gospel, Roman Catholicism fluctuates between asserting its Roman power and accentuating its Catholic embrace. In *Dominus Iesus* the Vatican restated its Roman understanding of the Catholic Church being the only and true church.[22] With *Fiducia supplicans*, the Vatican opens its Catholic embrace to same-sex couples.[23]

Fiducia supplicans is the icing on the cake of his pontificate. The main ingredients of Francis's Jesuit recipe have been two: we are "all brothers"[24] (Christians, non-Christians, atheists, and agnostics—everyone), and the Catholic Church is the "field hospital" for all. Now, there is also the icing on the cake.

Fiducia Supplicans is in open contrast to biblical teaching. Pope Francis is a shrewd Roman Catholic Jesuit who leads his church toward the most "catholic" form it has ever had but not toward the gospel of Jesus Christ.

---

22. Holy See, "Dominus Iesus."
23. Francis, "Fiducia Supplicans."
24. De Chirico, "Vatican File 181."

10

Miscellaneous

The New Saints and Pope Francis
(April 5, 2014, Number 78)

ON APRIL 27, TWO canonizations will take place in Rome. Two 20th-century popes will be proclaimed "saints" by the Catholic Church. John XXIII (Angelo Roncalli 1881–1963) and John Paul II (Karol Wojtyła 1920–2005) will be included in the canon, or list, of recognized saints. According to the *Catechism of the Catholic Church*, "By *canonizing* some of the faithful, i.e., by solemnly proclaiming that they practiced heroic virtue and lived in fidelity to God's grace, the Church recognizes the power of the Spirit of holiness within her and sustains the hope of believers by proposing the saints to them as models and intercessors."[1]

John XXIII and John Paul II were the two major popes of the last century. It was John XXIII who convened the Second Vatican Council, the most significant event in contemporary Roman Catholic history. Then it was John Paul II who re-launched Catholicism as a global player, after decades, if not centuries, of prevailing self-defensiveness. The fact that the church is canonizing the two together on the same day communicates a clear message concerning the present Pope. In a sense Francis wants to be identified with the "pastoral" afflatus of John XXIII while at the same time following the dynamism of John Paul II.

---

1. *Catechism of the Catholic Church*, 828.

The Pastor Pope

Perhaps the most defining mark of John XXIII was the "pastoral" tone of his pontificate. Gentle in spirit, meek in manners, approachable by the people, Roncalli was the first modern Pope to not be perceived as a king but instead as a pastor. His language was simple, and his human frame was humble. By no surprise, his main achievement, i.e., Vatican II, was meant to be a "pastoral" council. John XXIII did not want a rigidly "doctrinal" church that would judge the mistakes of the world but a loving "mother" who would offer protection and understanding for all.

Francis too is perceived as a "pastoral" Pope. Unlike his predecessor, the theologian Ratzinger, Francis continues to insist on the need for a change of attitude, leaving the doctrinal outlook of the church in the background of what he says. His main message is centered around his pastoral sensitivity. Like John XXIII, Francis wants to embrace the world as it is. He does not want to change any doctrine but wishes to draw nearer to the world. It is clear that John XXIII's shadow is behind Francis's way of interpreting his pontificate.

"To" and "From" the Ends of the Earth

John Paul II, however, is a more complex figure. In his long pontificate, this Pope travelled to the ends of the earth to take a strong Catholic identity and his energetic leadership to a polarized world (East/West and North/South). From the center of Catholicism, John Paul II went to the geographical peripheries to encourage Catholic renewal everywhere. Now, with the Argentinian Francis, the Pope who comes from the ends of the world, the church travels back to Rome to bring the enthusiasm, the energy, and the concerns of the peripheries. Francis is reversing John Paul II's journey. The direction of the movement is different (from periphery to center), but the energy that he is investing is similar. John Paul II reignited the Roman catholicity inside out, Francis is stirring the Catholic "mission" outside in. The common thread between the two is that something is moving in a significant way.

The canonizations of John XXIII and John Paul II will focus on two past popes, but they will also speak of the present Pope. The pastoral catholicity of the former and the shaking and shaping ability of the latter are marks of Pope Francis. In some important respects Francis is reflected in both of these predecessors, and this event will be a further opportunity to stress this identification.

"When Halfway Through the Journey of Our Life." Dante Between the Bible and Medieval Roman Catholicism (May 1, 2021, Number 188)

On the occasion of the seven hundredth anniversary of Dante Alighieri (1265–1321) there are several initiatives taking place around the world to celebrate this great medieval poet. Among them, Pope Francis wrote an apostolic letter to celebrate Dante as "prophet of hope and poet of mercy."[2] The magnitude of Dante's significance for Western civilization is too extensive to be properly handled in a short article and would deserve specific expertise that I have only in part. Here the focus will be to sample Dante's relationship with the Bible in the Comedy—his most known work—and to see how the Bible shapes its overall theological orientation. As Dante was led by Virgil (through the Inferno and Purgatory) and by Beatrice (through Paradise), in my journey I will be led by Giuseppe Ledda, *La Bibbia di Dante*,[3] since on my own I would get lost in the "dark forest" given the complexity of the task. Of course, the theological evaluations will be mine.

Where to start talking about the influence of the Bible on Dante? Perhaps making reference to numbers. There are about a thousand references to the Bible present in the Comedy. Sometimes they are direct quotations from the Latin Vulgate or in vernacular translations provided by Dante himself; other times they are allusions to characters or episodes of the biblical story intertwined in the events of the poem. The Bible is pervasively present and is one of the texts from which Dante drew constant inspiration. Scripture is a constitutive element of his religious imagery.

Bible Reminiscences at the Beginning of the Comedy

The beginning of the Comedy is universally known: "When half way through the journey of our life."[4] Dante immediately recalls a biblical text such as Ps 90:10. The fact that he does not speak only of his (Dante's) life

---

2. Piro, "Pope Francis Celebrates Dante."
3. See Ledda, *Bibbia di Dante*.
4. Dante, *Inferno*, I, 11.

but of "our life" (of all humanity) is connected to the verse of Ps of Moses according to which "the years of our life are seventy." For this reason, scholars believe that Dante was thirty-five years old when he wrote the Comedy. The point is that in calculating the duration of life, Dante uses a biblical parameter: seventy years. Furthermore, the first verses of Inferno speak of life as a "path." That of the journey is a biblical metaphor to describe life. Dante uses it to talk about his life and that of all humanity.

Beyond these indirect references, in the incipit there is a clear allusion, almost a reworking, of Isa 38:10, in which King Hezekiah, after being healed, writes, "In the middle of my days I must depart." As Hezekiah escaped death by being allowed to continue living, so Dante passes through a "forest dark" but comes out of it when he finds himself in front of an illuminated hill.

Dante had lost the "path which led aright." Within the metaphor of the journey, the "path" has very strong resonances in the Old Testament (e.g., the path of the righteous, Ps 1) and in the New Testament (Jesus as the only way, John 14:6). In the first verses Dante acknowledges that he has lost his way and that he has gone into a dark forest in sin and backsliding.

Arriving in front of the illuminated hill,[5] he looks up, echoing Ps 121:1, which says, "I lift my eyes to the hills, from where does my help come?" The gesture of looking up is the beginning of a change in the midst of a trial. Looking up, man can find the light of God to get out of the darkness of sin.

Starting the climb up the hill, Dante's journey is interrupted by the presence of three ferocious animals: a leopard, a lion, and a wolf.[6] For the poet they are representations of evil that obstruct the path and try to prevent it. Although not in the same order, they are the same animals found in Jer 5:6. Dante attributes to these animals a symbolic meaning of deadly sins, but the imagery from which the animal representation is drawn comes from the Bible.

Obstructed by the fairs, Dante rolls down and sees a figure with indistinct outlines to whom he asks for help with the words "have pity on me."[7] The reader of the Bible immediately recognizes the quotation from Ps 51:1: "Have mercy on me, O God," the most famous penitential psalm of the collection. It is the cry of the sinner who, in contrition and

---

5. Dante, *Inferno*, I, 16–18
6. Dante, *Inferno*, I, 31–54
7. Dante, *Inferno*, I, 65

repentance, invokes divine mercy to be forgiven. Dante will repeat the same quotation from Ps 51 in *Paradise* XXXII, 10–12. David, who exclaims that request for help from the Lord, becomes for Dante a model of a repentant sinner to inspire him on his journey as a penitent sinner.

As can be seen from these hints, from the first verses of the Comedy, it is clear that Dante's imagination is significantly shaped by biblical elements. Whether or not his overall vision is biblical is another matter: certainly it is steeped in direct and indirect references to the Bible, but this is not in itself a guarantee that his poem reflects a biblically oriented journey. Its biblical references are mediated by a medieval theology and spirituality which, although rich in biblical ideas, is at the same time marked by other points of reference far from Scripture.

Biblical Themes and Imagery in the Inferno

The Comedy is a journey into the realms of the afterlife. Dante imagines the world beyond death and, to do so, draws on classical and biblical sources in an original mix of settings and encounters. His journey starts from hell (Inferno), which is a biblically attested space even if he imagines it as a chasm in the shape of an inverted cone, a shape that has no biblical origin.

In the first canto of Inferno, Virgil explains to Dante that, having come out of the dark forest, one cannot climb the hill of happiness, except by taking another path through the kingdoms of the afterlife. It was forbidden to human beings, except for Aeneas (in the Aeneid) and Paul (according to an interpretation of 2 Cor 12:2–4, which in reality does not speak of hell but of heaven). In this double inspiration (classical and biblical), we find the sources of Dante's thought: on the one hand, the classical Greco-Roman heritage, and on the other, the biblical one interpreted according to the canons of medieval Christianity. Dante does not feel worthy to retrace the footsteps of these great characters of the past and objects by saying, "I'm not Aeneas, nor yet Paul am."[8] In the perplexity of his ability to face the journey, Dante echoes the doubt that Moses had when he said to God, "Who am I that I should go to Pharaoh?" (Exod 3:11).

Dante's Inferno is preceded by "limbo," a place not attested in the canonical gospels but in the apocryphal Gospel of Nicodemus. In this place that is neither hellish nor heavenly, he meets the virtuous non-Christians

---

8. Dante, *Inferno*, II, 32

who lived before Christianity. There he finds a string of biblical characters from the Old Testament: Adam, Abel, Noah, Moses, Abraham, David, Jacob, and others. Here Dante, while showing great familiarity with the biblical text, differs substantially from the Bible, which instead considers these believers before Christ as belonging to the great cloud of witnesses (Heb 12) and therefore destined for Paradise. A sacramental interpretation of baptism as necessary for salvation (and which these Old Testament believers had not received) makes Dante think that the saints of the Old Testament are not truly saved. This theology is outside of biblical teaching and is within medieval Roman Catholicism.

Entering hell, Dante shows off a poetic imagination imbued with many biblical elements. At canto XIX he meets the "simoniacs," churchmen who take their name from Simon, the magician who wanted to buy the power of God with money (Acts 8:20–21). The simoniacal church is seen by Dante as fornicating with kings[9] evoking the image of the "harlot" of Rev 17:1–8. The poet shows that he is imbued with Roman Catholicism in his theological vision but is at the same time very "free" to criticize the ecclesiastical institution, which he sees as guilty of serious compromises.

Continuing on his journey to hell, Dante meets other biblical characters such as Caiafa,[10] the high priest who condemned Jesus. At canto XXXIV there is Lucifer holding Judas—the traitor of Jesus—in his mouth. The pains that Dante assigns to each person is a parody of his sin, and their execution makes use of the technique of retaliation: what they caused in life with their sins, they now receive in return in their infernal existence.

Summing up, the punishment of hell seems to be a retribution for the evil works committed in life and is proportionated to the gravity of the same. When Dante speaks of divine grace, he associates it with sacramental grace and dilutes it in a view of the Christian life still encrusted with a work-based gospel. Far away is the biblical gospel of grace received by Christ alone by faith alone, which was preached by the apostolic church and which would be fully rediscovered by the Protestant Reformation three centuries after Dante.

---

9. Dante, *Inferno*, XIX, 108
10. Dante, *Inferno*, XXIII, 109–26

What Does Purgatory Have to Do With the Bible?

The second canticle of the Comedy is Purgatory. Through Dante's poetry this place (which is the fruit of the Roman Catholic religious imagination) has taken on a universally recognized literary guise. Purgatory is a child of medieval theology that broke off from the biblical vision of the afterlife, which added a state to that of the blessing of heaven for believers and the reprobation of hell for non-believers and adapted it to the need to have an "intermediate" place between hell and heaven. For the historian Jacques Le Goff, Dante's Purgatory is a "middle way placed at an unequal distance between the two extremes, which extends towards Paradise."[11]

In the prevailing conception of the Middle Ages (and which Dante makes his own in the Comedy), salvation is not a gift that is received by faith alone according to the imputed righteousness of Jesus Christ. Salvation for Dante is a path of continuous purification which, once earthly life is ended, continues in Purgatory and then finally reaches its completion in Paradise. Except for the saints (the heroes of the faith), for the "normal" Christians salvation is always "incomplete." As the readers of the Bible know, the gospel of Jesus Christ gives the believer a certainty which is not the fruit of personal arrogance but the result of the completeness of the Savior's work received by faith. Evidently, with his vision of Purgatory, Dante does not know the benefits of justification by faith based solely on the work of Christ alone: for this reason he must provide for an otherworldly "middle ground" through which Christians pass in order to be purified. For Dante, salvation is a mountain to be climbed from below with a view to progressive sanctification, not a divine declaration on the penitent sinner which clothes him with the righteousness of Jesus Christ.

One of the biblical metaphors that Dante uses in Purgatory to describe the Christian life is that of the exodus: life is a slavery from which one is liberated through a journey of purification. To underline the parallel between life and the exodus, it is no coincidence that the souls destined for Purgatory sing Ps 114:1, "When Israel went out from Egypt,"[12] evoking the idea that it is a journey back to God by us pilgrims.[13] Again, Dante mixes biblical elements with themes and trajectories present in medieval Christianity. They are more dependent on the theology of the time based on a conception of salvation by works and through penance

---

11. Le Goff, *Birth of Purgatory*, 401.
12. Dante, *Purgatory*, II, 46–48.
13. Dante, *Purgatory*, II, 63.

than on the biblical message centered on the perfect righteousness of Christ freely given to the believing sinner.

Dante's Purgatory has a mountain shape divided into seven terraces. In each of them the souls are purged of one of the seven deadly sins: pride, envy, anger, sloth, greed, gluttony, and lust. Only after they are purified will they be admitted to heaven. In this path of purification, in addition to abandoning vices, souls will have to embrace the Christian virtues that Dante identifies in the beatitudes contained in the Sermon on the Mount (Matt 5:1–12): humility, merciful love, meekness, diligence, detachment from earthly goods, temperance, and chastity. For Dante, each of these Christian virtues finds its supreme realization in Mary. The evangelical episodes of her life are considered illustrations of Mary's virtues that souls must learn. Mary is "humbler and loftier than any creature."[14] Also in this case, in line with the Roman Catholic Mariology of the Middle Ages, Mary is considered "more than a creature," endowed with the highest level of Christian virtues and the model par excellence of Christian life. It is true that Dante also recalls other biblical characters such as King David (humility), Stephen (meekness), and Daniel and John the Baptist (temperance). However, Mary surpasses everyone in that she eminently embodies the virtues/beatitudes that Jesus Christ proclaimed in the Sermon on the Mount. Even in this pervasive Mariology, Dante is more of a spiritual and cultural child of his time than a believer whose faith is shaped by the Bible.

The (Un)Biblical Paradise

After crossing the seven terraces of Purgatory, Dante and Virgil arrive in the earthly Paradise, which is located on the top of the mountain of Purgatory. Here Virgil, who has been the guide up to now, disappears, and Beatrice appears. She will accompany Dante on the remaining journey. Beatrice reflects divine beauty and is full of christological reminiscences, a sort of *alter Christus* (i.e., another Christ). She personifies the love that saves and encourages the poet to penance. In fact, in order to proceed Dante must undergo a further purification rite to become worthy to ascend to heaven. In the procession in which Dante takes part, he refers to elements of the books of Revelation and Ezekiel, as well as being inspired

---

14. Dante, *Purgatory*, XXXIII, 2.

by the story of the transfiguration in which the apostles taste an anticipation of the glory of Christ and are somehow overwhelmed by it.

Entering Paradise, Dante still refers to classical and biblical motifs, in this case from the poet Ovid and from the apostle Paul. In particular, it is Paul's abduction to third heaven that serves as a model for Dante. The intertwining of pagan and Judeo-Christian literature provides for the poet the categories within which he "sees," "feels," and experiences Paradise. Dante's poetics were born at the confluence of these currents (classical and biblical). He blended them together with his literary genius in the context of his medieval theological vision.

Arriving at the sky of the stars, Dante meets Peter, James, and John, who examine him respectively on the three theological virtues: faith, hope, and love. Once again, Dante must demonstrate that he knows and possesses these virtues. In heaven, one is not welcomed for the merits of Christ on the basis of the imputation to the sinner of his virtues received by faith alone but, in line with Roman Catholic theology, on the basis of a journey of sanctification that passes through successive stages in which one must demonstrate something infused and grown in himself. The canticle of Paradise is imbued with biblical references and Christian ideas, but the theological framework is not evangelical. Salvation is a mountain to climb and a state to deserve, not a confident response of faith to a gift already accomplished by Jesus Christ. In Dante sanctification effectively swallows and in the end cancels justification.

Towards the end of Paradise, Dante reaches a peak of Marian devotion, further demonstrating the profound but spurious character of the biblical influence on his poem. Mary is defined as "the face which to the Christ is most resemblant."[15] The climax is a Marian prayer placed in the mouth of Bernard of Clairvaux (a father of the medieval church much loved by Dante), which opens with the famous verses "O Virgin Mother, Daughter of thy Son, humbler and loftier than any creature."[16] The vision of Mary is followed by that of God, the unitary principle that gives meaning to the chaos of the universe, the divine Triunity and a special mention of the Son, who is seen in the image of a human being. A sort of Trinitarian architecture is also witnessed in Dante's choice to write in triplets, to write three canticles, each of which is composed of thirty-three chants,

---

15. Dante, *Paradise*, XXXII, 85–86.
16. Dante, *Paradise*, XXXIII, 1–2.

which also evoke the years of the life of Jesus Christ (even if Inferno, in reality, has an extra song that serves as a preface to the Comedy).

To the vision of God at the end of Paradise, language is placed in front of its limits, and Dante concludes by referring to theology as "high imagining," a lofty knowledge that cannot but resort to poetry in the face of the unspeakable. Compared to contemporary scholastic trends aimed at rationalizing or intellectualizing the discourse on God, Dante presents a poetic theology in which truth and beauty, proclaimed and experienced, go together.

The Comedy is a masterpiece that, in its extraordinary richness and complexity, reflects a culture mixed with those ingredients that made Italian culture in particular what it is: ingeniously absorbed by a religiosity that mixes the Bible and pagan culture, artistically interwoven into a spirituality that does not understand the gospel as a gift from God received by faith alone, strongly attracted to the figure of the "mother" (Mary) and the "woman" (Beatrice) in whom to look for love. It is this comedy that, from Dante onwards, is the canvas of Italian life.

"Go to Thomas!" Who Will Follow the Pope's Invitation? (November 1, 2021, Number 207)

Nothing could be more explicit: "Go to Thomas!" This warm invitation was issued by Pope Francis to participants of the International Thomistic Congress (September 21–24)[17] during an audience at the Vatican. In his address,[18] the Pope extolled the thought of Thomas Aquinas (1225–74) as a sure guide for Roman Catholic faith and a fruitful relationship with culture. Citing Paul VI[19] and John Paul II,[20] who had magnified the importance of Thomas's thought for the contemporary Roman church, Francis stood in the wake of recent popes in emphasizing superlative appreciation for the figure of Thomas while adding his own.

This is nothing new. For centuries, Roman Catholicism has regarded Thomas Aquinas as its champion. His voice is often considered the highest, deepest, and most complete of Roman Catholic thought and belief.

---

17. See Angelicum Thomistic Institute, "Eleventh International Thomistic Congress."
18. Francis, "Discorso del Santo Padre Francesco."
19. Paul VI, "Lumen Ecclesiae."
20. John Paul II, "Fides et Ratio."

Canonized by John XXII as early as 1323, he was proclaimed a doctor of the church by Pius V in 1567 to be the premier Roman Catholic theologian whose thinking would defeat the Protestant Reformation. During the Council of Trent, the *Summa theologica*[21] was symbolically placed next to the Bible as a testament to its primary importance in formulating the Tridentine decrees and canons against justification by faith alone and other Protestant doctrines. In the seventeenth century, he was considered the defender of the Roman Catholic theological system by Robert Bellarmine (1542–1621),[22] the greatest anti-Protestant controversialist who influenced many generations of Catholic apologists over the centuries. In 1879 Pope Leo XIII issued the encyclical *Aeterni patris*,[23] in which he pointed to Thomas as the highest expression of philosophical and theological science. The Second Vatican Council (1962–65) stipulated that the formation of priests should have Thomas as the supreme guide in their studies: "The students should learn to penetrate them (i.e., the mysteries of salvation) more deeply with the help of speculation, under the guidance of St. Thomas, and to perceive their interconnections."[24] Of recent popes, this has already been mentioned. Considering this, what could Pope Francis say but "go to Thomas!"

Francis indicated not only the need to study Thomas but also to "contemplate" the master before approaching his thought. Thus, to the cognitive and intellectual dimension, he added a mystical one. In this way, he caused Thomas, already a theologian imbued with wisdom and asceticism, to be seen as even more Roman Catholic. This mix best represents the interweaving of the intellectual and contemplative traditions proper to Roman Catholicism.

The International Congress had the exploration of the resources of Thomist thought in today's context as its theme. Thomism is not just a medieval stream of thought, but a system that is both solid and elastic at the same time. All seasons of Roman Catholicism have found it inspiring for the diverse challenges facing the Church of Rome, including the Reformation first, the Enlightenment project second, and now postmodernity. As a result of the Congress, we will continue to hear more about Thomas and Thomism, not only in historical theology and philosophy

21. De Chirico, "Vatican File 189."
22. De Chirico, "Bellarmine's Critique."
23. Leo XIII, "Aeterni Patris."
24. Second Vatican Council, "Optatam Totius," 17

but also in other fields of knowledge that were once far from previous interpretative traditions of Thomas.

In recent years, we have witnessed a growing fascination with Thomas Aquinas and Thomism by evangelical theologians, especially coming from the North American context. They seem to be attracted to the "great tradition" he represents. This phenomenon should be studied because it signals the existence of internal movements within evangelical theological circles. Protestant theology of the 16th and 17th centuries had a critical view of Thomas. In a sense, Thomas could not be avoided, given his stature and importance for theology, but he was read with selective and theologically adult eyes. Then, for various reasons, there has been a certain neglect not only of Thomas but with pre-Reformation historical theology as a whole. Today, in the face of the pressures coming from secularization and the identity crisis felt in some evangelical quarters, Thomas is perceived as a bulwark of "traditional" theology that needs to be urgently recovered. It is often overlooked that Roman Catholicism has considered Thomas as its champion in its anti-Reformation stance and also in its subsequent anti-biblical developments, such as the 1950 Marian dogma of the bodily ascension of Mary. Rome considers Thomas as the quintessentially Roman Catholic theologian and thinker.

"Go to Thomas!" is an invitation that even a growing number of practitioners of evangelical theology would take up. The point is not to uncritically study or absolutely avoid Thomas but rather to provide the theological map with which one approaches him. It is necessary to develop an evangelical map of Thomas Aquinas. If Rome considers Thomas its chief architect, can evangelical theology approach him without understanding that Thomas stands behind everything Roman Catholicism believes and practices?

11

Future Impact and Legacy

Secular Perceptions of Pope Francis
(January 6, 2014, Number 72)

WHAT OTHERS UNDERSTAND IS an important clue about what we are saying to them. It is true that the filter of the media is highly intoxicated and that it is able to manipulate everything according to its own interests. Interviews and speeches can be arranged by the media in such a way that they become something different than their original intentions and contents. However, what people are taking in is a combination both of what they want to hear and of what we allow them to hear.

In assessing the first months of Francis's pontificate, the secular media continues to communicate what their perception is concerning what the Pope has said up to this point. On the one hand there is a widespread fascination about his frugal style, charming personality, and engaging language. On the other, there is an appreciation for his "innovative" theology or lack of insistence on traditional tenets of Roman Catholic doctrine. Two recent comments about Francis's theology deserve some attention.

The Rejection of Church Dogma

Interestingly, on November 20, when *Time* initially named Francis as a candidate for the "Man of the Year" award, the website noted that he was nominated for his "rejection of church dogma." It was only after some pushback from the tweeting world that *Time* changed the description to read "rejection of luxury." In truth, Francis has never jettisoned any church dogma, but the perception of the secular media is worth considering. "Rejecting church dogma" is a gross overstatement, but deemphasizing, marginalizing, and putting doctrine in the background perhaps gets closer to the point. Francis is perceived as a Pope from whom dogma is less important than attitude, mercy more relevant than truth, and generosity of spirit more apt than the affirmation of traditional belief. Some of his statements (e.g., "Proselytism is a solemn non-sense," "Who am I to judge a homosexual person?," "Everyone has his own idea of good and evil and must choose to follow the good and fight evil as he conceives them") have become slogans with which secular people resonate well. They hardly represent a Christian view, and it is precisely for this reason that secularists find Francis's "gospel" a message that is far from church dogma. It is not an open rejection of it, but it is understood as being a significant distancing away from it.

After the dogmatic Benedict XVI, Francis is viewed as a less rigid Pope in terms of doctrine. He is seen as being more relaxed on defending the theological identity of his church and more committed to focusing on non-divisive issues. Roman Catholics should ask themselves whether him being considered for the "Man of the Year" honor is a real achievement or instead a matter that should raise concern.

The Abolition of Sin

There is yet another comment that reflects the widespread interpretations of Pope Bergoglio. The editor of the Italian newspaper *La Repubblica*, Eugenio Scalfari, who had met with Francis and published their conversation a couple of months ago, wrote an article (December 29) in which he argues that the greatest achievement of the Pope so far is that he has practically abandoned the traditional doctrine of sin. "He has *de facto* abolished sin." He is not saying that Francis has openly declared that the official Roman Catholic theology is wrong on its teaching on sin, rather he suggests that Francis sees mercy standing over sin to the point of practically overshadowing it and making it irrelevant. When he speaks about sin, he does so in reference to himself ("I am a sinner") or to the structural aspects of sin (e.g., the oppression of the poor) but never implying the idea of radical separation from God and divine judgement. He emphasizes that God is present in every person, and in so doing he downplays the tragic reality of sin. It is a *de facto* abolition.

The secularists applaud this development because they generally think that "sin" is the greatest obstacle for the modern conscience in coming to terms with the Christian religion. Whether or not this is a fair assessment of the Pope's views remains to be seen. It is, however, a matter of fact that his popularity with the media is based on the perception that the Pope is a dogmatically fluid and open-ended Christian leader. Is this an issue entirely dependent on the manipulation of the media or is it also a sign that Francis is actually saying confusing and misleading things? We are now back to where we started, i.e., what others understand is an important clue about what we are saying to them.

What Happens If Catholics Think the Pope Is a Heretic? (December 1, 2017, Number 144)

Roman Catholics as individuals and groups may have different opinions about the Pope. After all, the Church of Rome is not a monolith, and even popes polarize the assessments of the Catholic people. But what happens when negative voices become more frequent, more outspoken, more radical in their criticism, as seems to be the case in recent months? While public opinion is still heavily influenced by the overall positive image that Francis has and continues to consider him as a kind of "hero," within Catholic circles the "wait-and-see" approach toward some awkward aspects of his teaching is coming to an end. Groups of intellectuals, priests, and even cardinals are voicing their growing embarrassment and are doing it publicly and with a severe tone. In raising their concerns, what they point to are not some peripheral elements but important matters of doctrine. The irony is that the one who is supposed to guard the Roman Catholic deposit of faith is charged with allegations of introducing confusion, if not heresy.

Coming to Terms with Recent Criticism

There are at least three criticisms against Pope Francis that are worth considering. Let's briefly look at them chronologically.

In September 2016, four cardinals (two of whom have recently died) sent to the Pope five questions[1] (in Latin "dubia," doubts) concerning the interpretation of key parts of his summary document on the synod on the family, *Amoris lætitia*.[2] In the explanatory note, they give voice to the "grave disorientation and great confusion" that exist in the Catholic community. According to the cardinals, the contrasting interpretations of the Papal text arise from its ambiguity and the apparent contradictions with previous official teaching on the readmission of divorced people to the Eucharist. Although they asked the Pope to clear any ambiguity, Francis never responded and perhaps will never do so. Their doubts will remain unanswered.

In July 2017, more than two hundred Catholic priests and intellectuals from around the world wrote "a filial correction concerning the propagation of heresies"[3] to the Pope, thus elevating the tone of the criticism to the denouncing of doctrinal deviations. Their observations were no longer questions but real corrections made to the teaching of the Pope. The word "heresy" was evoked in looking at the demise of the traditional teaching on marriage and the sacraments, as they see happening, and severely threatening the future credibility of their church.

At the end of July then, Father Thomas Weinandy, a capuchin priest and former chief of staff for the U.S. Bishops' Committee on Doctrine and a current member of the Vatican's International Theological Commission, made public a letter sent to the Pope. In it, he argued that "a chronic confusion seems to mark your pontificate obscured by the ambiguity of your words and actions. This fosters within the faithful a growing unease. It compromises their capacity for love, joy and peace."[4] Moreover, Weinandy charges Francis with "demeaning" the importance of doctrine, appointing bishops who "scandalize" believers with dubious "teaching and pastoral practice," giving prelates who object the impression they will be "marginalized or worse" if they speak out, and causing faithful Catholics to "lose confidence in their supreme shepherd." This is hard language coming from a mainstream Roman Catholic theologian who has spent the whole of his life in the service of his church and the Vatican. What is happening in the Roman Catholic Church? Is Rome on the eve of an internal breaking point, with disastrous consequences?

1. Pentin, "Full Text and Explanatory Notes."
2. Francis, "Amoris Lætitia."
3. "Correctio."
4. Olson, "Fr. Thomas G. Weinandy," para. 9.

The Tensions Between the Roman and Catholic Components

These three criticisms are extremely serious and perhaps a tipping point in Catholic circles as far as the growing uneasiness towards Pope Francis is concerned. Various interpretations have been suggested in trying to understand what is happening. What might be useful in coming to terms with it, is to relate both Francis's apparent openness to change and ambiguity in teaching, on the one hand, and the angrier reactions of the traditionalists, on the other, to the inner and constitutive dynamics of Roman Catholicism.

Roman Catholicism is what it is because it inherently combines the "Roman" element with the "Catholic" one. Both are essential components of the synthesis offered by the Roman Catholic system. The genius of Roman Catholicism is its being at the same time Roman and Catholic, one and the other, one never at the expense of the other.

It is "Roman" in the sense that it is organically attached to the city and the Church of Rome and by extension to the institutions, canon laws, dogmas, hierarchy, and the political outlook associated with it. Much of this derives from a complex history marked by an imperial ideology.

It is "Catholic" in the sense of its being inclusive, global, embracing, and open to different movements, trends, and trajectories. The Roman elements provide stability and continuity; the Catholic element fosters development and renewal. Roman Catholicism is able to hold the tension deriving from its dual identity and to maintain it at a manageable balance.

What is happening with Pope Francis is to be understood against the background of the tensions between the Roman and Catholic poles within Roman Catholicism. Francis is strongly pushing the "catholic" agenda of Rome, embracing all, affirming all, expanding the traditional boundaries of the church.

Some traditionalist circles are reacting strongly because they see the danger of losing the Roman elements, represented by the well-established teachings and practices of the church. They see the Catholic swallowing the Roman. They see the risk of the Catholic taking precedence over the Roman and therefore severing the dynamic link that has characterized Roman Catholicism for centuries.

Whereas with the previous Pope (Benedict XVI), the overall balance was more in favor of the Roman than the Catholic, with Francis the Roman Catholic pendulum is swinging towards the catholicity of Rome.

Francis's critics believe that he has gone too far and want the pendulum to reverse towards more reassuring Roman elements.

Can There Be a Biblical Reformation in Roman Catholicism?

As we are celebrating five hundred years of the Protestant Reformation, with its call to the church to submit to the authority of Scripture and its recovery of the good news that we are saved by Christ alone through faith alone, it is appropriate to ask whether Rome is still grappling with the same issues that gave rise to it.

Luther took issue with the Pope and his theology and practice of dispensing God's pardon through indulgences. Luther's standard was the biblical gospel, and he challenged the church to embrace afresh the gospel. Rome responded by absorbing some of Luther's concerns about grace and faith within the sacramental system largely shaped around Roman elements and within its synergistic theology significantly marked by Catholic components, thus reinforcing the overall Roman Catholic synthesis rather than reforming it according to the Word of God.

Ever since, the Roman Catholic system has been swinging and bending one way or another to accommodate either progressive or traditional trends, either reiterating Roman emphases or introducing Catholic ones, and then rebalancing the whole. But the church was not reformed because it did not recognize the external and supreme authority of Scripture and the gospel of salvation by faith alone. As it stands, it will never be renewed according to the Word of God. It will certainly accommodate "Catholic" movements like the Charismatic renewal and "Roman" movements like the Marian groups and then re-fix the overall synthesis. It will even accommodate an emphasis on biblical literacy, as well as commend unbiblical devotions and beliefs: both-and, Roman and Catholic!

What is happening now with the criticism of Pope Francis is business as usual in the Roman Catholic Church: at times the pendulum swings one way before readdressing the overall balance. It could be argued that the Second Vatican Council (1962–65) was a great push towards the Catholic element and the reigns of John Paul II and Benedict XVI were subsequent attempts to moderate it in terms of reinforcing the Roman elements. With Francis the Catholic is again winning the day. These tensions will go on as long as Roman Catholicism exists. They are inner movements within the system. If one looks at Roman Catholicism as a system, then even the doubts of the cardinals, the criticism of priests and intellectuals, and even their charges of heresy against the Pope become easier to come to terms with. Roman Catholicism is both Roman and Catholic and will always be so.

Nothing is going to break abruptly and, more importantly, no biblical reformation is possible under these conditions. Roman Catholicism will be stretched and go through a stress test but will be able to handle both Francis's catholicity and his critics' insistence on the Roman component. The synthesis will be expanded, but the gospel will not be allowed to change Rome. This is the reason why the Reformation is not over.

"Confusion" and "Failure": Other Roman Catholic Blows Against Pope Francis (March 1, 2019, Number 159)

The turmoil in the Roman Catholic Church has reached a further disruption point. At the beginning of February, two independent but influential texts circulated widely that expressed strong criticism against Pope Francis. In Europe, the German Cardinal Gerhard Müller issued a *Manifesto of Faith*[5] that raised serious concerns over the downplaying of Roman Catholic identity under the present-day pontificate and suggested corrections to it. In the USA, the acclaimed journal *First Things* posted an article by R. R. Reno whose devastating thesis is evident from its title: "A Failing Papacy."[6] Both attacks came from high-profile Roman Catholic sources and show that the "Annus Horribilis"[7] of Rome is getting even worse. On both sides of the Atlantic, Pope Francis is under fire.

Away from Confusion but Where To?

Müller is the former Prefect of the Congregation for the Doctrine of the Faith (the highest Vatican authority in the area of doctrine after the Pope). He was named Prefect by Pope Benedict XVI in 2012 and has become known for his conservative views with regards to the interpretation of Catholic doctrine and morals. In doing so he collided with the open-ended and inclusive approach of Pope Francis, especially as to whether

---

5. Pentin, "Cardinal Müller."
6. Reno, "Failing Papacy."
7. De Chirico, "Vatican File 158."

or not to readmit people in "irregular" relationships to the Eucharist. Müller vocally opposed the relaxation of the Catholic attitude towards people living in relationships outside of marriage, as had been adopted by *Amoris lætitia*,[8] the 2015 Vatican document on the family that was strongly supported by the Pope. His criticism of the Pope is the reason Francis abruptly dismissed him in 2017, breaking the usual practice that the Prefect is confirmed in his office until retirement and even beyond. The fact that he who used to be the second or third in rank after the Pope in the Vatican hierarchy is now an outspoken opponent of him is a sign of the chaos that the Vatican is going through at the moment.

Over the last few years, Müller has become a reference point for those who are concerned with the direction that the Roman Catholic Church has taken under the leadership of Pope Francis. In the *Manifesto*, the German Cardinal talks of a "growing confusion" about church doctrine: "Today, many Christians are no longer even aware of the basic teachings of the Faith," the German cardinal laments, "so there is a growing danger of missing the path to eternal life." His concern has to do with the undermining of Roman Catholic traditional tenets happening under Pope Francis.

The *Manifesto* is a four-page document posted in multiple languages that calls people from around the world to sign it as a way of affirming Catholic identity in this time of "growing confusion." The target is clearly Pope Francis and his apparent lack of theological reliability. The *pars construens* is an attempt to recover Roman Catholic doctrinal stability and breadth from the 1992 *Catechism of the Catholic Church*,[9] which was promulgated by Pope John Paul II and drafted under the leadership of then Cardinal Joseph Ratzinger. While Francis is seen as causing confusion through his clumsy theology, John Paul II and Benedict XVI are seen as Roman bulwarks.

The *Catechism* is the traditional explanation of the Roman Catholic faith, beginning with the Triune God but centered on the sacramentality of the church, which prolongs the ministry of Christ and therefore administers God's grace through the sacraments. Rather than the biblical gospel, it is the "sacramental life" that shapes the Christian life according to the Cardinal. Rather than obedience to the biblical Jesus Christ, it is submission to the authority of the Roman Church that marks his

---

8. De Chirico, "Vatican File 116."
9. *Catechism of the Catholic Church.*

proposal. Müller's antidote to Francis's downgrading is the retrieval of traditional Catholicism: not a recovery of the gospel but the reaffirmation of Rome as the "visible sign and instrument of salvation realized in the Catholic Church." The solution is not qualitatively different from the problem it wants to solve.

A Failing Papacy?

On the other side of the Atlantic, the tone against Francis has reached an unexpected peak. The incipit of the aforementioned article in *First Things* is shocking if one considers its source:

> The current regime in Rome will damage the Catholic Church. Pope Francis combines laxity and ruthlessness. His style is casual and approachable; his church politics are cold and cunning. There are leading themes in this pontificate—mercy, accompaniment, peripheries, and so forth—but no theological framework. He is a verbal semi-automatic weapon, squeezing off rounds of barbed remarks, spiritual aperçus, and earthy asides (coprophagia!). This has created a confusing, even dysfunctional atmosphere that will become intolerable, if it hasn't already.[10]

And this is only the beginning. The article goes on to describe the situation of chaos that the Pope has brought to the Roman Church.

Given the North American provenance, an appropriate gut reaction to reading it is "Wow! What is happening in conservative Catholic circles?" These are not words written by an outmoded fundamentalist spitting his emotional anti-Catholicism. *First Things* is an authoritative voice of conservative Catholicism and a strong advocate of the Roman Catholic worldview. In reading this trenchant critique, one cannot help but think: how can a Catholic author write this and still affirm Francis as the Pope? How can a conservative Catholic who has said for decades that Roman Catholicism is unique and necessary because of the authoritative voice of the Pope now criticize what the Pope is teaching and doing? Isn't there a contradiction? More fundamentally, are we sure that Francis is the main problem? Or is it not the monarchial, political, and self-proclaimed infallible Papacy the issue at stake, biblically speaking?

Cardinal Müller sees the problem, but his solution is not better than it. *First Things* sees the problem but has no way to bring about a truly

---

10. Reno, "Failing Papacy," para. 1.

biblical reformation of the papacy. Seen from the outside, the battle between supporters and opposers of Pope Francis is of little significance if it does not lead to the recovery of the biblical gospel of salvation by faith alone and to a radical reorientation of the Roman Catholic Church.

Can the Roman Catholic Church Survive Two Popes?—One Catholic and One Roman (February 1, 2020, Number 172)

When Pope Benedict XVI resigned in 2013,[11] nobody could have imagined what has been happening since: the Roman Catholic Church has one reigning Pope (Francis), but also a former yet living Pope (Benedict) who still speaks, acts, and intervenes in ecclesiastical matters. There were hints that the prospect of having two living popes would cause some confusion, if not controversy. The fact that Benedict wanted to keep his title as Pope (only adding "Emeritus" to it), as well as his white Papal robe (a symbol of the Papal office) and his residence inside of the Vatican walls (the home of popes), indicated that, in spite of his pledge to remain silent for the rest of his days, the cohabitation between two popes would easily result in misunderstandings, even conflicts. The outcome has been an increasing polarization between Francis's fans *over against* Benedict's supporters and vice versa, certainly beyond the intentions of both.

One Pope, Two Popes?

In 2019 we had a preview of the present-day turmoil. The two popes spoke on the same subject, the sexual abuses committed in the Roman Church,[12] but with clearly different positions: Francis blamed "clericalism," an abuse of ecclesiastical power by the priests and religious people involved, whereas Benedict pointed to the collapse of Catholic doctrine and morality since the sixties and after the Second Vatican Council, a theological decay that according to him was at the root of the scandals. The two popes interpreted the malaise of their church and the possible solutions in radically different ways.

More recently, a power struggle rallying around Pope Francis and Pope Benedict erupted, with the "Francis party" pushing for changes in

11. De Chirico, "Vatican File 62."
12. De Chirico, "Vatican File 161."

areas such as the readmission of the divorced to the Eucharist[13] and the extension of the priesthood to married men, and the "Benedict party" resisting those changes, denouncing them as heresies,[14] confusions, and failures.[15] It was indeed an *Annus Horribilis*[16] (terrible year) for the Roman Church. Last but not least, we have now a popular movie entitled *The Two Popes*[17] telling a made-up story (with some truth in it) and making fun of the two characters and their unusual cohabitation in the Vatican. All of this was unthinkable seven years ago.

Pope Emeritus yet Outspokenly Concerned

The last episode in the tale of the two popes only happened a few days ago. Cardinal Robert Sarah, a prominent member of the traditionalist front, announced the imminent publication of a book written with Pope Benedict. The title of the book, *From the Depths of Our Hearts*,[18] is indicative of the highly emotional tone of its authors. The book itself is a heartfelt cry seasoned with theological acumen to maintain the traditional Roman Catholic doctrine and practice of the celibacy of the priests. It arises out of fears that after the 2019 Synod for the Pan-Amazon region, Pope Francis will allow some married men (*viri probati*, "proved men") to access the priesthood, thereby breaking a millennial rule of the Roman Catholic Church which prescribes her priests to be celibate. Sarah and Benedict staunchly defend the permanent validity of the celibacy of the priests and denounce any attempts at breaking it, even those painted as "exceptions" in extraordinary circumstances. It is true that after the press release by Cardinal Sarah there has been a backlash against Benedict appearing as co-author of the book, even though it looks like the Pope Emeritus had given at least tacit prior approval for the full manuscript. You can read the full story here.[19]

The theological arguments of the book deserve attention on their own merits because they show that traditional Roman Catholic theology

13. De Chirico, "Vatican File 116."
14. De Chirico, "Vatican File 144."
15. De Chirico, "Vatican File 158."
16. De Chirico, "Vatican File 158."
17. Thomas, "Two Popes."
18. Benedict XVI and Sarah, *From the Depths of Our Hearts*.
19. Pentin, "Unpacking the Benedict XVI."

is against progressive and liberal trends, not out of biblical concerns or standing under the authority of the Bible but in order to preserve traditional Roman Catholic teaching on the basis of the weight of church tradition and extra-biblical arguments (i.e., the "ontological" and "sacramental" nature of the priestly office). Because of its importance for gaining an insight into the traditional Roman Catholic way of theologizing, the book by Sarah and Benedict will be reviewed in a future Vatican File. What is of interest now are the standing questions that it brings.

An Unsettled Tension

One of the roles of the Pope has always been the maintenance of the balance between the Roman and the Catholic dimensions. Roman Catholicism is the ongoing tension between two fundamental aspects of the whole: the Roman side—with its emphasis on centralized authority, pyramidal structure, binding teaching and the rigidity of canon law—and the Catholic side, with its emphasis on the universal outlook, the absorption of ideas and cultures, and the inclusive embrace of practices into the Catholic whole. The resulting system is Roman Catholicism, at the same time Roman and Catholic. The human genius of Roman Catholicism, and one of the reasons for its survival across the centuries, has been its ability to be both, though not without tensions and risks of disruption.

Popes embody the Roman Catholic synthesis by holding together the Roman apparatus and the Catholic vision. Of course, they each do it differently, especially after the Second Vatican Council. John Paul II, for example, was a very Roman Pope but at the same time a very Catholic one. For example, he strongly defended traditional Roman Catholic teaching (e.g., by launching the 1992 *Catechism of the Catholic Church*[20]) but was second to none in promoting the universality of this church around the world (e.g., interreligious dialogue, traveling globally). Unlike John Paul II, who was both Roman and Catholic, Benedict XVI made the pendulum swing over the Roman pole. With his staunch conservativism in areas such as liturgy, morality, and the critical relationship with the secular world, Benedict appeared to be more Roman than Catholic. He seemed to be a rigid, centripetal, doctrinaire Pope. A *Roman* Pope. Many felt that his papacy, while strong in its Roman-centeredness and boundaries, was weak in its Catholic breadth and warmth.

---

20. See *Catechism of the Catholic Church*.

This criticism helps explain why a Pope like Francis was chosen to succeed him. With the election of Pope Francis, Rome seemed to be wanting the pendulum to move in the opposite direction in order to re-address the balance. Distancing himself from many Roman features of the office (e.g., his refusal of the pomp of the Vatican Curia, his blurred teaching that leans away from official teachings), Francis has embodied the role of a very Catholic Pope. His stress on "who are we to judge?,"[21] universal brotherhood with Muslims and other religions,[22] ecological concerns,[23] etc., made his papacy significantly shaped by the Catholic elements. The open-endedness of his teaching, coupled with the ambiguity of his language,[24] has created some interest in the secular West, which resonates with much of what he says on social issues. This is to say that he is a very *Catholic* Pope. Perhaps *too* Catholic and *too little* Roman for a growing number of Roman Catholics!

A Struggle to Re-Fix the Balance

Admitting the divorced to the Eucharist, fudging the traditional opposition to homosexuality, and extending the priesthood to married men have been perceived as the latest, dangerous "Catholic" moves of the Pope, which run contrary to the Roman tradition, risking its whole collapse! This is the highly emotional background behind the *From the Depths of Our Hearts*[25] book, part of which was written by Benedict himself in order to reinforce the "Roman" teaching on the celibacy of priests over against possible "Catholic" openings towards married men, which Francis seems to be in favor of.

The tension between the "Roman" Benedict and the "Catholic" Francis helps explain the present-day crisis. Past popes reigned without a Pope Emeritus around and therefore embodied in their own way the Roman Catholic synthesis. The next Pope would have fixed the synthesis differently. But now, with two very different popes living next to each other (with only one reigning but the other still lucid and active), the situation is very different. The overly Catholic attitude of Francis is compared and

21. De Chirico, "Vatican File 93."
22. De Chirico, "Vatican File 86."
23. De Chirico, "Vatican File 110."
24. De Chirico, "Vatican File 134."
25. See Benedict XVI and Sarah, *From the Depths of Our Heart*.

contrasted with the Roman outlook of Benedict, to the point of creating an unprecedented struggle between opposite parties. For some, Francis has become too Catholic to maintain a proper Roman Catholic synthesis. He is incapable of being the *Roman Catholic* (at the same time) Pontifex. Therefore, he needs the correction of a Roman Pope.

And yet, if this situation goes on unresolved, it will undermine the institution of the papacy as it was cleverly crafted throughout the ages. The "progressive" Pope will be counterbalanced by the "traditional" Pope, and the disruption of the system will be achieved. The papacy will be transformed into a two-party political system, as if it were an ordinary parliamentary monarchy. It will be the end of Roman Catholicism as it stands now.

This tension at the highest level of the Roman Catholic Church is not tenable in the long run. This is why it is highly probable that the status of Pope Emeritus (the one which Benedict enjoys now) will be revisited and regulated in order to end the temptation to think of the papacy as a "dual" responsibility, resulting in the ongoing confrontation of a Roman and a Catholic party. Roman Catholicism accommodates different positions and tendencies, but the Pope is thought of as being the one living synthesizer of the tension until the next one takes over and perhaps re-fixes the balance. The tale of two popes will not last long because Roman Catholicism is built on the conviction that its system is capable of keeping together its unchangeable Roman identity and its ever-increasing Catholicity. No biblical reformation is in view; it is only an internal struggle that is causing Rome to go through a stress test and some chaos until the Roman and the Catholic dimensions find a new, sustainable equilibrium.

Who Will Be the Next Pope? (September 1, 2021, Number 192)

There is a general perception that Pope Francis's pontificate has entered an irreversibly declining phase, a sort of late autumn that is a prelude to the end of a season. It is not just a question of age: yes, Pope Francis is elderly and in poor health. But aging aside, the pontificate finds itself navigating a descending parable. It started with the language of "mission" and "reform." Francis's reign, now nearly ten years old, was immediately engulfed in a thousand difficulties, particularly within the Catholic Church. Many of these problems were caused by the ambiguities of Francis himself, to the point that the push envisaged at the beginning turned out to be broken if not wholly inconclusive.

Given the predictable end of a season, the question is therefore legitimate: after Francis, who is next? Who will be the next Pope? This question is asked not by some bitter secularist or even a seasoned bookmaker but by the devout Roman Catholic scholar George Weigel, former biographer of John Paul II[26] and author, among other things, of a book in which he proposes a change in the meaning of the term "evangelical": from being a descriptor of the Protestant faith grounded on Scripture alone and faith alone to an adjective describing a fully-orbed Roman Catholicism.[27] Weigel is a bright intellectual and an exponent of the conservative American Roman Catholicism that has often been outspoken against Francis.[28]

In his book *The Next Pope: The Office of Peter and a Church in Mission*,[29] Weigel draws a composite sketch of the new Pope.[30] The next Pope will be a man who was either a child or very young during the years of the Second Vatican Council (1962–65). For the first time, Rome will have a Pope more "distant" from the controversies of the 1960s–1970s. For this reason, perhaps he will be more free from the interpretative wars over the council,[31] i.e., whether it was a council that continued with tradition or broke from it. However, as Weigel admits (but it doesn't take much acumen to recognize it), "there are profound divisions over Catholic doctrine and identity, praxis and mission, within the Church itself."[32] The next Pope will find these divisions on his desk. How will he deal with them?

According to Weigel, the next Pope will have to find inspiration from Leo XIII (1810–1903), whose papacy from 1878 to his death in 1903 generated a ferment in the life of the then tormented church: Leo anchored its life and thought to Thomist philosophy, developed its social doctrine, and launched a challenge to the modern world at the cultural level instead of adopting a defensive attitude towards it. The reverberations of this vitality were then channeled by John XXIII in convening

---

26. See, Weigel, *Witness to Hope*.

27. See, Weigel, *Evangelical Catholicism*. See also De Chirico, "Vatican File 56." See also De Chirico

28. De Chirico, "Vatican File 144."

29. Weigel, *Next Pope*.

30. Weigel, *Prossimo papa*.

31. De Chirico, "Vatican File 162."

32. Weigel, *Prossimo papa*, 9.

Vatican II and by John Paul II in the Great Jubilee of 2000. For the American scholar, this is the militant Roman Catholicism that the next Pope will have to embody and promote: faithful to its traditional doctrine, integral in its moral teaching, consistent in its ecclesial practices, made up of devout Catholics. For Weigel, taking inspiration from Leo XIII and John Paul II, the agenda of the new Pope needs to be the "new evangelization." Here is the way he puts it: the new Pope "will have to devote himself fully to the new evangelization as the great strategy of the Church of the 21st century."[33]

In order to "evangelize," the Roman Catholic Church must, according to Weigel, regain its identity as a sacramental and hierarchical church, combining this with its consolidated cluster of doctrines and practices handed down by tradition, i.e., the "fullness of the Catholic faith." Weigel warns Roman Catholicism against going down the bankrupt path of liberal Protestantism, which, by way of adapting to modern times, has lost its convictions and has also seen its churches empty. From his North American point of view, Weigel says that "the growing branches of Protestantism in the world are evangelicals, Pentecostals or fundamentalists,"[34] all characterized by "clear teaching and firm moral expectations." It is as if to say: Roman Catholicism can follow the path of liberal Protestantism, become "light" (that is, confused in doctrine and mixed with the world) and die, or it must recover its "full" identity and flourish again. For Weigel, "light Catholicism will lead to zero Catholicism,"[35] the loss of faith and a dissolutive process. For this reason, he hopes that the next Pope will be the expression of a full, convinced, devoted Roman Catholicism that aims at "evangelizing" (that is, Catholicizing) the world rather than being penetrated by the world.

This language of "light" versus "full" Catholicism helps explain why Weigel is critical of Francis. The present Pope is seen as embroiled in proposing a "light" form of Roman Catholicism: he speaks of "mission"[36] (e.g., in the apostolic exhortation *Evangelii gaudium*), but he works it out in a very different way from the "new evangelization." For Francis, mission is to go out to meet "all brothers" (i.e., Francis's latest encyclical argument for a universal brotherhood)[37] with mercy, highlighting

33. Weigel, *Prossimo papa*, 23
34. Weigel, *Prossimo papa*, 56
35. Weigel, *Prossimo papa*, 59
36. De Chirico, "Vatican File 145."
37. De Chirico, "Vatican File 181."

the unity that already exists among all human beings without lingering over differences. The strategy is to avoid facing disputes, not to challenge anyone, and to express mercy without a doctrinal backbone. Quite the opposite of what Weigel is hoping for. It is clear that Weigel's new Pope will have to make a vigorous shift away from Francis's trajectory.

Weigel often uses a kind of "evangelical" language to describe the Pope of his dreams. He speaks of fervor of spirit and solidity of convictions, all indicators not so much of doctrinal contents but of the experiences of the evangelical faith. At the same time, he speaks a very Roman Catholic language: he refers to salvation through baptism, Roman hierarchy, Papal primacy, and Marian devotions. As a traditionalist Catholic, Weigel believes that everything Roman Catholicism has collected throughout history (e.g., the Council of Trent, Vatican I, Marian dogmas, etc.) should be kept and nothing lost. All of this is very Catholic. He wants to make people believe that Roman Catholicism can (indeed must) also be "evangelical" without losing its Catholic tenets. He has in mind a Pope who is very traditional in doctrine (anti-evangelical) yet very passionate and committed like an "evangelical." This is the kind of Pope he hopes for.

When he was elected in 2013, Francis too was presented as very close to the "evangelical" ethos. Spontaneous prayer, experiential language, and a certain fervor in spirituality seemed to make him a different Pope. Many evangelicals were impressed,[38] only to discover some time later that Francis was and is also very Marian, universalist, Jesuit, and anti-evangelical. Now Weigel, indirectly criticizing Francis, hopes for an "evangelical" Catholic Pope, even if a very different Pope from the present one. Both Francis and Weigel have an experiential (non-doctrinal) meaning of "evangelical" in mind. They want to appropriate the evangelical ways of living out the faith, while remaining anchored to the traditional (Weigel) or "outgoing" (Francis) doctrine of Roman Catholicism. Both of them distort the evangelical faith and want to dissolve it in the dogmatic-institutional synthesis of Roman Catholicism.

Whoever is elected, the next Pope will unlikely be an "evangelical" if the word "evangelical" retains its doctrinal and historical meaning. The "evangel" is not the paramount commitment of the Roman Catholic Church. Therefore, its head will never be an "evangelical" Pope if the Roman Church will not undergo a reformation according to the "evangel."

38. De Chirico, "Vatican File 106."

New Cardinals for the Future Conclave
(October 1, 2022, Number 206)

When the reigning Pope creates new cardinals, it is because he is thinking not only of the Roman Catholic Church of today but, above all, that of tomorrow. Cardinals are those who, in addition to assisting the Pope with governing the universal church, meet in conclave and elect the successor once the reigning one has died or, as in the case of Pope Ratzinger, resigns. By the end of August, Pope Francis had created twenty-one new cardinals[39] (of which sixteen were electors, that is, still under eighty years of age). In doing so, he has appointed two-thirds of the voting college of cardinals (should the conclave meet today) from the beginning of his pontificate. Note that the majority required for the election of the Pope is just two-thirds. Most of the new cardinals and all those voting seem to belong to the pro-Francis area, that is, loyal to the line of the Pope and in continuity with his approach.

When it comes to electing Francis's successor, the overwhelming majority of the cardinals will have been created by Francis himself. Does this mean that they will vote for a "Franciscan" candidate, that is, one who carries out the agenda of the current papacy? It's not for sure. The history of the conclaves, including the last one, indicates that electoral majorities do not predictably follow in the way they were formed but can be constructed in an unexpected way. In any case, it is an indisputable element that Francis has now filled the conclave with cardinals of his appointment. On this point he followed not so much a "catholic" policy of choosing representatives of all the trends within Roman Catholicism (e.g., progressives, traditionalists, centrists . . .) but a partisan one: he chose cardinals who meet his personal theological and pastoral preferences.

The geographical origins of the new cardinals are different. In this regard, it should be noted that Pope Francis has chosen the new cardinals from the "peripheries" of the Roman Catholic world: think of the bishops of Singapore, Mongolia, and East Timor, small and decentralized episcopal sees that now become much more important. In Italy he appointed as cardinal the bishop of Como (a small diocese) while the nearby and large archdiocese of Milan still remains without a cardinal. In the USA he created as cardinal the bishop of San Diego (small in size) but left the much larger diocese of Los Angeles without. Pope Francis is like this:

---

39. Catholic News Service, "21 New Cardinals."

he is predictable in his willingness to unsettle established patterns that subvert expectations.

What does all this mean regarding the prospects of Roman Catholicism? Not much. Or rather: much as regards the internal dynamics in Rome but much less with regards to the expectation of a "turning point" of Roman Catholicism in an evangelical direction. Whether the next Pope is a "Franciscan" or a conservative, from the Southern Hemisphere or the Western world, elected by a narrow majority or by a large majority, in favor of synodality or centralizer, little of theological significance is going to change.

If the conclave would meet today, the most quoted candidates for the papacy are:

- Cardinal Luis Antonio Tagle (Philippines), who is thought of as being in line with Francis and represents the Roman Catholic Global South but is perhaps too young (being born in 1957);
- Cardinal Matteo Zuppi (Italy), close to Francis but with his own independent posture;
- Cardinal Peter Ërdo (Hungary), a good candidate of the conservative wing but European and therefore still from the "old" world;
- Cardinal Pietro Parolin (Italy), the current Vatican Secretary of State, in case the conclave ends up in a stand still and looks for a mediation between different groups.

Whoever the next Pope is, unless there is a surprise that stems from the extraordinary providence of God, he will remain within the logic of Roman Catholicism, which moves along the lines of ecclesiastical politics but whose agenda does not include a way towards a reformation according to the gospel. The true reformation requires abandoning all that Rome has added to the evangelical faith (Marian dogmas, sacraments, and practices that are not taught in Scripture, imperial and hierarchical structures, spurious if not really pagan devotions, etc.) to return to the biblical faith that is grounded in Scripture alone and centered on Christ alone. Unfortunately, everything that precedes the conclave does not seem to indicate any movement towards an evangelical reformation of the Roman Catholic Church but only another page in the long history of Roman Catholicism.

"The Next Pope Will Be John XXIV." Will He? (October 1, 2023, Number 220)

"On the Vietnam journey, if I don't go, John XXIV certainly will." In the traditional in-flight press conference[40] on the Papal plane returning to Rome from Mongolia (September 4), Pope Francis hinted at his possible successor. Being asked what his plans are for future international journeys, Francis showed awareness of his frailty due to age and poor health conditions. This is why he cannot plan long-term. He also indicated the name of a possible successor who could replace him after he is gone. Of course, he did not refer to a specific individual but to the Papal name he wished the next Pope could take.

The indication of the name "John XXIV" sheds light on the preferred portrait of the Pope of the future. It is worth noticing the possible names he did not refer to and the one he used during the interview.

"Francis II" was not mentioned for understandable reasons. A reigning Pope wishing his successor to follow his steps is legitimate, but indicating that he should choose his name would have been an abnormal form of egocentrism. In his ten-year tenure, Francis has shaped the next conclave[41] (i.e., the assembly of cardinals who will elect the next Pope) by nominating 70 percent of it. Most of the new cardinals are Francis's friends and like-minded people. Obviously, he wants the successor to follow in his footsteps, but wishing him to take the name "Francis II" would have been a *faux pas*.

"Benedict XVII" wasn't mentioned either. Despite formally polite coexistence, Francis has always thought of himself as breaking off the ecclesiastical trajectory of Pope Ratzinger. There has been a cleavage between the two on all grounds: doctrine, practice, style, language, strategy. After the death of Benedict XVI, Francis tried to limit his influence and close his era.[42] Certainly, Francis does not want Pope Ratzinger's staunchly "Roman" and traditional line to be revived after the end of his reign. He believes there is no place whatsoever for a "Benedict XVII" in the future of the Roman Catholic Church.

Furthermore, a "John Paul III" was not indicated as a desirable follow-up. John Paul II's legacy is surely tied to the relaunching of Rome's catholicity (i.e., the embracement of the world into Rome's sacramental

---

40. Vatican News, "Pope Francis Warns Church."
41. De Chirico, "Vatican File 206."
42. De Chirico, "Vatican File 218."

and institutional structures)—something that Pope Francis is also pursuing in his own way. However, John Paul II (now a "saint") was also the Pope who engaged in "culture wars" with the secularizing West, upholding traditional Roman Catholic moral identity markers (e.g., opposition to abortion, euthanasia, and homosexuality). He created an "us" versus "them" mentality in the relationship with the world, especially the secular West. This oppositional posture is very far from Pope Francis's more "catholic" and inclusivist strategy. He wants to underline that we are "all brothers"[43] and continue to be so despite professing different religions and having opposite ethical convictions. Francis does not want the Roman Church to be a polarizing agency but a place where differences exist in harmony.

"Paul VII" did not appear to Francis as a desirable successor either. While Francis often positively quotes Paul VI as the one who wrote the encyclical[44] calling the Roman Church to engage in "evangelization" (to be understood in the Roman Catholic sense of expanding the borders of the Roman Church), he apparently dislikes the black and white picture that Paul VI painted in dealing with moral issues such as the regulation of birth in his encyclical.[45] Paul VI created a chasm between the world and the church. On the contrary, Francis wants to eliminate all separation and treats differences, even the sharpest ones, as instances of human richness to be harmonized.

Neither "Francis II," "Benedict XVII," "John Paul III," nor "Paul VII." Why "John XXIV" then? Here are some possible explanations for why Pope Francis would like his successor to imitate or look like John XXIII. John XXIII is known as the "good Pope" who was approachable, kind, warm, and humble. Giuseppe Roncalli (1881–1963), John XXIII, was the Pope who convened the Second Vatican Council in 1959. The council only began in 1962, and John XXIII died during it. Vatican II is the watershed event[46] in the present-day Roman Catholic Church whereby Rome began to downplay its centuries-long insistence on the "Roman" sides of its identity (e.g., hierarchy, full adherence to the catechism, submission to the ecclesiastical authority) and to stress its "catholic" aspirations (e.g., inclusion, embracement, absorption). Francis thinks of himself as enacting and implementing this aspect of Vatican II.

43. De Chirico, "Vatican File 181."
44. Paul VI, "Evangelii Nuntiandi."
45. Paul VI, "Humanae Vitae."
46. De Chirico, "Vatican File 45."

Moreover, in the opening address to Vatican II,[47] John XXIII remarked that the Council had no doctrinal agenda but wanted to develop "a magisterium which is predominantly pastoral in character." Neither condemnations of the world nor theological definitions were to be expected. What ensued was a wholehearted affirmation of the goodness of the modern world. Francis likes to underline the pastoral nature of everything the church says and does. The pastoral dimension (warm, welcoming, accepting of all) is often referred to as if it were in opposition to the doctrinal one. Francis thinks of his pontificate as a "pastoral" attempt at building bridges instead of creating walls with the whole world, leaving doctrinal issues aside. He wants this "pastoral" emphasis to be kept and even increased by his successor. A John XXIII-like Pope is expected to promote universal fraternity in ecumenical, interfaith, and social relationships.

A final comment is in place. Unlike John Paul II, Benedict XVI, and Francis, John XXIII was an Italian Pope. Among the candidates to succeed Francis, Cardinal Matteo Zuppi, the Italian archbishop of Bologna and president of the Italian Bishops Conference, is at the top of the list. In recent months, Francis sent Zuppi to visit Ukraine, Russia, the US, and now China as his ambassador for peace in the Ukraine war. In so doing, he wanted to raise Zuppi's international profile. In many ways, Cardinal Zuppi resembles the portrait of "John XXIV": not known for his strong doctrinal views but recognized as a cardinal dedicated to dialogue, peace, and fraternity. Did Pope Francis intend to indirectly campaign for him?

---

47. Butler, "Pope John's Opening Speech."

Obituaries

Francis (1936–2025), the Pope So Close, So Far Away

ON MARCH 13, 2013, Jorge Mario Bergoglio became Pope Francis, marking a significant transition in the Roman Catholic Church. What he has stood for in his papacy, e.g., his affirming attitudes towards all, his noisy silence over traditional doctrine and his ambiguous language, his thoroughgoing Marianism, and his lack of clarity on several key issues, has caused many to puzzle. Some have acclaimed him as the "great reformer";[1] others have argued that he is bringing about a "revolution of tenderness and love."[2] Yet others too have found it difficult to square his words and actions into the established patterns of traditional Roman Catholicism.

Three Angles

Now that he passed away, there are at least three angles we could take to evaluate his papacy.

From the global point of view, he was elected to divert the attention of the Roman Catholic Church from the secularizing West (where Roman Catholicism is in decline) to the Global South (where in some places like Africa, it has potential to grow). His fifty-plus international journeys witnessed to his attention given to African and Asian countries. The

---

1. Ivereigh, *Great Reformer*.
2. Kasper, *Pope Francis' Revolution*.

appointments of cardinals were also made following a similar criterion. Under Francis the center of gravity shifted towards the Global South.

From the doctrinal viewpoint, his three encyclicals (e.g., *Laudato si* and *All Brothers*) and his apostolic exhortations (the most important ones being *The Joy of the Gospel* on mission and *Amor lætitia* on the family) indicate a shift of the Catholic magisterium towards becoming more "catholic" (i.e., inclusive, Global South, absorbing, focused on social issues) and less "Roman" (i.e., centered on Catholic distinctives). Francis has lowered the traditional Roman Catholic identity markers (sacraments, hierarchy) for all people (e.g., practicing, not practicing, believing, not believing, people in "disordered" lifestyles) to be included and to feel they "belong" to the church. When Francis talks about "mission," he has in mind this sense of inclusion, regardless of gospel criteria. Under Francis, the Roman Catholic Church has become more "catholic" than ever in its long history. As a matter of fact, in spite of his inclusiveness, Catholic churches are empty, and numbers are declining in the West.

Organizationally speaking, he has launched the "synodal" process whereby he wanted his church to be less centralized and with more participation from the peripheries. As Francis seemed committed to synodality on the one hand, his style of leadership appeared to be centralizing, moody and unpredictable, on the other.

Every Pope has had his internal enemies. John Paul II was not liked by some progressive circles. Benedict XVI was criticized every time he spoke. Francis received pushback from cardinals, theologians, and important sectors of Roman Catholicism, especially in the USA but also in Australia (e.g., the late Cardinal Pell) and Germany (e.g., Cardinal Müller).

They were concerned with the erosion of Roman Catholic identity based on traditional doctrines and practices being replaced with an "all brothers" kind of mindset where almost anything goes. Some mismanagement by Francis in financial and leadership decisions has also created an atmosphere of distrust in the Vatican.

Pope Francis and Evangelicals

When he was elected in 2013, Francis was presented as very close to the "evangelical" ethos. Spontaneous prayer, experiential language, the frequent use of Bible texts in his homilies, and a certain fervor in spirituality seemed to make him a different Pope. Many evangelicals were impressed,[3] only to discover sometime later that Francis was also very Marian,[4] tendentially universalist, a Jesuit who before becoming Pope had published nasty comments against Luther "the heretic" and Calvin "the schismatic."[5]

His approach to ecumenism was shaped as "walking together, praying together and working together" rather than in theological discussions seeking doctrinal agreement. His was a "spiritual ecumenism." He used the same approach with Liberal Protestants, Charismatics of various stripes, and Eastern Orthodox. His desire for unity reached out beyond Christian circles.

His *Document on Human Fraternity* (2019), signed with Muslim leaders, epitomized his insistence on the whole of humanity made by "brothers and sisters"[6] who are called to walk, work, and pray together, regardless of faith in Christ. Evangelicals should be aware that when Francis spoke of "unity," he did not have in mind unity in the gospel, by unity of the whole of mankind.

Francis has bluntly redefined what it means to be "brothers and sisters." He has extended "fraternity" to all those who live "under the sun," i.e., "the one human family." Muslims, Buddhists, agnostics, atheists, Protestants ... are all "all brothers."

That was his interpretation of what Vatican II meant with the church being "the sacrament of unity between God and mankind."[7] The redefinition of what it means to be brothers and sisters is an attempt to blur what the Bible expects us to distinguish. Our common humanity takes over the spiritual connotation of being "in Christ" as the basis for the shared fraternity. Francis pushed this unbiblical approach in his ecumenical endeavors and interfaith initiatives.

What's Next?

Now, Francis's pontificate is over. Whoever the next Pope is, unless there is a surprise that stems from the extraordinary providence of God, he will remain within the logic of Roman Catholicism, which moves along

---

3. De Chirico, "Vatican File 106."
4. De Chirico, "Vatican File 156."
5. De Chirico, "Vatican File 83."
6. De Chirico, "Vatican File 181."
7. Holy See, "Lumen Gentium," 1

the lines of ecclesiastical politics but whose agenda does not include a way towards a reformation according to the gospel. The true reformation requires abandoning all that Rome has added to the evangelical faith (Marian dogmas, sacraments and practices that are not taught in Scripture, imperial and hierarchical structures, spurious if not really pagan devotions, etc.) to return to the biblical faith that is grounded in Scripture alone and centered on Christ alone. Unfortunately, there is nothing that indicates any movement towards an evangelical reformation of the Roman Catholic Church but only another page in the long history of Roman Catholicism.

Roman Catholicism will be stretched and go through a stress test but will be able to handle both Francis's catholicity and his critics' insistence on the Roman component. The synthesis will be expanded, but the gospel will not be allowed to change Rome. This is the reason why the Reformation is not over.

Francis (1936–2025), the Pope who Made the Roman Church More "Catholic"

The Challenge of Change—the title of this book by David Willey,[8] BBC Vatican correspondent, expressed a widespread wish in Catholic circles when Cardinal Jorge Mario Bergoglio (1936–2025) was elected Pope in 2013 following the dramatic resignation by Pope Benedict XVI.[9] The Roman Catholic Church was experiencing a time of chaos (sexual scandals, financial corruption, negative attitudes by the media and public opinion), and Francis was elected "from the end of the world" to bring about change.

Pope Francis shook the Catholic world with a whirlwind of change: in symbols (wearing a silvery metal cross), in status (living in a simple apartment at Santa Marta), in language (speaking as a country priest), in posture (approachable by all), in tone (relational and warm), in style (undiplomatic and direct), in pastoral openness (blessing homosexual people and admitting divorced people at the Eucharist).

After few years of his pontificate, *New York Times* columnist Ross Douthat wrote *To Change the Church* (2018), a book that expressed concerns over the theological disruption that Pope had brought about and

---

8. Willey, *Promise of Francis*.
9. De Chirico, "Pope Benedict XVI."

the divisions that ensued.[10] Some traditionalist circles reacted strongly because they saw the danger of losing the Roman elements represented by the well-established teachings and practices of the church. High-rank Roman Catholic theologians did not dare to call him a "heretic."[11] They feared that the Catholic would swallow the Roman. The change he introduced became controversial, turning the high expectations of the beginning into the confusing developments that ended his pontificate.

Promise Turned into Puzzlement

Of eclectic and unfinished theological training, Argentine and non-academic, Francis immediately showed his frustration with the maintenance mood of the church, the rigidity of traditional schemes and patterns, and the clericalism of ecclesiastical culture.

The theological world of Francis was populated by words and expressions like "theology of the people,"[12] "missionary conversion,"[13] "mercy,"[14] "synodality,"[15] "ecological conversion,"[16] "fraternity and brotherhood."[17] Not all are new words; some of them are terms that have been already used in Roman Catholic teaching but were given a new nuance or a distinct significance by Francis. He also became the spokesperson of the world religions on issues like migration, the environment,[18] and peace—less so on issues like the protection of life. All of this in the context of his understanding of interfaith dialogue.

Francis emphasized vibes over doctrine. On how to promote Christian unity, Francis made his own the following strategy: "Let's do one thing: put all the theologians on an island and let them argue among themselves, and we shall move forward in peace."[19] For him theological conversations were almost a waste of time. His approach to ecumenism was shaped as "walking together, praying together, and working together"

10. Ross Douthat, *To Change the Church*.
11. De Chirico, "Vatican File 144."
12. De Chirico, "Vatican File 222."
13. De Chirico, "Vatican File 145."
14. De Chirico, "Vatican File 120."
15. Karr, "Synodality."
16. De Chirico, "Vatican File 166."
17. De Chirico, "Vatican File 86."
18. De Chirico, "Vatican File 166"
19. Bordoni, "Pope Prays for Christian Unity," para. 7

rather than in theological discussions seeking doctrinal agreement. His was a "spiritual ecumenism." He used the same approach with Liberal Protestants, evangelicals, Charismatics of various stripes, and Eastern Orthodox, as well as non-Christian faith communities. His desire for unity reached out beyond Christian circles.

Francis emphasized the unity of humankind over narrow ecclesial and even religious boundaries. His 2020 encyclical (the highest authoritative teaching of a Pope) *All Brothers*,[20] on universal fraternity, consolidated the idea that the church is inclusive of all on the basis of a common and shared humanity, not on the basis of repentance and faith in Jesus Christ. He regularly prayed with Muslims[21] and leaders of other faiths.

Francis emphasized inclusion rather than tradition. He encouraged his church to address the divorced and remarried Catholics, not according to the sheer "letter" of their traditional exclusion from communion but following the all-embracing "spirit" that looks for ways to include them on a case-by-case basis. This is the what his 2016 post-Synod on the family exhortation *Amoris Lætitia*[22] provided for.

Francis seemed embroiled in proposing a "liquid" form of Roman Catholicism.[23] What happened with Pope Francis is to be understood against the background of the tensions between the Roman and Catholic poles within Roman Catholicism. Francis strongly pushed the "catholic" agenda of Rome, embracing all, affirming all, expanding the boundaries of the church, and expanding its traditional boundaries.

Who Is Next: John XXIV?

Will the "change" brought about by Francis be advanced in the next Pope? On the Papal plane returning to Rome from Mongolia,[24] Pope Francis hinted at his possible successor. Of course, he did not refer to a specific individual but to the Papal name he wished the next Pope could take.

The indication of the name was "John XXIV."[25] This name sheds light on the preferred portrait of the Pope of the future. In his twelve-year

---

20. De Chirico, "Vatican File 181."
21. De Chirico, "Vatican File 139."
22. Francis, "Amoris Lætitia."
23. De Chirico, "Vatican File 200."
24. Vatican News, "Pope Francis Warns Church."
25. De Chirico, "Vatican File 220"

tenure, Francis has shaped the next conclave[26] (i.e., the assembly of cardinals who will elect the next Pope) by nominating 75 percent of it. Most of the new cardinals are Francis's friends and like-minded people.

Why "John XXIV" then? Here are some possible explanations for why Pope Francis would like his successor to imitate or look like John XXIII. John XXIII is known as the "good Pope" who was approachable, kind, warm, and humble. Giuseppe Roncalli (1881–1963), John XXIII, was the Pope who convened the Second Vatican Council in 1959. The council only began in 1962, and John XXIII died during it. Vatican II is the watershed event[27] in the present-day Roman Catholic Church whereby Rome began to downplay its centuries-long insistence on the "Roman" sides of its identity (e.g., hierarchy, full adherence to the catechism, submission to the ecclesiastical authority) and to stress its "catholic" aspirations (e.g., inclusion, embracement, absorption). Francis thought of himself as enacting and implementing this aspect of Vatican II. A John XXIII-like Pope is expected to promote universal fraternity in ecumenical, interfaith, and social relationships while preserving Catholic unity.

The change that Francis brought about did not promote an "evangelical" move in the Roman Church. He made his church more "catholic," less Roman but no more biblical. Whoever the next Pope will be, the need for a biblical reformation will be as relevant as ever.

---

26. De Chirico, "Vatican File 206."
27. De Chirico, "Vatican File 45."

Bibliography

Agasso, Jr., Domenico. "A Child Cries for the Death of His Father." *La Stampa*, Apr. 16, 2018. http://www.lastampa.it/2018/04/15/vaticaninsider/eng/the-vatican/a-child-cries-for-the-death-of-his-father-the-pope-he-was-good-man-he-is-with-god-DG03vN0K7IJe8lHt59VmFL/pagina.html.

———. "Pope Francis Warns Against Sovereignism: 'It Leads to War.'" *La Stampa*, Aug. 10, 2019. https://www.lastampa.it/vatican-insider/en/2019/08/09/news/pope-francis-warns-against-sovereignism-it-leads-to-war-1.37330049.

Alleanza Evangelica Italiana. "Orientamenti evangelici per pensare il cattolicesimo." Sep. 11, 1999. https://www.alleanzaevangelica.org/index.php/news/9-attualita-italia/89-orientamenti-evangelici-per-pensare-il-cattolicesim.

Allison, Gregg R. *Roman Catholic Theology and Practice: An Evangelical Assessment.* Wheaton, IL: Crossway, 2014.

Angelicum Thomistic Institute. "Eleventh International Thomistic Congress." 2022. https://angelicum.it/TI-romathomism2022/.

Awi Mello, Alexandre. *È Mia Madre: Incontri con Maria.* Rome: Città Nuova, 2018.

———. *Ella es Me Mamá.* Argentina: Editorial Patris Argentina, 2014.

Barth, Karl. *Church Dogmatics I/2: The Doctrine of the Word of God.* Translated by G. W. Bromiley et al. Edinburgh: T&T Clark, 2010. https://books.google.com/books?id=APXR1Eom_AkC&pg=PA145.

Benedict XV (Pope). "Maximum Illud." 1919. https://w2.vatican.va/content/benedict-xv/en/apost_letters/documents/hf_ben-xv_apl_19191130_maximum-illud.html.

Benedict XVI (Pope). "Address of His Holiness Benedict XVI." Sep. 23, 2011. https://www.vatican.va/content/benedict-xvi/en/speeches/2011/september/documents/hf_ben-xvi_spe_20110923_evangelical-church-erfurt.html.

———. "Verbum Domini." Sep. 30, 2010. https://www.vatican.va/content/benedict-xvi/en/apost_exhortations/documents/hf_ben-xvi_exh_20100930_verbum-domini.html.

———., and Robert Sarah. *From the Depths of Our Hearts: Priesthood, Celibacy, and the Crisis of the Catholic Church.* San Francisco: Ignatius, 2020.

Blanchard, Shaun. "The Reform Was Real: Continuity and Change at Vatican II." *Commonweal* 3 (2022). https://www.commonwealmagazine.org/reform-was-real.

Bordoni, Linda. "Pope Prays for Christian Unity with Ecumenical Delegation from Hong Kong." *Vatican News*, May 22, 2024. https://www.vaticannews.va/en/pope/news/2024-05/pope-ecumenism-hong-kong-christian-council-meeting.html.

Borghesi, Massimo. *Jorge Mario Bergoglio: Una Biografia Intellettuale*. Milan: Jaca, 2017.
Brockhaus, Hannah. "Pope Francis: Diverse Religious Identities Are 'A Gift from God.'" *Herald Malaysia Online*, Sep. 18, 2024. https://www.heraldmalaysia.com/news/pope-francis-diverse-religious-identities-are-a-gift-from-god/78294/4.
Burigana, Riccardo. *Un Cuore Solo: Papa Francesco e l'Unità della Chiesa*. Milan: Edizioni Terra Santa, 2014.
Butler, Christopher. "Pope John's Opening Speech to the Council." Vatican II—Voice of the Church, Oct. 11, 1962. https://vatican2voice.org/91docs/opening_speech.htm.
Caccaro, Alberto. *L'uomo Fa Una Differenza In Dio: La Questione Cristologica in Jacques Dupuis*. Brescia: Queriniana, 2024.
Cantalamessa, Raniero. "The Gate of Faith." Comboni2000, Dec. 11, 2022. https://comboni2000.org/2022/12/11/cantalamessa-the-gate-of-faith-first-sermon-advent-2022/.
Civiltà Cattolica. http://www.laciviltacattolica.it/.
CELAM (Consejo Episcopal Latinoamericano y Caribeño). "Concluding Document." 2007. https://www.celam.org/aparecida/Ingles.pdf.
———. "Documento de Puebla III Conferencia General del Episcopado Latinoamericano." 1979. https://www.celam.org/documentos/Documento_Conclusivo_Puebla.pdf.
Coppen, Luke. *Nient'altro che la Verità: La Mia Vita al Fianco di Benedetto XVI*. Milan: Piemme, 2023.
———. "'Nothing but the Truth': A Reader's Guide to Archbishop Gänswein's Memoir." *The Pillar*, Jan. 12, 2023. https://www.pillarcatholic.com/p/nothing-but-the-truth-a-readers-guide-to-archbishop-gansweins-memoir.
———. "The Pope's Great Evangelical Gamble." *Catholic Herald*, Jul. 23, 2015. https://thecatholicherald.com/the-popes-great-evangelical-gamble/.
Correctio Filialis. "Correctio Filialis de Haeresibus Propagatis." Jul. 16, 2017. http://www.correctiofilialis.org/wp-content/uploads/2017/08/Correctio-filialis_English_1.pdf.
Costaldo, Chris. "Why I Am Disappointed with Pope Francis." Chris Costaldo (blog). https://chriscastaldo.com/why-i-am-disappointed-with-pope-francis/.
Coulter, Dale M. "The Pope, Protestantism, and Reformation." *First Things*, Nov. 2, 2016. https://firstthings.com/the-pope-protestantism-and-reformation/.
Dante Alighieri. *The Divine Comedy of Dante Alighieri, Vol. 1 (Inferno)*. Translated by Courtney Langdon. Cambridge: Harvard University Press, 1918.
De Chirico, Leonardo. "Bellarmine's Critique of Protestantism: Tridentine Roman Catholicism vs. the Reformation." Forum of Christian Leaders, May 17, 2021, video, 37:34. https://foclonline.org/talk/bellarmines-critique-protestantism-tridentine-roman-catholicism-vs-reformation.
———. *A Christian's Pocket Guide to Mary: Mother of God?* Fearn, Scotland: Christian Focus, 2017.
———. *A Christian's Pocket Guide to the Papacy*. Fearn, Scotland: Christian Focus, 2015.
———. *Engaging with Thomas Aquinas: An Evangelical Approach*. London: Apollos, 2024.
———. *Evangelical Theological Perspectives on Post-Vatican II Roman Catholicism*. Oxford: Peter Lang, 2003.
———. *Jubilee: Much More and Much Better than a Holy Year*. N.p.: GCD, 2025.

———. "Is the Pope Catholic?" *Unio Cum Christo* 9 (2023) 101–18.
———. "Leonardo De Chirico on Pope Francis." Interview by Skyler Hamilton, *Distinctive Christianity*, Apr. 28, 2025, podcast, mp3, 1:21:28. https://app.redcircle.com/shows/3beb896e-70f7-43c3-a701-02f9b9cc8299/ep/56d3fabb-54ab-42d7-aca5-a14bf4c478ca.
———. "Not by Faith Alone?: An Analysis of the Roman Catholic Doctrine of Justification from Trent to the Joint Declaration." In *The Doctrine on Which the Church Stands or Falls*, edited by Matthew Barrett. Wheaton, IL: Crossway, 2019.
———. "Pope Benedict XVI (1927–2022): His Life and Legacy." Gospel Coalition, Dec. 31, 2022. https://www.thegospelcoalition.org/article/pope-benedict-xvi/.
———. "Robert Bellarmine and His Controversies with the Reformers: A Window on Post-Tridentine Roman Catholic Apologists." *European Journal of Theology* 31 (2022) 21–42. https://www.aup-online.com/content/journals/10.5117/EJT2022.1.003.CHIR.
———. *Same Words, Different Worlds: Do Roman Catholics and Evangelicals Believe the Same Gospel?* London: IVP, 2021.
———. *Tell Your Catholic Friend: How to Have Gospel Conversations with Love.* Brentwood, TN: B&H, 2025.
———. "Vatican File 1. Vatican Efforts Towards New Evangelization?" Reformanda Initiative, Oct. 18, 2010. https://vaticanfiles.org/en/2010/10/1-vatican-efforts-towards-new-evangelization/.
———. "Vatican File 45. What Happened at Vatican II." Reformanda Initiative, Sep. 14, 2012. https://vaticanfiles.org/en/2012/09/45-what-happened-at-vatican-ii/.
———. "Vatican File 56. Left Without Words: How Roman Catholicism Is Reshaping the Evangelical Vocabulary." Reformanda Initiative, Apr. 1, 2013. https://vaticanfiles.org/en/2013/04/56-left-without-words/.
———. "Vatican File 58. Hurrah to Madonna: Pope Francis and the Re-Marianization of the Papacy." Reformanda Initiative, May 10, 2013. https://vaticanfiles.org/en/2013/05/58-hurrah-to-madonna/.
———. "Vatican File 61. Lumen Fidei: The First Encyclical by Pope Francis." Reformanda Initiative, Jul. 8, 2013. https://vaticanfiles.org/en/2013/07/61-lumen-fidei-the-first-encyclical-by-pope-francis/.
———. "Vatican File 62. A Church with Two Popes." Reformanda Initiative, Jul. 22, 2013. https://vaticanfiles.org/en/2013/07/62-a-church-with-two-popes/.
———. "Vatican File 64. Between Trent and Aparecida: The Trajectory of Pope Francis." Reformanda Initiative, Aug. 26, 2013. https://vaticanfiles.org/en/2013/08/64-between-trent-and-aparecida-the-trajectory-of-pope-francis/.
———. "Vatican File 65. The Pope Francis' Dogma: 'God Is Present in Every Person's Life.'" Reformanda Initiative, Sep. 20, 2013. https://vaticanfiles.org/it/2013/09/65-the-pope-francis-dogma-god-is-present-in-every-persons-life/.
———. "Vatican File 67. The World Entrusted to Mary: Why?" Reformanda Initiative, Oct. 15, 2013. https://vaticanfiles.org/en/2013/10/67-the-world-entrusted-to-mary-why/.
———. "Vatican File 69. The Joy of the Gospel: A Window into Francis' Vision." Reformanda Initiative, Dec. 2, 2013. https://vaticanfiles.org/en/2013/12/69-the-joy-of-the-gospel-a-window-into-francis-vision/.
———. "Vatican File 72. Secular Perceptions of Pope Francis." Reformanda Initiative, Jan. 6, 2014. https://vaticanfiles.org/en/2014/01/72-secular-perceptions-of-pope-francis/.

———. "Vatican File 80. 'Without Mary the Heart Is an Orphan': Another Instance of Francis' Marianism." Reformanda Initiative, May 16, 2014. https://vaticanfiles.org/en/2014/05/80-without-mary-the-heart-is-an-orphan-another-instance-of-francis-marianism/.

———. "Vatican File 83. What Francis Really Thinks of the Reformation (and of Calvin in Particular)." Reformanda Initiative, Jun. 23, 2014. https://vaticanfiles.org/en/2014/06/83-what-francis-really-thinks-of-the-reformation-and-of-calvin-in-particular/.

———. "Vatican File 86. Redefining Fraternity: At What Cost?" Reformanda Initiative, Aug. 11, 2014. https://vaticanfiles.org/en/2014/08/86-redefining-fraternity-at-what-cost/.

———. "Vatican File 87. The Marian Message of Pope Francis to Korea." Reformanda Initiative, Aug. 22, 2014. https://vaticanfiles.org/en/2014/08/87-the-marian-message-of-pope-francis-to-korea/.

———. "Vatican File 93. Who Are We to Judge?: The Synod on the New Forms of the Family." Reformanda Initiative, Oct. 31, 2014. https://vaticanfiles.org/en/2014/10/93-who-are-we-to-judge-the-synod-on-the-new-forms-of-the-family/.

———. "Vatican File 101. Holy Mother of God! Three Times!" Reformanda Initiative, Feb. 15, 2015. https://vaticanfiles.org/en/2015/02/101-holy-mother-of-god-three-times/.

———. "Vatican File 106. Should Evangelicals Love Pope Francis?" Reformanda Initiative, Apr. 13, 2015. https://vaticanfiles.org/en/2015/04/106-should-evangelicals-love-pope-francis/.

———. "Vatican File 109. Jubilee of Mercy (and Indulgences)." Reformanda Initiative, Jun. 1, 2015. https://vaticanfiles.org/2015/06/109-jubilee-of-mercy-and-indulgences/.

———. "Vatican File 110. A 'Green' Pope?" Reformanda Initiative, Jul. 1, 2015. https://vaticanfiles.org/en/2015/07/110-a-green-pope/.

———. "Vatican File 111. We Are Not Puritans, Are We?" Reformanda Initiative, Aug. 1, 2015. https://vaticanfiles.org/en/2015/08/111-we-are-not-puritans-are-we.

———. "Vatican File 116. After the Synod on the Family, What?" Reformanda Initiative, Dec. 1, 2015. https://vaticanfiles.org/en/2015/12/116-after-the-synod-on-the-family-what/.

———. "Vatican File 120. An Atonement-Free Mercy?" Reformanda Initiative, Mar. 1, 2016. https://vaticanfiles.org/it/2016/03/120-an-atonement-free-mercy/.

———. "Vatican File 131. After Lund, What Remains of the Protestant Reformation?" Reformanda Initiative, Nov. 9, 2016. https://vaticanfiles.org/2016/11/131-after-lund-what-remains-of-the-protestant-reformation/.

———. "Vatican File 131. Is Pope Francis Making the Catholic Church Protestant?" Reformanda Initiative, Dec. 1, 2016. https://vaticanfiles.org/it/2016/12/131-is-pope-francis-making-the-catholic-church-protestant/.

———. "Vatican File 132. 'The Only Creature Without Sin'—Pope Francis on the Immaculate Conception of Mary." Reformanda Initiative, Jan. 1, 2017. https://vaticanfiles.org/en/2017/01/132-the-only-creature-without-sin-pope-francis-on-the-immaculate-conception-of-mary/.

———. "Vatican File 134. The 'Uncertain Teaching' of Pope Francis." Reformanda Initiative, Mar. 1, 2017. https://vaticanfiles.org/en/2017/03/134-the-uncertain-teaching-of-pope-francis/.

———. "Vatican File 139. Would You Ever Ask Muslims to Pray for You? Pope Francis Did." Reformanda Initiative, Jul. 1, 2017. https://vaticanfiles.org/en/2017/07/139-would-you-ever-ask-muslims-to-pray-for-you-pope-francis-did/.

———. "Vatican File 140. Is the Roman Catholic Church Now Committed to 'Grace Alone'?" Reformanda Initiative, Aug. 1, 2017. https://vaticanfiles.org/2017/08/140-is-the-roman-catholic-church-now-committed-to-grace-alone/.

———. "Vatican File 144. What Happens if Catholics Think the Pope Is a Heretic?" Reformanda Initiative, Dec. 1, 2017. https://vaticanfiles.org/en/2017/12/144-happens-catholics-think-pope-heretic/.

———. "Vatican File 145. Mission. Did Pope Francis Say Mission?" Reformana Initiative, Jan. 1, 2018. https://vaticanfiles.org/en/2018/01/145-mission-pope-francis-say-mission/.

———. "Vatican File 156. She Is My Mamá?: Pope Francis and Mary." Reformanda Initiative, Dec. 1 2018. https://vaticanfiles.org/it/2018/12/156/.

———. "Vatican File 158. The Annus Horribilis (Terrible Year) of the Roman Catholic Church." Reformanda Initiative, Feb. 1, 2019. https://vaticanfiles.org/en/2019/02/vf158/.

———. "Vatican File 159. 'Confusion' and 'Failure': Other Roman Catholic Blows Against Pope Francis." Reformanda Initiative, Mar. 1st, 2019. https://vaticanfiles.org/en/2019/03/vf159/.

———. "Vatican File 161. Are There Two Popes of the Roman Catholic Church?" Reformanda Initiative, Apr. 19, 2019. https://vaticanfiles.org/en/2019/04/vf161/.

———. "Vatican File 162. Deciphering Vatican II: A New Book Especially Helpful for Evangelicals." Reformanda Initiative, May 1, 2019. https://vaticanfiles.org/en/2019/05/vf162/.

———. "Vatican File 166. Pope Francis Fears for the Planet, but Where Is the Gospel?" Reformanda Initiative, Sep. 1, 2019. https://vaticanfiles.org/en/2019/09/166-pope-francis-fears-for-the-planet-but-where-is-the-gospel/.

———. "Vatican File 181. 'All Brothers': The Unbearable Cost of Roman Catholic Universalism." Reformanda Initiative, Nov. 1, 2020. https://vaticanfiles.org/en/2020/11/181-all-brothers-the-unbearable-cost-of-roman-catholic-universalism/.

———. "Vatican File 182. The Dogma of the Bodily Assumption of Mary, 70 Years After." Reformanda Initiative, Dec. 1, 2020. https://vaticanfiles.org/en/2020/12/vf182/.

———. "Vatican File 183. What Francis Really Thinks of the Reformation and of Calvin in Particular." Reformanda Initiative, Jun. 23, 2014. https://vaticanfiles.org/2014/06/83-what-francis-really-thinks-of-the-reformation-and-of-calvin-in-particular/.

———. "Vatican File 189. A Biography of Thomas Aquinas' Summa Theologiae. Is It Also a Radiography of Roman Catholicism?" Reformanda Initiative, Jun. 1, 2021. https://vaticanfiles.org/en/2021/06/189/.

———. "Vatican File 200. Who Is Afraid of 'Liquid' Roman Catholicism?" Reformanda Initiative, Apr. 1, 2022. https://vaticanfiles.org/en/2022/04/200/.

———. "Vatican File 205. One Roman (Vatican) Stop After a Catholic (German) Push." Reformanda Initiative, Sep. 1, 2022. https://vaticanfiles.org/en/2022/09/205/.

———. "Vatican File 206. New Cardinals for the Future Conclave." Reformanda Initiative, Oct. 1, 2022. https://vaticanfiles.org/en/2022/10/vf206/.

———. "Vatican File 218. In a Double Move, Francis Closes the Ratzinger Era. For Now." Reformanda Initiative, Aug. 1, 2023. https://vaticanfiles.org/en/2023/08/vf218/.

———. "Vatican File 220. 'The Next Pope will be John XXIV': Will He?" Reformanda Initiative, Oct. 1, 2023. https://vaticanfiles.org/en/2023/10/220/.

———. "A Window into the Theological Vision of Pope Francis." *Christian Research Journal* 38.6 (2015) 12–19.

Dianich, Severino. *Magistero in Movimento: Il Caso Papa Francesco*. Bologna: EDB, 2016.

Douthat, Ross. *To Change the Church: Pope Francis and the Future of Catholicism*. New York: Simon & Schuster, 2018.

Dupuis, Jacques. *Christianity and the Religions: From Confrontation to Dialogue*. Maryknoll, NY: Orbis, 2002.

———. *Jesus Christ at the Encounter of World Religions*. Maryknoll, NY: Orbis, 1991.

———. *Toward a Christian Theology of Religious Pluralism*. Maryknoll, NY: Orbis, 2002.

Economy of Francesco. https://francescoeconomy.org/.

Fernández, Víctor Manuel. *Il Progetto di Francesco: Dove vuole portare la Chiesa*. Bologna: EMI, 2014.

Fournier, Keith A. "He Went to Find Brothers: Message of Pope Francis to Evangelical/Pentecostal Brother John and the Church at Caserta." Catholic Online, Jul. 31, 2014. https://www.catholic.org/news/international/europe/story.php?id=56355.

Francis (Pope). "Act of Veneration to the Immaculate Conception at the Spanish Steps. Prayer of His Holiness Pope Francis." Dec. 8, 2016. https://www.vatican.va/content/francesco/en/prayers/documents/papa-francesco_preghiere_20161208_immacolata.html.

———. "Ad Theologiam Promovendam." Nov. 1, 2023. https://press.vatican.va/content/salastampa/it/bollettino/pubblico/2023/11/01/0760/01668.html.

———. "Address of His Holiness: 'Catholic Junior College.'" Sep. 13, 2024. https://www.vatican.va/content/francesco/en/speeches/2024/september/documents/20240913-singapore-giovani.html.

———. "Address of His Holiness, Parque Eduardo VII, Lisbon." Aug. 3, 2023. https://www.vatican.va/content/francesco/en/speeches/2023/august/documents/20230803-portogallo-cerimonia-accoglienza.html.

———. "Address of His Holiness Pope Francis, Christuskirche Parish." Nov. 15, 2015. https://w2.vatican.va/content/francesco/en/speeches/2015/november/documents/papa-francesco_20151115_chiesa-evangelica-luterana.html.

———. "Address of His Holiness Pope Francis, Synod Hall." Oct. 24, 2015. https://www.vatican.va/content/francesco/en/speeches/2015/october/documents/papa-francesco_20151024_sinodo-conclusione-lavori.html.

———. "Address of Pope Francis, Archbishop's House, Rio de Janeiro." Jul. 28, 2013. https://www.vatican.va/content/francesco/en/speeches/2013/july/documents/papa-francesco_20130727_gmg-episcopato-brasile.html.

———. "Address of Pope Francis, Patriarchal Church of St. George, Istanbul." Nov. 30, 2014. https://www.vatican.va/content/francesco/en/homilies/2014/documents/papa-francesco_20141130_divina-liturgia-turchia.html.

———. "Address of Pope Francis to the Member of the Pontifical Biblical Commission, Hall of the Popes." Apr. 12, 2013. https://www.vatican.va/content/francesco/en/speeches/2013/april/documents/papa-francesco_20130412_commissione-biblica.html.

———. "Address of the Holy Father, Ankara." Nov. 28–30 2014. https://www.vatican.va/content/francesco/en/speeches/2014/november/documents/papa-francesco_20141128_turchia-presidenza-diyanet.html.
———. "Address of the Holy Father Pope Francis, Papal Basilica of St. Mary Major." May 4, 2013. https://www.vatican.va/content/francesco/en/speeches/2013/may/documents/papa-francesco_20130504_santo-rosario.html.
———. "Al Colloquio Internazionale Sulla Complementareità tra Uomo e Donna." Nov. 17, 2014. https://www.vatican.va/content/francesco/it/speeches/2014/november/documents/papa-francesco_20141117_congregazione-dottrina-fede.html.
———. "All'Associazione Medici Cattolici Italiani." Nov. 15, 2014. https://www.vatican.va/content/francesco/it/events/event.dir.html/content/vaticanevents/it/2014/11/15/medicicattolici.html.
———. "Amoris Lætitia." Mar. 19, 2016. http://vatican.va/content/dam/francesco/pdf/apost_exhortations/documents/papa-francesco_esortazione-ap_20160319_amoris-laetitia_en.pdf.
———. *Chi sono i gesuiti*. Bologna: EMI, 2014.
———. "Christus Vivit." 2019. http://www.vatican.va/content/francesco/en/apost_exhortations/documents/papa-francesco_esortazione-ap_20190325_christus-vivit.html#PART_FOUR.
———. "Dilexit Nos." Oct. 24, 2024. https://www.vatican.va/content/francesco/en/encyclicals/documents/20241024-enciclica-dilexit-nos.html.
———. "Discorso del Santo Padre." Nov. 10, 2015. https://www.vatican.va/content/francesco/it/speeches/2015/november/documents/papa-francesco_20151110_firenze-convegno-chiesa-italiana.html.francesco_20151110_firenze-convegno-chiesa-italiana.html.
———. "Discorso del Santo Padre Francesco ai Partecipani al Congresso Tomistico Internazionale, Promosso dalla Pontificia Accademia de San Tomasso d'Aquino." Sep. 22, 2022. https://www.vatican.va/content/francesco/it/speeches/2022/september/documents/20220922-congresso-tomistico.html.
———. "Epistula Data Valthero S.R.E. Cardinali Brandmüller." Nov. 19, 2013. https://www.vatican.va/content/francesco/la/letters/2013/documents/papa-francesco_20131119_brandmuller-450-chiusura-concilio-trento.html.
———. "Evangelii Gaudium." Nov. 24, 2013. https://www.vatican.va/content/francesco/en/apost_exhortations/documents/papa-francesco_esortazione-ap_20131124_evangelii-gaudium.html.
———. "Fiducia Supplicans." Dec. 18, 2023. https://press.vatican.va/content/salastampa/it/bollettino/pubblico/2023/12/18/0901/01963.html#en.
———. "Fratelli Tutti." Oct. 3, 2020. https://www.vatican.va/content/francesco/en/encyclicals/documents/papa-francesco_20201003_enciclica-fratelli-tutti.html.
———. "Full Text: Pope Francis' In-Flight Presser from Sweden." Interview by Greg Burke, *Catholic News Agency*, Nov. 1, 2016. http://www.catholicnewsagency.com/news/full-text-pope-francis-in-flight-presser-from-sweden-66035/.
———. "Full Text of Pope Francis' In-Flight Press Conference from Bangladesh." National Catholic Register (blog), Dec. 3, 2017. http://www.ncregister.com/daily-news/full-text-of-pope-francis-in-flight-press-conference-from-bangladesh.
———. "General Audience Catechesis." Zenit, Nov. 5, 2014. http://www.zenit.org/en/articles/full-text-of-pope-s-general-audience-catechesis-nov-5th.

———. "General Audience, Saint Peter's Square." Feb. 3, 2016. https://www.vatican.va/content/francesco/en/audiences/2016/documents/papa-francesco_20160203_udienza-generale.html.

———. "Homily of His Holiness Pope Francis, Basilica of the Shrine of Our Lady of the Conception of Aparecida." Jul. 24, 2013. https://www.vatican.va/content/francesco/en/homilies/2013/documents/papa-francesco_20130724_gmg-omelia-aparecida.html.

———. "Homily of His Holiness Pope Francis, Lund." Oct. 31, 2016. https://w2.vatican.va/content/francesco/en/homilies/2016/documents/papa-francesco_20161031_omelia-svezia-lund.html.

———. "Homily of Pope Francis, World Cup Stadium (Daejeon)." Aug. 15, 2014. https://www.vatican.va/content/francesco/en/homilies/2014/documents/papa-francesco_20140815_corea-omelia-assunzione.html.

———. "Homily of His Holiness Pope Francis, Vatican Basilica." Jan. 1, 2015. https://www.vatican.va/content/francesco/en/homilies/2015/documents/papa-francesco_20150101_omelia-giornata-mondiale-pace.html.

———. "Homily of Pope Francis, Vatican Basilica." Oct. 1, 2019. https://www.vatican.va/content/francesco/en/homilies/2019/documents/papa-francesco_20191001_omelia-vespri-mesemissionario.html.

———. "Interreligious Meeting, Plain of Ur." Mar. 6, 2021. http://www.vatican.va/content/francesco/en/speeches/2021/march/documents/papa-francesco_20210306_iraq-incontro-interreligioso.html.

———. "Interview with Pope Francis." Interview by Antonio Spadaro. Aug. 19, 2013. https://www.vatican.va/content/francesco/en/speeches/2013/september/documents/papa-francesco_20130921_intervista-spadaro.html.

———. "Laudato Si'." May 24, 2015. https://www.vatican.va/content/francesco/en/encyclicals/documents/papa-francesco_20150524_enciclica-laudato-si.html.

———. "Letter to a Non-Believer." Sep. 4, 2013. https://www.vatican.va/content/francesco/en/letters/2013/documents/papa-francesco_20130911_eugenio-scalfari.html.

———. "Lumen Fidei." Jun. 29, 2013. https://www.vatican.va/content/francesco/en/encyclicals/documents/papa-francesco_20130629_enciclica-lumen-fidei.html.

———. "Meeting with the Bishops of Asia. Address of Pope Francis, Shrine of Haemi." Aug. 17, 2014. https://www.vatican.va/content/francesco/en/speeches/2014/august/documents/papa-francesco_20140817_corea-vescovi-asia.html.

———. "Meeting with the Participants of the Fifth Convention of the Italian Church. Address of the Holy Father." Nov. 10, 2015. https://www.vatican.va/content/francesco/en/speeches/2015/november/documents/papa-francesco_20151110_firenze-convegno-chiesa-italiana.html.

———. "Message for World Mission Day 2019." 2019. https://www.vatican.va/content/francesco/en/messages/missions/documents/papa-francesco_20190609_giornata-missionaria2019.html.

———. "Message of the Holy Father Francis to Participants in the International Meeting for Peace." Sep. 22–24, 2024. https://www.vatican.va/content/francesco/en/messages/pont-messages/2024/documents/20240917-messaggio-pace-parigi.htmls

———. "Misericordiae Vultus." 2015. https://www.vatican.va/content/francesco/en/bulls/documents/papa-francesco_bolla_20150411_misericordiae-vultus.html.

———. "An Open Dialogue with Unbelievers." *Le Repubblica*, Sep. 11, 2013. https://www.repubblica.it/cultura/2013/09/11/news/the_pope_s_letter-66336961/.
———. "Pope Francis to Chorus: Popular Piety Is the Immune System of the Church." *Rome Reports*, Nov. 11, 2018. https://www.romereports.com/en/2018/11/26/pope-francis-to-chorus-popular-piety-is-the-immune-system-of-the-church/.
———. "Querida Amazonia." 2020. http://www.vatican.va/content/francesco/en/apost_exhortations/documents/papa-francesco_esortazione-ap_20200202_querida-amazonia.html.
———. "Recital of the Holy Rosary for the Conclusion of the Marian Month of May." May 31, 2013. https://www.vatican.va/content/francesco/en/speeches/2013/may/documents/papa-francesco_20130531_conclusione-mese-mariano.html.
———. "Spes Non Confundit." 2024. https://press.vatican.va/content/salastampa/it/bollettino/pubblico/2024/05/09/0374/00781.html#ing.
———. "Video Message of His Holiness Pope Francis to Participants in the Meeting." Nov. 21, 2020. http://www.vatican.va/content/francesco/en/messages/pont-messages/2020/documents/papa-francesco_20201121_videomessaggio-economy-of-francesco.html.
———. "Video Message of Pope Francis for the Third Festival of the Social Doctrine of the Church Held in Verona." Nov. 21–24, 2013. https://www.vatican.va/content/francesco/en/messages/pont-messages/2013/documents/papa-francesco_20131121_videomessaggio-festival-dottrina-sociale.html.
———. "Videomessaggio del Santo Padre Francesco ai Partecipanti al 'Global Compact on Education.'" Oct. 15, 2020 https://press.vatican.va/content/salastampa/it/bollettino/pubblico/2020/10/15/0527/01219.html.
———., and Ahmad Al-Tayyeb. "A Document on Human Fraternity for World Peace and Living Together." Feb. 4, 2019. https://www.vatican.va/content/francesco/en/travels/2019/outside/documents/papa-francesco_20190204_documento-fratellanza-umana.html.
Gänswein, Georg. *Neint'altro che verità: La mia vita al fianco di Benedetto XVI*. Milan: Piemme, 2023.
Ghirlanda, G. "'Praedicate Evangelium' Sulla Curia Romana." *La Civiltà Cattolica* 4123 (2022) 41–56.
Giuffrida, Angela. "Vatican Scrambles After Pope Appears to Deny Existence of Hell." *The Guardian*, Mar. 30, 2018. https://www.theguardian.com/world/2018/mar/30/vatican-scrambles-to-clarify-popes-denial-that-hell-exists.
Global Compact on Education. https://www.educationglobalcompact.org/en/.
Goodwin, Thomas. *The Heart of Christ in Heaven Toward Sinners on Earth*. Edinburgh: Banner of Truth, 2022.
Gutiérrez, Gustavo, and Gerhard L. Müller. *An der Seite der Armen: Theologie der Befreiung*. Augsburg: Sankt Ulrich, 2004.
Hagenskord, Bernd. "Pope Urges German Church to Walk Together, Moved by the Spirit." *Vatican News*, Jun. 29, 2019. https://www.vaticannews.va/en/pope/news/2019-16/pope-francis-letter-german-church-synodality.html.
Harris, Elsie. "Be Like Mary—Say Yes to God, but Not Halfway, Pope Francis Says." *Catholic News Agency*, Dec. 8, 2016. http://www.catholicnewsagency.com/news/be-like-mary-say-yes-to-god-but-not-halfway-pope-francis-says-65203/.
Higher Committee of Human Fraternity. https://www.forhumanfraternity.org/.

Holy See. "Audience to the General Assembly of the Pontifical Mission Societies." Jun. 3rd, 2023. https://press.vatican.va/content/salastampa/it/bollettino/pubblico/2023/06/03/0419/00936.html#ing.

———. "Catechism of the Catholic Church." 1993. https://www.vatican.va/archive/ENG0015/_INDEX.HTM.

———. "Communique: Holy Father Approves Recommendations of the Future of the IOR." Jul. 4, 2014. https://press.vatican.va/content/salastampa/it/bollettino/pubblico/2014/04/07/0244/00548.html.

———. "Conference on the Encyclical Letter 'Fratelli Tutti' of the Holy Father Francis on Fraternity and Social Friendship." Apr. 10, 2020. https://press.vatican.va/content/salastampa/en/bollettino/pubblico/2020/10/04/201004a.html.

———. "Decree on the Granting of the Indulgence During the Ordinary Jubilee Year, 2025." May 13, 2024. https://press.vatican.va/content/salastampa/en/bollettino/pubblico/2024/05/13/240513f.html.

———. "Dichiarazione della Santa Sede." Jul. 21, 2022. https://press.vatican.va/content/salastampa/it/bollettino/pubblico/2022/07/21/0550/01133.html.

———. "Dominus Iesus." 2000. https://www.vatican.va/roman_curia/congregations/cfaith/documents/rc_con_cfaith_doc_20000806_dominus-iesus_en.html.

———. "Erklärung des Heiligen Stuhls." Jul. 21, 2022. https://press.vatican.va/content/salastampa/it/bollettino/pubblico/2022/07/21/0550/01133.html#de.

———. "Instruction Dignitas Personae on Certain Bioethical Questions." 2008. http://www.vatican.va/roman_curia/congregations/cfaith/documents/rc_con_cfaith_doc_20081208_dignitas-personae_en.html.

———. "Instruction on the Respect for Human Life in its Origin and on the Dignity of Procreation: Replies to Certain Questions of the Day." Feb. 22, 1987. http://www.vatican.va/roman_curia/congregations/cfaith/documents/rc_con_cfaith_doc_19870222_respect-for-human-life_en.html.

———. "Iuvenescit Ecclesia." May 15, 2016. http://www.vatican.va/roman_curia/congregations/cfaith/documents/rc_con_cfaith_doc_20160516_iuvenescit-ecclesia_en.html.

———. "Lumen Gentium." Nov. 21, 1964. https://www.vatican.va/archive/hist_councils/ii_vatican_council/documents/vat-ii_const_19641121_lumen-gentium_en.html.

———. "Pontifical Academy of Theology." https://www.vatican.va/content/romancuria/en/pontificie-accademie/pontificia-academia-theologica.html.

———. "Praedicate Evangelium." Mar. 19, 2022. https://press.vatican.va/content/salastampa/it/bollettino/pubblico/2022/03/19/0189/00404.html.

———. "Udienza ad una Delegazione di Leader Musulmani della Gran Bretagna." Apr. 5, 2017. https://press.vatican.va/content/salastampa/it/bollettino/pubblico/2017/04/05/0220/00498.html.

———. "Unitatis Redintegratio." Nov. 21, 1964. https://www.vatican.va/archive/hist_councils/ii_vatican_council/documents/vat-ii_decree_19641121_unitatis-redintegratio_en.html.

Istituto di Formazione Evangelica e Documentazione. "Orientamenti evangelici per pensare il cattolicesimo." Alleanza Evangelica Italiana, Sep. 10–11, 1999. https://www.alleanzaevangelica.org/index.php/news/9-attualita-italia/89-orientamenti-evangelici-per-pensare-il-cattolicesimo.

Ivereigh, Austen. *The Great Reformer: Francis and the Making of a Radical Pope*. New York: Henry Holt and Company, 2014.

———. *The Great Reformer: Francis and the Making of a Radical Pope*. New York: Picador, 2015.

John Paul II (Pope). "Evangelium Vitae." Mar. 25, 1995. https://www.vatican.va/content/john-paul-ii/en/encyclicals/documents/hf_jp-ii_enc_25031995_evangelium-vitae.html.

———. "Familiaris Consortio." Nov. 22, 1981. https://www.vatican.va/content/john-paul-ii/en/apost_exhortations/documents/hf_jp-ii_exh_19811122_familiaris-consortio.html.

———. "Fides et Ratio." 1998. https://www.vatican.va/content/john-paul-ii/en/encyclicals/documents/hf_jp-ii_enc_14091998_fides-et-ratio.html.

———. "Redemptoris Missio." 1990. https://www.vatican.va/content/john-paul-ii/en/encyclicals/documents/hf_jp-ii_enc_07121990_redemptoris-missio.html.

———. "Veritatis Splendor." Aug. 6, 1993. https://www.vatican.va/content/john-paul-ii/en/encyclicals/documents/hf_jp-ii_enc_06081993_veritatis-splendor.html.

Kantor, Jodi. "In Law School, Obama Found Political Voice." *New York Times*, Jan. 28, 2007. http://www.nytimes.com/2007/01/28/us/politics/28obama.html.

Karr, Reid. "No One Excluded: A Key (But Problematic?) Concept for the Synodal Catholic Church." Reformanda Initiative, Nov. 8, 2022. https://www.reformandainitiative.org/resources/no-one-excluded.

———. "Synodality and Its Ambiguous Path." Reformanda Initiative, Nov. 1, 2023. https://www.reformandainitiative.org/resources/evangelical-reflections-on-the-instrumentum-laboris-of-the-synodal-church-reflection-2-rn3n2-bll6n-289r9-pj2lc.

———. "Synodality, Reform, and the Roman Catholic Church of the Third Millennium." Reformanda Initiative, May 30, 2023. https://www.reformandainitiative.org/resources/synodality-reform-and-the-roman-catholic-church.

Kasper, Walter. *Mercy: The Essence of the Gospel and the Key to Christian Life*. Mahwah, NJ: Paulist, 2014.

———. *Pope Francis' Revolution of Tenderness and Love: Theological and Pastoral Perspectives*. New York: Paulist, 2015.

Kelly, Jack. "Pope Francis Partners with Corporate Titans to Make Capitalism More Inclusive and Fair: Is This For Real or Just Corporate Virtue Signaling?" *Forbes*, Dec. 9, 2020 https://www.forbes.com/sites/jackkelly/2020/12/09/pope-francis-partners-with-corporate-titans-to-make-capitalism-more-inclusive-and-fair-is-this-for-real-or-just-corporate-virtue-signaling/?sh=deef4be4c7b1.

Lafont, Ghislain. *Petit Essai Sur Le Temps du Pape François*. Paris: Cerf, 2017.

Lausanne Movement. "The Cape Town Commitment." 2010. http://www.lausanne.org/content/ctc/ctcommitment.

———. "The Lausanne Covenant." 1974. https://www.lausanne.org/content/covenant/lausanne-covenant.

Ledda, Giuseppe. *La Bibbia di Dante*. Turin: Claudiana, 2015.

Le Goff, Jacques. *The Birth of Purgatory*. Chicago: University of Chicago Press, 1986.

———. *La Nascita del Purgatorio*. Turin: Einaudi, 1982.

Leo XIII (Pope). "Aeterni Patris." 1897. https://www.vatican.va/content/leo-xiii/en/encyclicals/documents/hf_l-xiii_enc_04081879_aeterni-patris.html.

———. "Providentissimus Deus." 1893. https://www.vatican.va/content/leo-xiii/en/encyclicals/documents/hf_l-xiii_enc_18111893_providentissimus-deus.html.

LifeSiteNews. "Full Text of 4 Cardinals' Letter to Pope Francis with Explanatory Notes and 5 Questions." Nov. 14, 2016. https://www.lifesitenews.com/news/full-text-of-4-cardinals-letter-to-pope-francis-with-explanatory-notes-and.

The Local. "Pope Francis Praises British Muslim Leaders, Asks Them to Pray for Him." Apr. 5, 2017. https://www.thelocal.it/20170405/pope-francis-meets-british-muslim-leaders-praises-their-contribution.

Lewis, C. S. *English Literature in the Sixteenth Century*. Oxford: Clarendon, 1954.

———. *Studies in Medieval and Renaissance Literature*. Cambridge: Cambridge University Press, 1980.

Lo Sapio, Luca. *Bioetica Cattolica e Bioetica Laica Nell'era di Papa Francesco*. Novara: Utet, 2017.

Lutheran World Federation. "Joint Declaration on the Doctrine of Justification by the Lutheran World Federation and the Catholic Church." 1999. https://lutheranworld.org/resources/publication-joint-declaration-doctrine-justification.

Magister, Sandro. "The Pope in Mission Territory. But the Only One Talking About Jesus Is a Buddhist." *L'Espresso*, Nov. 28, 2017. https://www.pro-memoria.info/wp/wp-content/uploads/The-Pope-in-Mission-Territory_-But-the-Only-One-Talking-About-Jesus-Is-a-Buddhist-Magister.pdf.

Maradiaga, O. A. R. *Praedicate Evangelium. Una Nuova Curia per Un Tempo Nuovo*. Rome: Pubblicazioni Clarettiane, 2022.

Mission 4.7. https://www.mission4point7.org/.

Monergism. "John Calvin to Cardinal Sadoleto, 1 September 1539." https://www.monergism.com/john-calvins-letter-cardinal-sadoleto-1539.

Montagna, Diane. "Pope Francis Blocks German Bishops' Intercommunication Proposal." LifeSite, Jun. 4, 2018. https://www.lifesitenews.com/news/cdf-sends-letter-on-behalf-of-pope-francis-to-german-bishops-regarding-inte/.

Müller, Gerhard L. *Provera per i Poveri: La Missione della Chiesa*. Rome: Libreria Editrice Vaticana, 2014.

Naro, Massimo. *Protagonista è l'Abbraccio: Temi Teologici nel Magistero di Francesco*. Venice: Marcianum, 2021.

Nichols, Alan. "Occasional Paper: An Evangelical Commitment to Simple Lifestyle." Lausanne Movement, 1980. http://www.lausanne.org/content/lop/lop-20.

Obama, Barack. *The Audacity of Hope: Thoughts on Reclaiming the American Dream*. New York: Crown, 2006.

O'Donnell, Norah. "Pope Francis Tells 60 Minutes in Rare Interview: 'The Globalization of Indifference Is a Very Ugly Disease.'" CBS News, Dec. 30, 2024. https://www.cbsnews.com/news/pope-francis-interview-60-minutes-transcript.

Olson, Carl E. "Fr. Thomas G. Weinandy Explains His Critical Letter to Pope Francis." *Catholic World Report*, Nov. 1, 2017. http://www.catholicworldreport.com/2017/11/01/fr-thomas-g-weinandy-explains-his-critical-letter-to-pope-francis/.

O'Malley, John W. *Trent: What Happened at the Council*. Cambridge, MA: Belknap Press of Harvard University Press, 2013.

Packer, J. I. *Among God's Giants. The Puritan Vision of the Christian Life*. Eastbourne, UK: Kingsway, 1991.

Paul VI (Pope). "Enchiridion Indulgentiarum." 1968. https://www.vatican.va/roman_curia/tribunals/apost_penit/documents/rc_trib_appen_doc_20020826_enchiridion-indulgentiarum_lt.html.

———. "Evangelii Nuntiandi." Dec. 8, 1975. https://www.vatican.va/content/paul-vi/en/apost_exhortations/documents/hf_p-vi_exh_19751208_evangelii-nuntiandi.html.

———. "Humanae Vitae." Jul. 25, 1968. https://www.vatican.va/content/paul-vi/en/encyclicals/documents/hf_p-vi_enc_25071968_humanae-vitae.html.

———. "Indulgentiarum Doctrina." 1967. https://www.vatican.va/content/paul-vi/en/apost_constitutions/documents/hf_p-vi_apc_01011967_indulgentiarum-doctrina.html.

———. "Lumen Ecclesiae." 1974. https://www.vatican.va/content/paul-vi/it/apost_letters/documents/hf_p-vi_apl_19741205_lumen-ecclesiae.html.

The Pillar. "'Ad Theologiam Promovendam': A Brief Guide for Busy Readers." Nov. 6, 2023. https://www.pillarcatholic.com/p/ad-theologiam-promovendam-a-brief.

Pentin, Edward. "Cardinal Müller Issues 'Manifesto of Faith.'" National Catholic Register (blog), Feb. 8, 2019. http://www.ncregister.com/blog/edward-pentin/cardinal-mueller-issues-manifesto-of-faith.

———. "Fr. Lombardi: Latest Scalfari Article on Pope 'In No Way Reliable.'" National Catholic Register (blog), Nov. 2, 2015. http://www.ncregister.com/blog/edward-pentin/fr.-lombardi-latest-scalfari-article-on-pope-in-no-way-reliable/.

———. "Full Text and Explanatory Notes of Cardinals' Questions on 'Amoris Laetitia.'" National Catholic Register (blog), Nov. 14, 2016. https://www.ncregister.com/blog/full-text-and-explanatory-notes-of-cardinals-questions-on-amoris-laetitia.

———. "Unpacking the Benedict XVI-Cardinal Sarah Book Fiasco." National Catholic Register (blog), Jan. 15, 2020. https://www.ncregister.com/blog/edward-pentin/unpacking-the-benedict-cardinal-sarah-book-fiasco.

Piro, Isabella. "Pope Francis Celebrates Dante: Prophet of Hope and Poet of Mercy." Vatican News, Mar. 25, 2021. https://www.vaticannews.va/en/pope/news/2021-23/pope-francis-apostolic-letter-dante-anniversary.html.

Pius IX (Pope). "Divino Afflante Spiritu." Sep. 30, 1943. https://www.vatican.va/content/pius-xii/en/encyclicals/documents/hf_p-xii_enc_30091943_divino-afflante-spiritu.html.

———. "Ineffabilis Deus." Papal Encyclicals, Dec. 8, 1854. https://www.papalencyclicals.net/pius09/p9ineff.htm.

———. "On Revelation." In Decrees of the First Vatican Council. Papal Encyclicals, Jun. 29, 1868. https://www.papalencyclicals.net/councils/ecum20.htm.

Pongratz-Lippitt, Christa. "Germany's 'Synodal Path' Is a Model for the Global Church, Says Observer." LaCroix International, Oct. 12, 2021. https://international.la-croix.com/news/religion/germanys-synodal-path-is-a-model-for-the-global-church-says-observer/15036.

Pontifical Biblical Commission. "Inspiration and Truth of Sacred Scripture." Feb. 22, 2014. https://www.vatican.va/roman_curia/congregations/cfaith/pcb_documents/rc_con_cfaith_doc_20140222_ispirazione-verita-sacra-scrittura_it.html.

Pontifical Council for Interreligious Dialogue. "Towards a Genuine Fraternity Between Christians and Muslims." 2014. https://www.usccb.org/resources/Ramadan-English-2014.pdf.

Catholic News Agency. "Pope Beatifies 124 Korean Martyrs, Praising Their Witness to Christ." Aug. 15, 2014. https://www.catholicnewsagency.com/news/30299/pope-beatifies-124-korean-martyrs-praising-their-witness-to-christ.
Vatican Archives. "Pope Francis' Prayer Intentions for January 2016." Jan. 6, 2016, YouTube video, 1:31. https://www.youtube.com/watch?v=-6FfTxwTX34.
"Pope Francis Warns Church Against Ideologies in Church and World." Vatican News, Sep. 4, 2023. https://www.vaticannews.va/en/pope/news/2023-09/pope-francis-mongolia-return-press-conference-synod-ideologies.html.
Prodi, Paolo. *Il Paradigma Tridentino: Un'epoca della Storia della Chiesa.* Brescia: Morcelliana, 2010.
Reeves, Michael. "The Joint Declaration on the Doctrine of Justification: A Curtain on the Reformation?" Reformanda Initiative, Jul. 15, 2019. http://reformandainitiative.org/the-joint-declaration-on-the-doctrine-of-justification-a-curtain-on-the-reformation/.
Reformanda Initiative. "Is the Reformation Over?: A Statement of Evangelical Convictions." Nov. 9, 2016. http://isthereformationover.com/.
———. "Reformanda Initiative." 2020. https://www.reformandainitiative.org.
———. "Vatican Files—Evangelical Theological Perspectives on Roman Catholicism." Apr. 2025. https://vaticanfiles.org.
Reno, R. R. "A Failing Papacy." *First Things*, Feb. 1, 2019. https://www.firstthings.com/article/2019/02/a-failing-papacy.
Return to Tradition (blog). "Unofficial Full English Translation of Francis' Revolutionary Motu Proprio Ad Theologiam Promovendam." Nov. 3, 2023. https://returntotradition.org/unofficial-full-english-translation-of-francis-revolutionary-motu-proprio-ad-theologiam-promovendam-plus-breaking-news-report-on-text/.
Rorate Cæli (blog). "Bombshell: Pope to His Favorite Journalist: 'All the Divorced Who Ask Will Be Admitted [to Communion].'" 2015. http://rorate-caeli.blogspot.com/2015/11/bombshell-pope-to-his-favorite.html.
Sansonetti, V., ed. *Francesco e Maria: L'amore di Papa Bergoglio per la Madonna.* Milan: Rizzoli, 2014.
Scalfari, Eugenio. "The Pope: How the Church Will Change." *La Repubblica*, Oct. 1, 2013. https://www.repubblica.it/cultura/2013/10/01/news/pope_s_conversation_with_scalfari_english-67643118/.
Second Vatican Council. "Decree on Priestly Training, 'Optatam Totius.'" Oct. 28, 1965. https://www.vatican.va/archive/hist_councils/ii_vatican_council/documents/vat-ii_decree_19651028_optatam-totius_en.html.
———. "Dogmatic Constitution on Divine Revelation, 'Dei Verbum.'" Nov. 18, 1965. http://www.vatican.va/archive/hist_councils/ii_vatican_council/documents/vat-ii_const_19651118_dei-verbum_en.html.
———. "Dogmatic Constitution on the Church, 'Lumen Gentium.'" Nov. 21, 1964. http://www.vatican.va/archive/hist_councils/ii_vatican_council/documents/vat-ii_const_19641121_lumen-gentium_en.html.
Spadaro, Antonio, "A Big Heart Open to God: An Interview with Pope Francis." *America*, Sep. 30, 2013. https://www.americamagazine.org/faith/2013/09/30/big-heart-open-god-interview-pope-francis.
———., and Carolos Maria Gali. *La Riforma e le Riforme Nella Chiesa.* Brescia: Queriniana, 2017.

Synod of Bishops. "The Amazon: New Paths for the Church and for an Integral Ecology. Final Document." http://www.vatican.va/roman_curia/synod/documents/rc_synod_doc_20191026_sinodo-amazzonia_en.html.

———. "The Final Report of the Synod of Bishops to the Holy Father, Pope Francis." Oct. 24, 2015. https://www.vatican.va/roman_curia/synod/documents/rc_synod_doc_20151026_relazione-finale-xiv-assemblea_en.html.

Thomas, Huw. "The Two Popes: Jonahtan Pryce's 'Emotional Moment' in Vatican." BBC, Dec. 18, 2019. https://www.bbc.com/news/uk-wales-50837607.

Tornielli, Andrea. "Never Be Afraid of Tenderness." *La Stampa*, Dec. 15, 2013. https://www.lastampa.it/vatican-insider/en/2013/12/15/news/never-be-afraid-of-tenderness-1.35947042/.

———. "Transcript: Pope Francis' Remarks to the United Nations." *Los Angeles Times*, Sep. 25, 2015. http://www.latimes.com/nation/la-na-pope-francis-remarks-to-united-nations-20150925-story.html.

———. "Transcript: Pope Francis' Speech to Congress." *Washington Post*, Sep. 24, 2015. https://www.washingtonpost.com/local/social-issues/transcript-pope-franciss-speech-to-congress/2015/09/24/6d7d7ac8-62bf-11e5-8e9e-dce8a2a2a679_story.html.

United Nations. "Department of Economic and Social Affairs: Sustainable Development." https://sdgs.un.org/goals.

Valli, Aldo Maria. "Il Dilemma del Successore di Francesco: Continuare a Essere il Cappellano dell'Onu o Tornare a Confermare i Fratelli Nell Fede?" Aldomariavalli (blog), Jan. 7, 2021. https://www.aldomariavalli.it/2021/01/07/il-dilemma-del-successore-di-francesco-continuare-a-essere-il-cappellano-dellonu-o-tornare-a-confermare-i-fratelli-nella-fede.

Vatican News. "COVID-19: Faithful Respond to Pope's Invitation to Pray on 14 May." *Vatican News*, May 12, 2020. https://www.vaticannews.va/en/church/news/2020-05/covid-19-faithful-respond-to-popes-invitation-to-pray-may-14.html.

———. "Il Cardinale Cantalamessa: Dio Ha Molti Modi per Salvare." Dec. 2, 2022. https://www.vaticannews.va/it/vaticano/news/2022-12/cardinale-cantalamessa-dio-molti-modi-salvare.html.

Wehner, Peter. "Why Evangelicals Should Love the Pope." *New York Times*, Apr. 4, 2015. https://www.nytimes.com/2015/04/05/opinion/sunday/why-evangelicals-should-love-the-pope.html.

Weigel, George. *Evangelical Catholicism: Deep Reform in the 21st-Century Church*. New York: Basic, 2015.

———. "Liquid Catholicism and the German Synodal Path." *First Things*, Feb. 16, 2022. https://www.firstthings.com/web-exclusives/2022/02/liquid-catholicism-and-the-german-synodal-path.

———. *The Next Pope: The Office of Peter and a Church in Mission*. San Francisco: Ignatius, 2020.

———. *Il Prossimo Papa: L'ufficio di Pietro e la Missione della Chiesa*. Verona: Fede & Cultura, 2021.

———. *Witness to Hope: The Biography of Pope John Paul II*. New York: Cliff Street, 1999.

Wells, David F. *The Courage to Be Protestant*. Grand Rapids: Eerdmans, 2008.

———. *Revolution in Rome*. Downers Grove, IL: InterVarsity, 1972.

Wenham, John. *Christ and the Bible*. Grand Rapids: Baker, 1994.

Wikipedia. "*Salus Populi Romani*." https://en.wikipedia.org/wiki/Salus_Populi_Romani.

Willey, David. *The Promise of Francis: The Man, the Pope, and the Challenge of Change.* New York: Gallery, 2015.

Wooden, Cindy. "Pope Francis Asks German Bishops to Set Aside Plan on Communion for Non-Catholic Spouses." *Catholic News Service*, Jun. 4, 2018. https://www.americamagazine.org/faith/2018/06/04/pope-francis-asks-german-bishops-set-aside-plan-communion-non-catholic-spouses.

World Council of Churches. "Baptism, Eucharist and Ministry." 1982. https://www.oikoumene.org/resources/documents/baptism-eucharist-and-ministry-faith-and-order-paper-no-111-the-lima-text.

World Evangelical Alliance. "On the Care of Creation." 2008. https://www.worldevangelicals.org/pdf/WEA_Statement_GA2008_Care_of_Creation_draft_A_Oct_22.pdf.

Zenit. "Pope Francis' Meditation at 3rd Word Retreat of Priests (Part II)." Jun. 17, 2015. http://www.zenit.org/en/articles/pope-francis-meditation-at-3rd-world-retreat-of-priests-part-ii.

Zernike, Kate, and Jeff Zeleny. "Obama in Senate: Star Power, Minor Role." *New York Times*, Mar. 9, 2008. http://www.nytimes.com/2008/03/09/us/politics/09obama.html?pagewanted=all&_r=0.

www.ingramcontent.com/pod-product-compliance
Lightning Source LLC
Chambersburg PA
CBHW071234230426
43668CB00011B/1439